FIELD & STREAM
THE TOTAL OUTDOORSMAN SKILLS & TOOLS

FIELD & STREAM
THE TOTAL OUTDOORSMAN SKILLS & TOOLS

T. EDWARD NICKENS
AND THE EDITORS OF
FIELD & STREAM

weldonowen

CONTENTS

◉ CAMPING

1 Sleep Under the Stars
2 Make Guylines Shine
3 Strengthen a Tent with Picket Stakes
4 Fix a Tired Tent Pole
5 Use Garbage Bags as Sand Spikes
6 Turn Back Every Tick and Chigger
7 Fix Torn Mosquito Netting
8 Make a Bug Blotter
9 Survive a Lightning Strike
10 Make Contact with Your Touchscreen
11 Fix Misbehaving Zippers

» **THE ICON: SVEA 123 STOVE**

12 Divvy Up KP
13 Accessorize Dutch Oven Cooking
14 Spice Up a Camp Kitchen
15 Clean Pots with a Six-Pack Ring
16 Dice It Up
17 Draw a Pocketknife Like a Gunslinger
18 Switch Up a Pocket Clip
19 Remember Four Knife Nevers
20 Choose a Kid's First Knife
21 Re-Waterproof Your Rain Shell
22 Try Before You Buy
23 Pack a Poop Tube
24 Use a Come-Along
25 Get Hitched
26 One-Hand a Bowline
27 Turn a Weak Fire into a Hot Inferno
28 Pack a Complete Camp Kitchen
29 Sleep Like a Log in Sweltering Summer Heat
30 Tab a Tent
31 Hang Gear Inside a Wall Tent
32 Sleep Tight with a Pool Noodle

33 Roll Out the Home Turf
34 Make Rainy Days Fly
35 Defunk Skunk Gunk
36 Remove Porcupine Quills from a Dog
37 Bring Batteries Back to Life
38 Sanitize Disgusting Hydration Bladders
39 Portage Canoe and Gear
40 Carry a Backpacking Boat Anchor
41 Dry Boots with a Hot Rock
42 Keep Gear Dry
43 Make a Backwoods Energy Drink
44 Bake Camp Biscuits
45 Pack Lunch in a Water Bottle
46 Cook Campfire Brownies with an Orange
47 Trick Out a Mud-Proof ATV
48 Buck a Log with an Axe
49 Split Camp Wood with a Tire
50 Haul Firewood with a Web Strap
51 Roll a Paper Log
52 Dig a Dakota Fire Hole
53 Burn Your Gear Into a Hot Inferno
54 Hang a Pot Over a Fire Three Ways
55 Make a Summer Fire
56 Know Your Axes and Hatchets
57 Name Those Parts
58 Choose Your Weapon
59 Sharpen a Machete
60 Finish a Blade with a Leather Strop
61 Sharpen an Axe
62 Give Your Knife a Spa Treatment
63 Sharpen Using a Sharpie
64 Prepack for Camping
65 Organize a Giant Duffel

66 Whip Finish a Rope
67 Go Beyond Duct Tape
68 Carry a Tight Roll of Duct Tape
69 Protect Lantern Globes with Duct Tape
70 Show a Lantern Some Love
71 Rig a Canoe with Painter Lines
72 Rig a Pack on the Spot with Paracord
73 Make a Camp Table with Paracord
» MY TOOL: THE CANOE BARREL

FISHING

74 Supercharge a Lure with a Nail
75 Hack Your Plastics
76 Make a Wooden Dowel Popper
77 Avoid Treble
78 Make a Custom Fly Rod
79 Mark Fly Lines
80 Float a Line with an Earplug
81 Fish a Greased Leader
82 Dampen Line Twist
83 See Red (or Not)
84 Know Your Canoe
85 Pull Off a Cheap Canoe-Camp Trip
86 Master the Bimini Twist
87 Rig a Killer Cane Pole

88 Patch Grip Potholes
89 Organize Hooks with Safety Pins
90 Have a Midday Quickie
91 Master the Palomar Knot
92 Be a 21st-Century Angler
93 Hit Nothing But Net
94 Skin a Cat with Your Toolbox
95 Measure Fish with Your Wallet
96 Clean Fish in 40 Seconds
97 Rubberize Your Reel Handle
98 Replace Drag Washers
99 Rope-Tape Your Grip
100 Change Bearings
101 Fly-Cast to a Moving Target
102 Get a Fly to the Bottom of Things
103 Do the Chuck 'n' Duck
104 Make a Spin-Fly Mash-Up Outfit
105 Stroke Like a Pro
106 Use the Miracle of Minicell Foam
107 Weave a Canoe Seat with Duct Tape
108 Rock a Bent-Shaft Paddle
109 Dry Wet Waders
110 Patch Waders on the Stream
111 Fish a Bush Hook
112 Hold On Tightly

113 Take Jaw-Dropping Fish Vids
114 Keep a Worm Box
115 Catch Bait with a Blade of Grass
116 Make a Plywood Bait Farm
117 Catch Bait Leeches with a Coffee Can
118 Make a Kick Seine
119 Rig a Pork Rind
120 Master the Arbor Knot
121 Bail a Boat with a Jug
122 Fish a Cricket Anywhere, Any Time
123 Use Salt to Keep Eggs on a Hook
124 Upgrade Your Live Baits
125 Troll the Backcountry Downrigger
126 Troll at a Snail's Pace
127 Fix Any Flat
128 Troll a Fly
129 Keep Muck Out of Your Truck
130 Pack a Fly Vest Three Ways
131 Store Fishing Line
132 Rig an On-the-Stream Fish Stringer
133 Feather a Spinning Reel 50 Feet
134 Convert to Manual Shift
135 Make Your Own In-Line Spinners
136 Widen Your Gathering Guide
137 Master the World's Fair Knot
138 Remove Hooks with a Popsicle Stick
139 Build a Predator Rig
140 Protect Hair-Thin Trout Tippets
141 Set a Spool Brake

142 Strip into a Hamper
143 Improve Fly Line Memory
144 Pack a Bag for a Smallie Assault
145 Survive the Frog Chomp
146 Tie the Nickens Know-Nothing
147 Dye Bucktail Lures and Flies
» THE ICON: ZEBCO 33
148 Fish Like a Japanese Stream Warrior
149 Catch a Dinosaur with a Rope
150 Shoot Docks for Crappie
151 Give Redbreast Sunnies the Slip
152 Make Your Own Sand Spikes
153 Throw a One-Two Punch for Smallies
154 Hammer a Bream Bed
155 Grill Fish with a Tree Branch
156 Get Minty Fresh with Minnows
157 Chill It with Dry Ice
158 Trick Trout with the Right Stick
159 Filter Fish-Frying Oil
160 Prank Social Media Pals
161 Master the Orvis Knot
162 Trick Lunkers with a Lantern
163 School a Kid on Fly Fishing
» MY TOOL: MAD RIVER EXPLORER DUCK HUNTER CANOE

⊛ HUNTING

164 : Stick it to Downed Game

165 : Hoist a Deer

166 : Take a Killer Selfie

167 : Decoy a Pronghorn Antelope

168 : Pack String Wax Every Hunt

169 : Customize Your Bow Sight

170 : Read a Bloody Arrow

171 : Pimp Your .22

172 : Use Snap Caps Three Ways

173 : Ruin a Rifle by Being an Idiot

174 : Make a European Mount Duck Skull

175 : Tune a Duck Call

176 : Brush Up a Duck Canoe

177 : Use a Dog Whistle to Call a Mallard Drake

178 : Use a POV Camera

179 : Use GPS to Record Game Trails

180 : Control a Spinning Turkey

181 : Know Trail Cam Lingo

182 : Fine-Tune Trail Cams

183 : Turn a Pistol into a Shotgun

184 : Target Shop at Walmart

185 : Use an Old Tire to Teach a New Dog Tricks

186 : Train a Dog to Scent Trail

187 : Make a Canine First Aid Kit

188 : Teach a Dog to Dive for Ducks

189 : Store a Duck in Pantyhose

190 : Tune Shotgun Swing with a Flashlight

191 : Disappear with Zip Ties and Clothespins

192 : Turn Away Ticks

193 : Understand Knife Shapes and Grinds

194 : Master the Ground-Blind Shot

195 : Use Superglue

196 : Use Confidence Decoys to Arrow a Deer

197 : Shoot Tighter Groups at Every Distance

198 : Drill for the Scampering Squirrel

199 : Call Squirrels with Stuff in Your Junk Drawer

200 : Be the Tripod

201 : Build a Rabbit Gum

202 : Mount a Rack on a Rock

203 : Track a Blood Trail

204 : Light Up a Hunt

205 : Rig a Deer Drag

206 : Fool Wood Ducks with a Spinning Dove Decoy

207 : Make the Awesomest Duck Whistle
     on the Planet

208 : Translate a Quack

209 : Snag Decoys in Deep Water

210 : Glass the Grid

211 : Homebrew Deer Scents

212 : Stick a Call to Your Coat

213 : Make a Drag Rag

214 : Maintain a Mount

215 : Make Jerky with a Pencil

216 : Pack a Field-Dressing Kit

217 Camo Paint a Gun Stock
218 Clean a Trigger with a Toothbrush
219 Hold Binoculars Rock Steady Three Ways
220 Fix Stock Dings with an Iron
» THE ICON: SCHRADE SHARPFINGER
221 Double Your Range with a Bipod
222 Use Binoculars as a Spotting Scope
223 Make a PVC Rifle Rest
224 Know the Anatomy of an AR
225 Get Out of a Jam
226 Make a Tater Tree
227 Make a Handy Bandolier
228 Clean a Blackpowder Gun with a Guitar
229 Use Spit to Shoot a Blackpowder Rifle
230 Stop Ramrod Blisters
231 Make a Buck Bed with a Chain Saw
232 Steer Deer with Buckets
233 Prune an Apple Tree for Deer
234 Make Your Own Scent Dripper
235 Shoot from a Layout Blind
236 Know Your AR Big-Game Cartridges
237 Earn the Rifleman's Merit Badge
238 Brighten Your Rifle Sight
239 Shoot with Two Eyes
240 Save Your Eardrums for a Quarter
241 Shoot a Double Gun for Plantation Quail
242 Remove a Recoil Pad
243 Build a Gunsmith Box
244 Make a DIY Target Stand
245 Make a Trail Tape Dispenser
246 Stop Gun-Sling Slip
247 Flag a Duck
248 Cook a Duck with a Stick
249 Make a Duck Hunter's Floating Table
250 Cold-Proof Your Shotgun
251 Put More Spring in Your Semiauto Shotgun

252 Make Exploding Flash Targets for an Olympic-Style Shoot
253 Shoot Old-School
254 Try a Blackpowder Pellet
255 Take a Blackpowder Powder
256 Know Your Blackpowder Projectiles
257 Use a Lineman's Belt
258 Make Your Own Scent-Killer
259 Mount a Meat Grinder for Easier Grinding
260 Protect Your Turkey-Call Striker
261 Hunt on Snowshoes
262 Keep Hunting Clothes Clean in Camp
263 Re-Proof Waxed Cotton
264 Silence Your Zipper
265 Keep Calls Clean
266 Make a Frog Gig
267 Prepare Your Frogs
268 Mark Your Pot Call
269 Make Your Own Layout Blind
270 Shoot a Super-Modern Arrow
271 Get the Perfect Nock Fit
272 Call a Turkey with a Peacock
273 Tune Up a Box Call
274 Blow a Wingbone Yelper
275 Make a Cinder Block Pit Cooker
276 Keep Wild Game Fresh
» MY TOOL: KIMBER MODEL 84M

⊛ SURVIVAL

277 Know Your Topo
278 Evaluate a Bubbly Compass
279 Treat a Snake Bite
280 Create a Whirling Propeller of Signal Light
281 Save Your Backtrail on a GPS
282 Sharpen a Serrated Knife
283 Superglue a Cut

284 : Check a Knife for Nicks

» : THE ICON: SPACE BLANKET

285 : Rate an Insect Sting

286 : Prepare for Anaphylaxis

287 : Call for Rescue with a Nut

288 : Send a Maritime Distress Signal

289 : Hurl a Rope

290 : Free a Grounded Boat

291 : Carve a Fuzz Stick for a Fast Firestarter

292 : Make Fire Wick at Home

293 : Improvise Snowshoes

294 : Stay Found for Less than 10 Bucks

295 : Survive a Stranding

296 : Test a Knife with a Newspaper

297 : Escape from Wildfire

298 : Make a Wicked Slingshot

299 : Maintain a Knife Clip

300 : Start a Fire with a Flare

301 : Remove a Fish Hook

302 : Catch Fish with a Trigger Snare

303 : Construct a Fish Weir

304 : Stop Bleeding

305 : Pack a 1-Day Survival Kit

306 : Pack a 3-Day Survival Kit

307 : Pack a 1-Week, Multiperson Survival Kit

308 : Beat the Bugs

309 : Make a Swiss Seat

310 : Rig the Z-Drag

311 : Make Waterproof Matches

312 : Stay Alive with Toilet paper

313 : Make a Survival Faucet

314 : Scrounge Up Survival Wire

315 : Shave the Day

316 : Reuse a Shotshell

» : MY TOOL: PERSONAL LOCATOR BEACON

317 : Spray a Bear into Retreat

318 : Spark Fire with a Knife

319 : Tie the Knot that Fixes All

320 : Prevent a Gutpile Mauling

321 : Open a Can without a Can Opener

322 : Make a Duct Tape Butterfly Bandage

323 : Cook Fish on a Log

324 : Make a Duct Tape Bowl

NEVER STOP LEARNING, NEVER STOP HAVING FUN

It's a small thing, a basic elemental skill, but there are few things that give me more satisfaction than starting a campfire the way I was taught to many years ago by my outdoor mentors. Finding natural tinder from the woods around you, gathering armloads of kindling, and piling up a stack of good, dry wood. Finally you arrange the material in a way that one strike of a waterproof match ignites a flame that slowly builds into the kind of fire that heats your body, warms your spirit, and creates a deep bed of coals for cooking your supper–preferably fresh fish or game.

One of the fundamental rewards of hunting, fishing, camping, and paddling is that these activities are built upon the kinds of atavistic skills that are too often neglected in our increasingly plugged-in world. From outwitting game animals with calls and camo to fooling fish with a bit of feather tied around a wire hook, and everything in between, being a total outdoorsman depends on skills, competence, and self reliance.

It can take a lifetime to acquire these skills, and the mission of this book is to not only help you learn them but also inspire you to use them. One of the core principles of *Field & Stream* is that the more you know, the more fun you can have. Every season, every day, brings a new opportunity in the fields, woods, rivers, lakes, and oceans that make up the world of the total outdoorsmen. It's easy to stick with what you know, but it's much more rewarding and a heck of a lot of fun if you're always pushing yourself to try something new.

I can think of no better guide to becoming a well-rounded sportsman than the author of this book, T. Edward Nickens. From first descents down Alaskan rivers to hunting ducks with his son in the local swamp, Nickens has done it all and written about it in his long career as an outdoor journalist and adventure writer.

One more thing about Nickens and *Field & Stream*: While we value the fundamental, old-school skills that are a part of these sports, we make it our mission to look forward as well as backward. So this book is full of not just the tried and true but also the cutting edge and innovative. We believe that being a total outdoorsman is not just mastering what the basics, but evolving and embracing new tools, techniques, and tactics. If you master half of what is in this book, I promise you that you'll not only be a better hunter and fishermen, but you'll have more success and have more fun doing it.

ANTHONY LICATA
Editor, *Field & Stream*

I FOUND IT ON A RIDGE TOP

where heavy rains the day before had scoured the top layer of turned earth in the muddy field furrows. I was headed for a deer stand, barely looking at the ground, but the object's leaflike profile caught my eye. Some primordial corner of my brain recognized the angles, the edges, instantly. It was a stone point, perched on a tiny pedestal of red-clay dirt, a gift left by the ancients and unwrapped by time.

The white-quartz edges were still sharp. A lance point—an old one—it dated from the Archaic Period that predated the development of the bow and arrow. And yet, I could lash the point to a straight sapling and kill a deer with it today, perhaps 5,000 years after some hunter stalked this very same ridge top.

I believe whoever made that stone point—whoever hunted with it—would have had much in common with you and me. He would have appreciated tools—sporting gear, fishing tackle, ropes and packs, and knives and bows. And not just for the sake of having tools, but because tools would've helped him feed his family and move quietly in the wild and stay alive when things turned rough. That long-ago hunter would have been obsessed with knowing how to use tools. Just like I am. Just like you are.

He would have liked this book. No doubt, he would have some great ideas for these next few hundred pages.

This is a book about sporting tools. It's a book packed with essential skills about how to use stuff, fix stuff, improvise stuff, and improve the stuff you already own to create better hunting, fishing, and camping experiences. A lot of the skills in this book I wrote for *Field & Stream*'s annual Total Outdoorsman issue, published every May. A few of the tips come from the magazine's accomplished staff and field editors, and we've even pulled a few of our favorite reader's tips. But the majority of these skills are brand new. They've never been published—until now.

A lot has changed since that ancient hunter moved in moccasins across that river bluff, spear in hand. Corn and soybeans clad the hill these days, not beech and oaks. Many hunters now carry a daypack crammed with gear my native predecessor could not imagine—GPS units, LED headlamps, laser rangefinders.

No doubt he would have scoffed at the surgical gloves I wear while field-dressing deer to keep blood out of any nicks and cuts. I don't want to think about what he would say about a spinning-wing decoy. He would have drooled over my knives, though, and he would have marveled at the modern riflescope. No question about that.

I'll tell you what would blow his mind: my basement. Honestly, I'd be embarrassed for a guy who killed deer with little more than a stick tipped with a sharp rock to see the mountains of gear I've amassed. Barrels bristling with fly rods and canoe paddles. Storage bins bulging with camouflage clothing. A pair of gun safes. Trolling motors.

Bags of soft-plastic baits. Duck decoys stuffed into every corner.

My collection will be nothing out of the ordinary to anyone holding this book. Your garage is likely no different from my basement. We're gear-heads. We love tools, and there's not a thing wrong with that. But owning tools isn't the same as knowing how to use them. There's nothing worse that some yahoo who shows up with the latest, greatest gear but can't cast close to the pond bank. Or hit the broad side of an elk. Or sharpen a hatchet. Or cinch down the tent fly. Or stop the bleeding from a buddy's gashed leg.

Gear is just stuff that gets in the way—unless you know how to use it, fix it, improve it, and improvise with it.

This is a book for folks who want to learn new ways to do all of that with hunting, fishing, camping, and survival tools. It's not a what-to-buy book. You won't find a single gear review in here. This is a book that will make you a better hunter, angler, paddler, game cook, and camp companion. It's a book for people who love stuff for the right reason: They love the stuff that gear allows them to do.

T. EDWARD NICKENS
Editor-at-Large, *Field & Stream*

EVERYTHING WE NEED

We make quite a scene at the airport: two adults, two teenagers, four carry-ons, and eight pieces of checked baggage, each of which weighs within ounces of the 50-pound-per-bag maximum. It's all there: everything a family of four will need for a week-long camping trip in the big American West.

We've done it enough times now to have it down to a science. A 48-quart cooler is packed with a stove, a lantern, and cookware. Every man, woman, and child has his or her own duffel of clothes and personal gear, fishing rods, and summer reading. There are two backpacks loaded with tents, sleeping bags, and pads, and my beloved canoe barrel packed with breakables. Once on the ground, we rent a van and buy cheap camp chairs and a square of indoor/outdoor carpet. We hit a grocery store. And just like that we're off for a week of camping and fishing and hiking. Two adults, two teenagers, and pushing 400 pounds of gear.

Every year we make the trip, I spend the night before we leave cinching straps and triple-checking gear lists and wondering if it's worth all the work and hassle. And every year, as we pack up camp the night before we fly home, I know the answer. Yes. A thousand times, yes.

There is simply not a more American pastime than camping. And despite the fact that we've upgraded from birch bark canoes and Conestoga wagons to jetliners and $40,000 pickup trucks, the spirit is still there, still true: pack up a semblance of home, move it to some distant riverbank or mountain ridge, and reassemble. Raise the tent, hang the grub, lay the fire. Set up camp. Pair a camping trip with a rod or gun, and the fun factor rockets. Now there's fresh trout on the fire, and elk quarters hanging in the dark timber.

Of course, having the right gear is a big part of the difference between a string of miserable nights in the woods and an unforgettable week in the wild.

And the right stuff doesn't necessarily mean the newest stuff or the most expensive gear. It can mean knowing how to get the most of some of the most basic tools you own.

Consider the tent guyline, the cord that attaches the rain fly to the tent stakes. It's a piece of cord, really, so what else is there to know? Plenty, which is the point of this book. Learn to tie a taut-line hitch at the end of the guyline and you can cinch the rain fly tight in front of a storm. Replace all your old manufacturer-supplied guyline cord with reflective cord and you'll never again trip on those dark midnight trips to the groover. Learn how to rig a guyline picket stake and your tent fly will never again loosen when the winds start to howl. Those are three examples of how you can rig and modify one overlooked piece of gear.

I'm an unapologetic gear hog, and I admit that I have a hoarder's tendency to keep just about everything. My basement is crammed with camping

gear that spans a half-century, from my dad's old lensatic compass to a set of GPS-enabled two-way radios. Even in the woods, I'm the guy who brings it all. I was never one to drill holes in my toothbrush to shave a few ounces from my backpack's weight. I'd rather sweat a bit more up the ridge so I can kick back with real coffee than make do with instant swill. I'd rather have two headlamps because you never know. Most likely, I'll be the guy with the gun-cleaning kit stashed in the boat bag, and you'll come looking for me when your canoe turns over.

But we can't forget attitude and aptitude. Good gear and know-how have a hard time trumping a whiny disposition when the trail turns tough. A positive frame of mind invites on-the-fly innovation and makes the most of every situation. A gracious spirit is thankful for every night spent under the stars—no matter how rocky and rooty the ground under your back. Your brain and your heart are your most important tools.

Once, during an 8-day paddling and fishing trip down Ontario's remote Palisade and Allanwater rivers, my buddy Scott Wood and I had to put in a monstrous day. We broke camp early and paddled 22 miles, with a 3-mile lake crossing and mucky overgrown portages. We were still on the go at 11 P.M., with no food for eight hours and daylight fading fast, yet we had our largest rapid to run. At the base of Black Beaver Rapids, we dragged the boat to shore as an orange moon rose through spectral fire-blackened forest, too exhausted to cook supper. We stamped down a rough bivvy 10 feet from the water, running tent guylines to blueberry shrubs, and collapsed in the sleeping bags as northern lights arced overhead, wholly unappreciated. We had a few more days on the river, and I spent the few fitful minutes before sleep triple-checking the map and wondering if it was worth all the hassle.

In the morning we limped out of the tents to find the blueberry plains sheathed in frost, a world so glittery and serene, I half-expected unicorns to come prancing through the valley. We caught a breakfast walleye, cleaned it on the bottom of an overturned canoe, fried it hot and fast and washed the fish down with pure, cold water from the river and handfuls of blueberries. And just like that—I was ready to do it all again.

Worth it every time.

SLEEP UNDER THE STARS

Growing up we slept under the stars, sans tent or tarp, to prove how tough we were, but now I sleep in the Big Scary Open because I get a huge kick out of nodding off to shooting stars and waking to the first rays of the sun. And it's super cool to sleep with frost sheathing your sleeping bag. If you're squeamish about dozing off without the protection of a nylon cocoon, try it my way: Spread out a space blanket first, then a super-comfy sleeping pad. Having a spread of ground cloth between you and the bare ground is a mental comfort, and it also means you can spread your arms and thrash around a bit without actually wallowing in the dirt. I wear a toboggan to hold in extra body heat and keep a flashlight tucked in a boot near my head so I can find it quickly. If it makes you feel better, the other boot can hold a knife, handgun, pepper spray, or ninja death stars.

2 MAKE GUYLINES SHINE

In 30 minutes you can replace all your old tent guylines with reflective cord, and never again trip over them while stumbling around during a middle-of-the-night pee, during which you stub your right big toe so badly that the nail splits and the toe swells and you can't wear wading boots for two days. Listen to me.

3 STRENGTHEN A TENT WITH PICKET STAKES

This supercharged guyout plan kicks in when the wind cranks up to 25 mph. Picket stakes boost the holding power of tent stakes, so use them on the guylines attached to the side of the tent that faces the wind.

STEP 1 Drive the first stake into the ground at the desired location, and attach it to the tent guyline. To make a picket-stake line, tie an overhand loop in one end of a 16-inch length of parachute cord. Attach the p-cord to the first stake by threading the running end through the overhand loop and cinching it tight against the stake.

STEP 2 Drive a second stake—this will be the picket stake—into the ground 8 to 12 inches from the first stake so that it's in a straight line with the guyline. Wrap the running end of the p-cord around the picket stake twice, then tie it off with two half hitches.

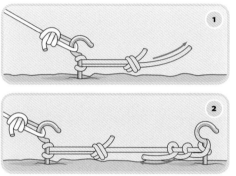

5 USE GARBAGE BAGS AS SAND SPIKES

It's always been a challenge to anchor a tent or tarp on beaches, river sandbars, and other places where tent stakes won't hold. The solution: bag it. Fill garbage bags or empty stuff sacks with sand, tie a knot in the opening, then tie the tent's stake loops and rain fly guylines to them. For high winds, burying the bags will provide a rock-solid stake point. And stuffing sand bags along the inside tent edge will help batten down the hatches.

4 FIX A TIRED TENT POLE

It ranks among the most humiliating of outdoor snafus: When you pull the tent poles from the stuff sack, where they have been lovingly stored since portable CD players were all the rage, the pole sections fall to your feet like pick-up-sticks, the shock cord holding them together slack and limp.

It's always best to replace old shock cord as it starts to lose its elasticity, not when it is gone forever. In most cases, elastic bungee cord is threaded through the pole sections and held in place with a stopper knot that jams against a washer or some other stop inside each terminal pole section. A few tent models require a kit if the shock cord goes south, but most can be handled with nothing more than new bungee.

First, remember to keep the pole sections in their original order throughout this process. Access the cord by prying off a pole tip. Remove the old cord.

Tie an overhand knot in one end of the new cord.

Thread the cord through the poles one section at a time, joining the sections together as you make progress. If the bungee bunches up while being pushed, cut a straight length of coat hanger wire, attach to the end of the bungee, and feed the wire through the poles. When finished, pull the bungee cord fairly tight, but leave some slack. Tie another stopper knot, but don't cut off the excess yet. You may need to experiment with the cord length to get the tension right. You want enough to hold the poles together, but not so much that the cord is stretched too tightly when you decouple the sections.

6 TURN BACK EVERY TICK AND CHIGGER

It's taken me decades of tinkering to perfect this system, but I've cut my number of tick and chigger bites by 90 percent or better with a tactical approach to applying bug dope and modifying clothing. The advent of roll-top and sponge-top insect repellents also helps keep the required dosage to a minimum. Here's the drill.

Start with the strategic placement of high-percentage DEET bug dope. I rarely use anything less than 30 percent, and when the chigger infestations are at their worst, I use 100-percent DEET without hesitation. The idea is not to slather your entire body with the strong stuff, but to minimize use by drawing hard chemical lines to turn back the insect hordes. Run a stripe of dope around each leg on the upper thighs, below the bottom edge of your underwear, and another one below the knee. Now lift up your shirt, pull the pants waistband down an inch or two, and apply another stripe of bug dope around your waist an inch above the top of where your pants ride. The idea is to prevent a tick and chigger recon squad from crawling up or down. Now tuck pant hems into socks and run a band of duct tape around the seam. Apply more DEET to boots, socks, and pants legs below the knees.

Exposed areas around your neck need bug dope, as do wrists. A double stripe below and above the elbow will keep creepies from crawling up your arms. Designate a hat as your bug-dope-friendly brim. Apply dope to the crown. Last, run a stripe of repellent along the edge of the hat brim. This helps produce a vapor barrier of bug dope in front of your face, but keeps the chemicals out of your eyes.

tick

chigger

7 FIX TORN MOSQUITO NETTING

Having a properly sealed mosquito net can spell the difference between a healthy safari and a bout of malaria—or at least, a good night's sleep and one full of itches and welts.

For straight tears less than 2 inches long, thread a needle and stitch the rip closed. If you have extra netting in a repair kit, reinforce with a netting patch cut ½ inch larger than the tear. In the field, any makeshift thread will work: dental floss, fishing line, or even plant fibers. You can always pretty it up with nylon sewing thread back home.

For jagged, Frankenstein rips large enough for bats to fly through, heavier lifting is required. First, pull the edges of the tear together and tape with masking tape (A). (Duct tape is too sticky.) Then tape a strip of paper over the tape to serve as extra backing (B). On the other side, brush on a layer of silicone-based repair adhesive (C). Give it two days to cure, then remove the paper backing. Dust the patch with body powder (D) to knock back the stickiness and prevent it from picking up dirt or sticking to the rest of the tent.

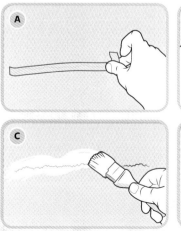

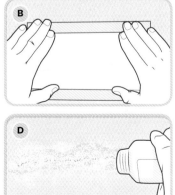

8 MAKE A BUG BLOTTER

Duct tape makes a fine insect blotter. Wrap a few strips around your hand and blot the bugs trapped inside the tent. Better than smashing them into the tent fabric.

9 SURVIVE A LIGHTNING STRIKE

There are lots of snappy sayings to help you remember lightning safety: When the thunder roars, get indoors! If you can see it, flee it! But what do you do when you're caught outdoors with almost nowhere to hide? The National Outdoor Leadership Schools, or NOLS, and other experts, recommend the following.

IF YOU ARE CLOSE TO YOUR VEHICLE OR AN ENCLOSED STRUCTURE Get inside something—your car, a house, a barn. Open shelters such as picnic shelters provide little to no protection.

IF YOU ARE CAMPING Avoid open fields and ridge tops during seasons when thunderstorms are prevalent. Stay away from fence lines, metal and tall, isolated trees. Tents provide no protection. If you are in dangerous open terrain during a thunderstorm, leave the tent and assume the "lightning crunch" (described in the last paragraph).

IF YOU ARE IN OPEN COUNTRY Avoid the high ground and contact with dissimilar objects, such as water and land, boulders and land, or single trees and land.

Head for ditches, gullies, or low ground. Spread out at least 50 feet apart and assume the "lightning crunch."

IF YOU ARE ON THE WATER Head inside a boat cabin, which offers a safer environment. Stay off the radio unless it is an emergency. Drop anchor and get as low in the boat as possible. If you're in a canoe on open water, get as low in the canoe as possible and as far as possible from any metal object. If shore only offers rocky crags and tall isolated trees, stay in the boat.

IF YOU CANNOT FIND SHELTER Some experts believe that the "lightning crunch" provides little to no protection for a direct or close strike, but at this point, some action is better than nothing. Stand on an insulated pad or bag of clothes. Do not stand on packs; the metal in frames and zippers could increase chances of a lightning strike. Put your feet together and balance on the balls of your feet. Squat low, wrap your arms around your legs, tuck your head, close your eyes and cover your ears. Maintain the position until danger passes.

10 MAKE CONTACT WITH YOUR TOUCHSCREEN

Most of us bring along a smartphone on our camping trips. When it's cold, however, the device is impossible to use with gloves, which block the transfer of electrical energy from your skin to the capacitive touchscreen. You can buy touchscreen-compatible gloves, outfitted with small, conductive fingertip dots. Or you can save 40 bucks and take pride in being a postmodern mountain man by sewing a few stitches of conductive thread to the tips of your own mitts. All you need is a pair of old-school gloves, a sewing needle, and a couple feet of conductive thread.

STEP 1 Thread a sewing needle with 18 inches of conductive thread. Double the thread, and tie an overhand knot in the end.

STEP 2 If possible, turn the glove finger inside out to start the stitching. (If your glove is too thick to turn it inside out, trim the excess thread as close as possible to the knot, and start from the outside.) Make 4 to 5 parallel stitches, keeping the threads as close as possible. You want enough exposed thread to conduct the electricity from your skin, but not so much as to make the active touchscreen dot too large. On the inside of the glove, create a half-inch bird's nest of thread to help transfer the electric charge.

STEP 3 Tie the thread off by slipping the needle through the last two stitch loops and snugging down with a knot. Trim the thread with a 3-inch tail on the inside of the glove. This will serve as a kind of antenna to help pick up electricity.

Turn the glove right-side-out and you are smartphone-app ready. Now you can text your pal about the bruiser buck headed his way. The one you could have shot had you not been playing Fruit Ninja.

11 FIX MISBEHAVING ZIPPERS

When it comes to gear failure, temperamental zippers top the list of easy-to-fix issues. Problems with a $5 zipper can turn a $550 tent into a heap of useless nylon. Broken or stuck zippers are often easy to fix, though, and here's how.

CLEAN THE MACHINE If a zipper is just dirty and so gunked up the pull doesn't want to slide, scrub with hot water and a toothbrush, then give a worn zipper some spa love with Gear Aid Zip Care. If you're in the field, lubricate a zipper with a few strokes of a graphite pencil, bar soap, or a smear of lip balm. You'll want to clean thoroughly once at home.

DIY PULL TABS Replace broken or missing zipper pulls with a short loop of reflective tent guyline cord or old fly line. Use a double fisherman's knot to provide a smooth, grippy connection.

FIX SLIDER SLIPPAGE A loose slider fails to stitch a zipper's teeth together. Fix with needle-nose pliers. Crimp each side of the slider very slightly, alternating between sides, and check after each round of crimping so you don't overdo it.

PREVENT TOOTH DECAY Sometimes an individual zipper tooth goes out of whack. Gently squeeze it back into formation with pliers.

CLEAR THE PATH If you've wedged a wad of fabric between the zipper pull and the teeth, you'll need to either tug the fabric gently from the zipper pull's jaws, or move the zipper pull past the point where the fabric bunches up. A squirt of window cleaner can help. Test a small swatch of the fabric first to make sure the window cleaner doesn't stain, then soak the zipper pull and fabric with window cleaner. It acts as a cleaner and lubricant that will make removing the fabric wad much easier.

When it comes to backpacking stoves, the Svea 123 is the origin of the species. Strip away all the most modern elements from today's cutting-edge stoves—the piezo-electronic ignitions, the adaptors for French press coffee makers, the USB ports that enable you to charge a phone while heating gruel—and this is what you'll have: a tough, compact, light means of applying heat to a pot.

You might expect that from a Swedish company known for building blowtorches. The Svea 123 hit the market in 1955, just as backpacking was hitting the American mainstream. At the time, of course, it was positively futuristic. The stove featured a pressurized naphtha fuel tank that could be preheated with a small amount of fuel, which meant the contraption would fire up in unholy cold. At full speed, it will boil a liter of water in 7 minutes, depending on altitude. Made of solid brass, with a minimum of moving parts, there was little to break. With an empty tank, the Svea 123 weighed only 18 ounces. It found a place beside external-frame backpacks, Goodyear-welt boots, and egg-grate foam pads as a tool revered by backpackers, alpinists, and even long-distance motorcycle riders.

Happily, the Svea 123 is still a viable gear option. More modern versions come with a self-cleaning fuel needle, but otherwise, they are near-exact copies. Mine dates from the late 1960s, and I remember when my dad bought it at a sporting goods store where campstoves and lanterns shared shelf space with World War II patches, bullets, and German battle helmets.

Pulling out the stove these days makes a statement, and I'm not referring to its retro lines. On high, or anywhere near it, the Svea 123 absolutely roars—like a jet takeoff roars. Subtle it is not, and it elicits a horror-stricken *what the #@+*! is that*? double take from some modern-gear weenies. But it burns hot, it lights every time no matter the conditions, and you can drop this stove off a cliff and cook breakfast at the bottom.

12 DIVVY UP KP

Assigning kitchen duty is no fun at home, and it's a drag at a hunting or fishing camp, too. There are plenty of solutions, and here are two that work.

HAVE A LOTTERY
Each night of the season or trip has a number, and whatever number you draw, you're responsible for the evening meal, from preparation to clean-up. Have it catered, if you want to. Just don't ask for help.

USE THE BUDDY SYSTEM Assign 2-person teams for Kitchen Patrol: one to cook, one to clean. That way, no one misses out on the entire evening's festivities.

13 ACCESSORIZE DUTCH OVEN COOKING

Dutch oven cooking is a camp staple. Here are six items that will make it easier to channel your inner iron chef.

TONGS Useful for placing coals on top of an oven lid and turning food items during the cooking process.

LID LIFTER Cowboys call it a "gonch hook"—a lid lifter raises the lid while preventing it from tipping and dumping coals into your casserole.

SMALL WHISK BROOM Use to brush coals from a lid.

CHIMNEY STARTER FOR CHARCOAL Gets coals roaring fast, and prevents the need for lighter fluid.

HEAVY LEATHER GLOVES OR FIRE GLOVES Great for handling hot pots and lids.

PLASTIC PUTTY KNIFE Good for scraping away burned bits of food without scratching the oven finish.

15 CLEAN POTS WITH A SIX-PACK RING

If you forget to pack a pot scrubber to clean your dishes, remove the plastic rings from a few six-packs of canned beverages, stack and fold them as shown, and bundle them tightly together with a zip tie. It's very effective at scraping off food residue baked onto pans. Just make sure to dispose of the plastic rings properly at home.

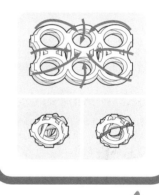

14 SPICE UP A CAMP KITCHEN

Empty Tic-Tac boxes make the best camp spice bottles in the world. Mark the contents with a permanent marker. They're small enough that you can carry an entire spice rack in a very small package.

16 DICE IT UP

I always pack a couple of flexible cutting boards on camping trips. They weigh next to nothing, stuff anywhere, and makes slicing and dicing— and cleaning fish—a snap.

17 DRAW A POCKETKNIFE LIKE A GUNSLINGER

Folding knives are hugely popular, but there are choices when it comes to how to carry a clip-mounted knife and how to draw it quickly and ready for action.

DEPLOY THE KNIFE TIP DOWN Many prefer a tip-down carry for safety reasons. If the blade were to open slightly in your pocket, a tip-down carry will help prevent an accident slicing of your fingertips. Assisted opening knives should be carried tip-down. To deploy, reach into your pocket with your thumb on the inside of the knife, two fingers on the outside at the clip position, and draw. As the knife comes out of your pocket, grasp the pivot point between thumb and forefinger, and use the middle finger to catch the edge of the pocket clip and rotate the handle slightly into your palm, keeping your thumb on the opening stud or hole. You're ready to open the knife.

DEPLOY THE KNIFE TIP UP The tip-up position allows for very rapid deployment of flipper knives. To deploy from tip-up, reach into the pocket and slide your thumb down the handle almost to the pivot point, with other fingers on the clip side of the handle.

One slick modification for tip-up knives, such as many Spyderco knives with opening holes, is to use a zip tie to create a quick opening feature. Insert a small zip tie through the opening hole and cinch down tightly so that the protruding side of the zip tie is on the same side of the knife as the clip. Cut the tails off flush. (You might need two small zip ties to prevent each from wiggling around.) Now as you pull the knife from your pocket, pull back slightly so the zip ties catch on the back corner of the pocket seam, pulling the knife open. Practice the move and it can be impressively instantaneous.

18 SWITCH UP A POCKET CLIP

Many folding knives come with pocket clips that can be placed on either side of the handle, either tip-up or tip-down. Where and how you carry a knife is personal preference, but keeping a clip tightly screwed in place is critical.

Many clips are attached with the 6-sided star screws called Torx screws. Designed to prevent cam-out, Torx screws can be screwed down very tightly, but you'll have to have the proper size of Torx bit for the job. Add a tiny drop of blue Loctite, which is a medium strength threadlocker that will prevent clip screws from loosening.

19 REMEMBER FOUR KNIFE NEVERS

Keep these tips in mind, and your favorite blade will last as long as you do—or even longer.

NEVER store a knife in a leather sheath; it can cause rusting or discoloration.

NEVER use water to clean a horn handle. Horn absorbs moisture and can splinter.

NEVER use hot water to clean a wood handle. If the wood is cracked or dried, rub it with olive oil.

NEVER touch the blade or metal parts after oiling. This can leave behind salt and acids, which can cause oxidation.

20 CHOOSE A KID'S FIRST KNIFE

How old is old enough for a knife? Some will consider it heresy, but I used a rotary tool to grind the blade on a Swiss Army knife down to butter-knife dull, and let my 5-year-olds putter around camp with it at will. That sparked plenty of early conversations about knife safety and has paid off now that they are teenagers.

General-purpose folders will whittle a stick, clean a panfish, and help take the hide off a deer. While shopping, look for features that make certain designs safer for smaller hands, and don't drop a pile of cash on a kid's knife.

For ages 10 and younger, look for a locking main blade. Some newer models of Swiss Army knives have been updated with locks, and they still have all the cool stuff—tweezers, toothpick, screwdrivers —with an ergonomic handle for an even surer grip.

For kids 11 to 13, blades shorter than 3 inches are still stout enough to cut through a squirrel. Look for jimping at the base of the blade spine to help provide control, and find a knife with a fat handle that will fit smaller hands well. I like indentations deep enough to serve as a finger guard.

For those 14 and older, flipper opening mechanisms create a nifty blade guard when the knife is open. Older kids will also appreciate a backup locking mechanism for an added measure of safety.

21 RE-WATERPROOF YOUR RAIN SHELL

Rain should roll off your shell in beads. If it doesn't, you need to restore the fabric's DWR, or durable water repellent, finish. Otherwise the outer fabric will "wet out" and prevent sweat vapor from passing through.

Wash with a mild powder detergent like Dreft, or a specialized outerwear formula such as Nikwax Tech Wash, and dry on medium setting. If water beads up, you're done. If not, iron the garment with a warm iron. Heat redistributes the DWR coating throughout the fabric. Still wetting through? Apply a new coating of spray-on DWR. Brands to consider: Nikwax and Granger's. Cabela's sells a cleaning kit with both detergent and DWR packaged together.

22 TRY BEFORE YOU BUY

What can 5 minutes of serious study tell you about the gear you're about to buy? Plenty. Just ignore the stares of other shoppers, and think twice about buying from a store that won't let you put their products through the ringer.

A SLEEPING BAG Roll the bag out on the floor, and climb in. Sit up and try to touch your toes. If you bind, opt for a longer size. Next, lie back down. Zip the bag open and closed three times from the inside, and three times from the outside. If the zipper hangs up, keep looking.

B BOOTS Shop in the late afternoon, when your feet are swollen. Wear the sock combination you prefer in the field. Lean forward and slide your index finger between heel and boot. There shouldn't be more than a $1/2$-inch gap. Next, kick the wall. If your toes hit the front of the boot, keep shopping.

C FLY ROD Wiggling a rod won't tell you much, so walk into the store with a reel loaded with your favorite line, with leader attached, and a few flies with the hook points snipped off. Ask if you can try a few casts in the parking lot, on a nearby lawn, or off the loading dock out back. They'll let you.

D BACKPACK Load it with a volume similar to a typical day's worth of hunting gear, stuff one more spare vest inside, and sling it on. Raise your arms overhead to make sure the sternum strap doesn't cut across your throat. The hip belt should ride on the hips, not above the navel. Test zippers for binding.

23 PACK A POOP TUBE

"Pack it in, pack it out." That's the leave-no-trace mantra of many wilderness areas, and it's not just talking about candy bar wrappers. Packing out your own poop is actually required in some backcountry regions, and it's not as gross as you think. The elegant solution, devised by big-wall climbers who spend days aloft, is called the Poop Tube.

STEP 1 Cut a length of 4-inch-diameter PVC pipe to size. For a three-day trip, 6 to 10 inches should suffice. Better too long than too short. This is irrefutable.

STEP 2 Glue a solid cap to one end of the tube, and a threaded fitting to the other. Attach a tether of parachute cord to the tube and a screw cap.

STEP 3 When duty calls, bring along a plastic grocery bag. Reach behind your back, grab one handle of the bag in each hand, pull the handles toward your hips, and get 'er done.

STEP 4 Tie the bag, then deposit into the Poop Tube.

A come-along is a hand-operated winch with a mechanical brake, and it will help unstick a stuck truck, pull a boat or ATV up a steep ramp, and winch a tree out of the trail. Come-alongs come in various sizes, rated from 1 to 4 tons, and rule #1 is use enough gun. These devices are slow and require some pretty serious muscle power, but they will get you out of a bad spot when there's no one else around.

Before you start, tick off a few safety items. Make sure the come-along is adequate for the pulling load. Wear leather work gloves and safety glasses.

STEP 1 Attach the stationary hook—the one affixed to the come-along frame—to a fixed object such as a tree or vehicle that will handle the load of the pulling operation. Release the drum safety lever and pull out the cable. Always retain at least 2 full cable wraps on the drum.

STEP 2 Connect the pulling hook to the load. It's best to use some type of attachment—a chain, eyebolt, or sling—to provide a secure connection between the hook and the load.

STEP 3 Engage the drive pawl with the drum ratchet. Make sure the ratchet lock is engaged before you begin to crank on the come-along.

STEP 4 Pump the handle back and forth in order to wind cable onto the drum.

STEP 5 Before releasing the come-along, make sure the load is stable and supported and won't move when tension is released. To release the come-along, release the ratchet lock, disengage the drive pawl, and pull out the cable.

25 GET HITCHED

The quick-release highwayman's hitch seems perfectly devised for the (sometimes guilty) pleasures of summer. It's just right for tying a johnboat off to an overhanging branch. And this get-gone-quick hitch is the go-to knot for when you sneak a canoe into the city lake at night (we'd never condone this) for some late bass action (we've heard only "rumors" of big fish) and just might need to boogie out of there fast (we do know that short, choppy strokes are better for a quick start—just sayin').

STEP 1 Place a loop under the fixed post, pole, branch, or railing. Form another loop in the standing line.

STEP 2 Pull this second loop over the post and under the first loop.

STEP 3 Make a loop in the end of the line...

STEP 4 And thread it through the loop formed at the top of the knot. Pull the standing line to set the knot. To release, pull the end of the free line.

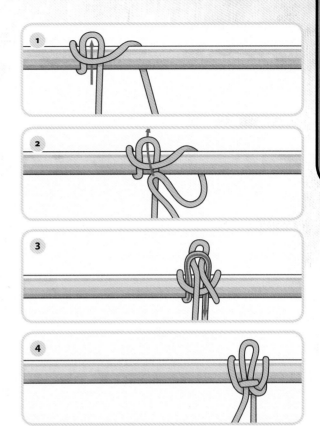

26 ONE-HAND A BOWLINE

This is a neat trick that needs some practice to get right. Start with the rope around your back, grasping its running end, then work your way through these steps.

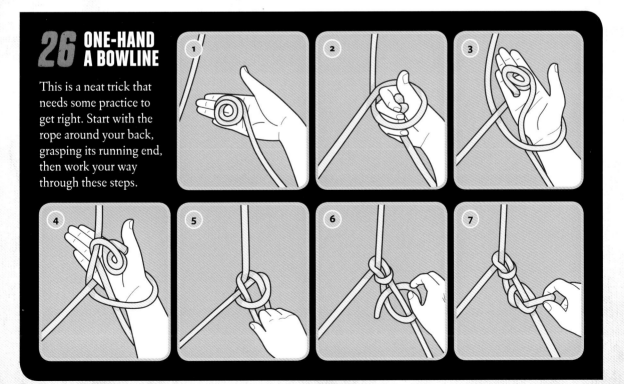

27 TURN A WEAK FIRE INTO A HOT INFERNO

You need a fire to keep warm, cook dinner, and gather round for spooky stories. Make sure yours is a blazing bonfire, not a fickle flame.

GO WITH PAPER It cools off little old ladies at church dinners, and it'll get your fire going in a pinch: Grab a paper plate and start fanning. Make sure to get on ground level so the breeze doesn't create a mushroom cloud of ash, and keep it up at medium speed.

PUMP IT UP You won't believe this trick until you see it. Hose down a meager coal with air from a battery-powered pump like those used to inflate air mattresses. Just remember to go easy—too much of a breeze will stifle a fire, not supercharge it.

PERFORM SURGERY Attach 3 feet of surgical tubing to a 5-inch length of copper tubing for a precision instrument that can turn a puff into a fire blast. Place the copper tube near the cinders, and blow gently for as long as you can. Just be careful not to inhale through the tube.

28 PACK A COMPLETE CAMP KITCHEN

The best way to make sure you always have what you need in the camp kitchen is to put together a complete set of cooking gear, pack it in an old cooler or plastic tote, and stow it in the basement or garage. The worst thing you can do: raid the camp kitchen just because you can't find the home kitchen spatula. Here's what you need to cook for a family or small group.

STOVE
(1) 2- or 3-burner camp stove

COOKWARE
(2) Pot set
(3) No. 10 Dutch oven
(4) Large fry pan
(5) Dutch oven lid lifter
(6) Measuring/mixing cup
(7) Pot grabber
(8) Coffee pot or French press and extra mugs

UTENSILS
(9) Opinel Knife No. 8
(10) Opinel Knife No. 10
(11) Mixing and serving spoons
(12) Spatula
(13) Metal tongs
(14) Stackable plates/cups set

CLEAN-UP
(15) Camp sink
(16) Biodegradable soap
(17) Quick-dry towels
(18) Pot scrubbers
(19) Trash bags

MISCELLANEOUS
(20) Strike-anywhere matches
(21) Charcoal chimney
(22) Bottle opener
(23) Corkscrew
(24) Spices, assorted
(25) Can opener
(26) Military can opener for backup
(27) Collapsible water container
(28) Plastic tablecloth and clips
(29) Aluminum foil
(30) Fire gloves
(31) Flexible cutting boards
(32) Thermacell

29 SLEEP LIKE A LOG IN SWELTERING SUMMER HEAT

It's a cruel twist, but for years my summer camping trips made for blissful daytime memories and miserable nights. There were sweltering tents. Happy campers singing 'round the fire so late the coyotes even howled for them to shut up. And then the endless snoring. Many mornings I greeted a gorgeous dawn sleep-deprived and grouchy.

Then I figured out the system for the best summer night's sleep ever. I bugged out of the communal snuggle-up-to-the-campfire scene and went solo with a sweet one-man tent. While everyone else fought with snoring tentmates and fitful sleep close to the festivities, I tucked my selfish little shelter into some leafy nook half a football field away. Nite-nite, suckers.

Here's my setup. I like tents with a body made almost entirely of mesh to hold summer bugs at bay but let summer breezes right in. Since I'm a big tosser and turner, I like a sleeping bag with an integrated sleeping pad. They're so sturdy even a sumo wrestler could not push me off the pad. And because it breathes so well, I like my bag to be lightly filled with lightweight down—even in summer—and I prefer a pad that blows up to a comfy $3\frac{1}{2}$ inches thick.

Add a pair of soft earplugs and a half dose of melatonin, and I'm good till morning's light.

30 TAB A TENT

Make tent line tighteners with soda can pull tabs. Thread the cord through the tab, loop it around the tent stake, and tie it back to the tab. Slide to make adjustments.

31 HANG GEAR INSIDE A WALL TENT

If your wall tent has an interior frame, you can hang many items with inexpensive shower-curtain hooks. Place the hooks over the horizontal poles, and hang pots and pans.

32
SLEEP TIGHT WITH A POOL NOODLE

I'm not afraid to admit it: Sleeping on a camp's top bunk without a rail makes me a little nervous. I'm a thrasher in the sack, and the thought of plummeting off the side of the bed keeps me up at night. The answer to this sleepy-time conundrum: a pool noodle. Wedge a pool noodle under a fitted sheet on the edge of the bed closest to the abyss. Now when you roll over, that pool noodle is just enough to keep you from going over the side, knocking your noggin at the bottom of your fall.

33
ROLL OUT THE HOME TURF

A piece of indoor-outdoor carpeting makes a fine front porch for any tent. It keeps the dirt out and doubles as a changing-room floor if you have a large tent vestibule.

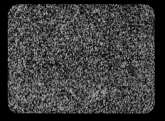

34
MAKE RAINY DAYS FLY

Sleeping pads make perfect game boards, and there's no better way to pass time during a downpour than with a rousing brain-smash of chess. Or a spirited tic-tac-toe challenge, if you'd rather. Come up with a friendly competition—the winner, for example, gets first crack at the best trout hole on the creek.

At home, use a warm wet rag to clean the pad of dirt, sweat, grime, and smashed-in candy bars. While the pad is drying, pull out your favorite board games, a ruler or protractor (remember those?), and a quiver of permanent markers.

Sketching out a chess and checkers board is as easy as drawing squares and coloring between the lines. Backgammon is a bit more complicated, but no big deal. And there's always tic-tac-toe. If you have kids, a boiled down board of Chutes and Ladders isn't that difficult to draw. And you could go hardcore and sketch out Monopoly if you like. The game pieces for these games aren't terribly heavy or bulky, and for checkers and backgammon, pebbles or trout flies will suffice. Die-hard chess fans should snip out cardboard cutouts and store in a pack pocket for a rainy day.

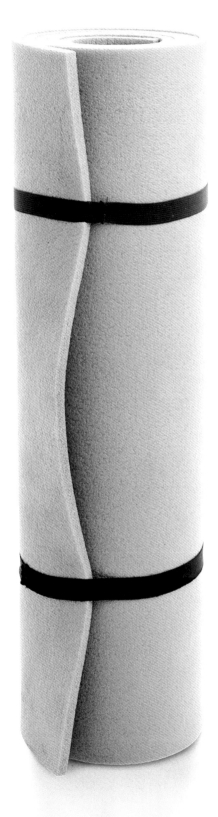

One enduring myth regarding skunks is that they spray urine. They do not. They spray an oily, foamy matrix of thiols and thioacetates such as bifurtryphenoliate that smells every bit as bad as you've heard. All carnivores have scent glands and ducts, but only the skunks have evolved overly enlarged scent glands attached to an aimable nipple tucked near the rectum and manipulated by a group of highly controllable muscles. (And you thought they just stank.)

That nipple works in two modes. A skunk can send out an atomized burst of redolent mist that covers a relatively large area, or the animal can employ what famed skunk researcher Jerry Dragoo (he was born with very little sense of smell) calls "the .357 magnum tactic": one compact stream of stink juice. A skunk's funk is accurate to 10 feet out and ballistically viable for another 15 more. And they have plenty of time to practice. Baby skunks arrive with chambered rounds and can spray the stuff before their infant eyes open.

Happily, skunks don't open fire willy-nilly but engage in highly ritualistic behaviors prior to the main event. Stumble up on one and it might stomp its feet. It might bluff charge. Or stand up and hiss. You've been warned. If all that—plus the fact that it is, after all, a skunk—doesn't convince you to hit the dirt, the skunk will likely spin around, raise its tail (or not) and open fire.

If you're hit, you will quickly find out who your good friends are, and it's a good bet you won't have many. Deskunkifying will be a lonely task. Begin by bathing with a solution of one pint hydrogen peroxide, 1/4 cup baking soda, and a teaspoon of dishwashing liquid. Lather, rinse, repeat. Again and again, most likely. If you're close to civilization, try a commercial application such as Nature's Miracle Skunk Odor Remover.

During this process, try to ponder what an impressive creature the skunk is—an efficient predator, beautiful to behold, and packing one evil olfactory boot knife. Don't hate them because they're putrescible.

36 REMOVE PORCUPINE QUILLS FROM A DOG

Removing skunk funk from a dog, pulling ingested fly line from a Lab's anus hand-over-hand, one revolting inch at a time—firsthand experience is mine, proud to say. But for porky quills, the expert is Dr. T. J. Dunn, DVM, who figures he's de-quilled upwards of 400 dogs at his Rhinelander, Wisconsin, practice. Dunn says a dog with a dozen or so quills stuck in the nose, chin, or lips is a DIY job: Drape a towel over the dog's eyes and grasp the quills firmly with pliers. "A lot of the time the dog feels that sensation and instinctively backs away," Dunn reports. "The quills will pop out almost on their own, and you can get 2 or 3 at a time." Spread the pain over an hour or two if needed, giving the dog a break, a

walk, and a dose of tasty treats in between treatments.

For hounds pin-cushioned with more quills, or quills embedded in the mouth, tongue, or near the eyes, the dog needs a veterinarian and anesthesia. If a vet is miles of rough woods or days away, try trimming the quills with scissors to reduce their chances of catching on brush or clothing. But leave plenty sticking out for the vise-grips to come.

37 BRING BATTERIES BACK TO LIFE

When batteries give way in frigid conditions, there are ways to give them temporary new life. You won't get enough juice to do battle on a level of Angry Birds, but you could get enough to lock down your location on a GPS or send a text.

HAVE A HOT POCKET First, remove batteries from the device if possible. Warm them next to your body. Armpits work well, as do chest pockets if you are generating body heat. Overnight, toss batteries into the foot of a sleeping bag. They should be ready to fire up come dawn.

PACK HEAT If you have a granulated, air-activated hand warmer, place the hand warmer and batteries inside a closed pouch or a pocket. Better yet, duct-tape the hand warmer directly to the batteries.

TAKE A SOLAR SHOWER Fill a plastic zip-seal bag with dark materials—a black T-shirt, dark leaves, or a swath of black foam padding all work. Place the batteries on top of the material, seal the bag, and place it in direct sunlight. The sun will heat the dark materials, trapping the resulting warm air inside the bag. The batteries should heat up sufficiently for a few seconds or minutes of emergency use.

38 SANITIZE DISGUSTING HYDRATION BLADDERS

Store a hydration bladder improperly during those weeks and months between hunting and fishing seasons, and you'll wind up with a world-class mildew, mold, and gunk farm. To clean a bladder, mix a solution of $1/2$ teaspoon of bleach to 1 quart of warm water. Stir well, then pour into the bladder. Shake the bladder to coat all sides, and use a cotton swab to clean the cap threads. Hold the bladder over a sink and squeeze the bite valve to clean out the tubing. Empty the bleach solution, rinse twice, then flush with a solution of 1 teaspoon of baking soda to 1 quart of water. Flush with tap water a few more times.

To store between seasons, make a bladder hanger from a coat hanger. Cut off one of the arms that extends from the hook to the tip of the hanger. Thread the bladder on the hanger rung, and hang to dry and store. If it will be a few months before you use the bladder, store in a freezer.

39 PORTAGE CANOE AND GEAR

I thought I knew how to pack for a canoe trip—then I went paddling with a few Canadian friends. They made me look like some pioneer hawking fry pans in the backcountry.

Start with a monstrous portage pack, such as the indomitable Boundary Pack. Loaded like a standard backpack, there's still room for tackle bags and vests, daypacks, maps, and all the other crap that winds up strewn from bow to stern. Unless we plan to use our paddles as makeshift hiking staffs, we lash them, along with fishing rods, to the underside of the canoe seats.

Next, it's Canadian clean-and-jerk time. One paddler shimmies into the lightest portage pack and single-mans the canoe on his shoulders. The other paddler double-packs, with the heaviest pack on his back, and front-carries a lighter one by threading arms backwards through the shoulder harness. To be honest, with such a load, I sometimes peter out halfway down the trail. But there's a substantial psychic reward in at least humping the bulk of the gear partway in one giant effort.

40 CARRY A BACKPACKING BOAT ANCHOR

If you portage a canoe much or haul one into distant fishing holes, you know how much precious room a heavy folding anchor takes up in a pack. Solution: a basketball net. Tie off the bottom with a short piece of rope. When you need it, fill it with a few rocks, and tie off the other end with an anchor line.

41 DRY BOOTS WITH A HOT ROCK

You almost made it across the creek—but now your feet are soaked, your boots are sloshing, and you're headed for misery, if not frostbite. There are no quick fixes to drowned boots, so don't hold off. As soon as you're in camp, strip off socks and shoes and get to work. Propping boots in front of the fire is one solution, but it's hard on rubber, hell on leather, and leaves a boot's inner workings still moist enough to soak your last dry pair of socks. Here's how to dry them from the inside out.

STEP 1 Remove the insoles and set them aside. Pack boots with absorbent material: paper towels or newspaper if you have them, dry leaves and grasses if you don't. Remove the materials and repeat until you've gotten as much moisture out as possible.

STEP 2 Heat rocks in boiling water or near the fire, then carefully place in spare socks or a bandana. Test the stones for 10 seconds to make sure they don't scorch the material, then fill up the boot. Or pour boiling water into water bottles or smaller spice bottles. Tuck the smaller bottles into the boot foot, and stand a full-sized water bottle in the shank.

STEP 3 While your boots are cooking, work on the insoles. Press them between spare clothing, paper towels or dried grasses, and squeeze hard to express water. Toss them in the bottom of your sleeping bag for the final overnight finish.

STEP 4 If you can't resist the temptation to prop boots and insoles by the fire, go easy. Fire-baked leather will crack and synthetic material can melt. Insoles can harden in the heat without much of a visual warning. If you can't press your hand to the warmed boot and leave it there, move it back from the fire.

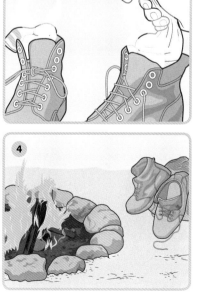

42 KEEP GEAR DRY

There are lots of reasons to store camp foods in vacuum bags. Cuts of meat and poultry lie more or less flat, so they take up less room in a cooler. Vacuum bags don't permit food smells to permeate. And vacuum bags are watertight, so it's no big deal if your sealed-tight cheese goes swimming in the cooler slop.

But don't stop with the cold cuts. Use vacuum bags to keep these items dry, handy, and safely stored in duffels and day packs.

- Strike-anywhere matches
- Spare ammunition
- Change of thermal underwear and socks
- Maps
- Batteries
- Hunting and fishing licenses
- Toilet paper
- Trail snacks
- Items you don't want to rattle while hunting on the move (spare game calls, compasses, survival items)

43 MAKE A BACKWOODS ENERGY DRINK

Smooth and staghorn sumac are found across most of eastern America, and the tall clusters of red berries produce a tart drink—like Kool-Aid gone wild. Look for the shrubby trees in open sun; the upright berry clusters are on the tips of leafy branches. (Stay away from poison sumac. It prefers wet, boggy soils, and the white to pale green berries hang down like grape clusters.) Sumac-Aid is best made with summer berries that are fully ripened, but before heavy rains dilute their potency.

STEP 1 Collect six to eight clusters—called panicles—of sumac berries. Examine closely for spiders and bugs.

STEP 2 Place the panicles in a pitcher and add ½ gallon of cold water. Wash your hands, then reach in the pitcher and agitate the berries to rub off the red coverings that contain most of the flavoring.

STEP 3 Let steep for up to two hours—taste occasionally to monitor tartness. Strain through cheesecloth.

STEP 4 Add maple syrup, honey, or sugar to taste. Serve chilled or over ice.

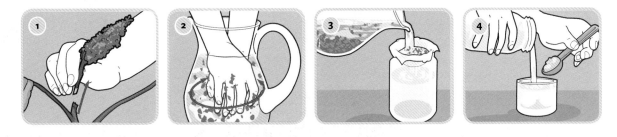

44 BAKE CAMP BISCUITS

Use a pair of foil pie pans as a makeshift backcountry camp oven. Lightly grease the bottom and sides of each. Place the biscuits in one pie pan, leaving ½ inch or so of space between the batter and the sides. Invert the other pie tin on top, and wrap the whole shebang in heavy-duty aluminum foil. Cook on a grill over coals or on the coals themselves. Figure 15 minutes, and flip them at the midpoint. Reusable. Recyclable. Sustainable.

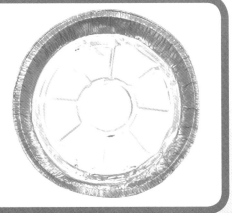

45 PACK LUNCH IN A WATER BOTTLE

Breakfast is simple. Dinner is meat. Lunch? It's always a problem. You don't want to take the time to cook. You don't want to pull out half your gear to prepare a meal. And you don't want yet another bagel and salami. Here's the solution: At home, grab a wide-mouth water bottle. Loosely roll up a few tortillas and place them inside, letting them unroll so they lie against the sides. Add a vacuum-packed foil pouch of tuna or chicken. Toss in a hunk of cheese and a small spice bottle filled with black beans. Presto! All the makings of a backcountry wrap, in a bombproof container.

46 COOK CAMPFIRE BROWNIES WITH AN ORANGE

We're not turning our backs on the venerable S'more, but there's nothing wrong with a little camp-goodie variety. Baking brownies inside a hollowed-out orange creates a moist, citrus-scented dessert, and you don't even have to hold a stick.

Start by cutting one end off the oranges and hollowing out the pulp, all the way down to the white pith on the insides of the peels. Add a bit of fresh-squeezed orange juice to prepared brownie mix, and spoon the batter into the orange peels until three-quarters full. Place the orange top back on and wrap with two layers of heavy-duty foil.

Cook in ashes—not in flames—by inserting the oranges into hollowed out pockets of coals, and shovel a few coals all the way over the top. Make a few extras so you can pull them out after 10 minutes or so and test for doneness.

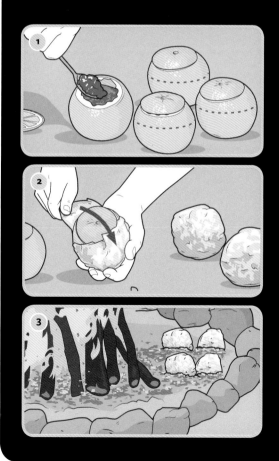

47 TRICK OUT A MUD-PROOF ATV

Unless you live in the desert, your ATV's biggest challenge is likely to be good old-fashioned mud. While ATVs are trail-worthy right off the factory floor, you can take your machine's performance up several notches with shade-tree mechanic skills and a modest cash investment. "If you can change the oil in your truck, you can handle most of this," says Rick Sosebee, an off-road guru and the ATV blogger on fieldandstream.com. Here are Sosebee's five ATV upgrades that will boost your machine's mud-eating potential in half-a-day's work.

PULL HARD You're going to get stuck. Be prepared with a winch whose pulling power is rated at least twice the weight of your machine. That way you'll have plenty of reserve for uphill tugs. Make sure the components are sealed for a waterproof unit; water resistant is not good enough.

GEAR UP Recalibrate the CVT (continuously variable transmission) with an upgrade kit. "This changes the engagement of the transmission so the motor ramps up into a higher power range before engaging the drive," Sosebee says. The result: less spin, more get up and go-through-the-muck. Many kits are available with the tools required. It's a three-hour job, give or take, and any hobbyist grease monkey could pull it off.

DO TREAD ON THESE Upgrade to a mud tire. Look for a lug at least 1 inch deep and in an open pattern with plenty of spacing between the lugs. Sosebee particularly likes a broken-chevron pattern, in which the two sides of a V come in from the right and left and cross at the centerline of the tire.

STOP GAPS To keep grime out of differentials, extend a hose from the differential vent up to the steering bracket. You can cap it with an inexpensive fuel filter to double the protection. While you're at it, remove CVT covers and run a $1/4$-inch bead of silicone around the rims, then replace. It's a snap. "If you can caulk cracks around your house to keep air from coming in," Sosebee says, "you can caulk CVT covers to keep water out."

GET A GRIP Many factory grips are too smooth for real mud work. Look for a honeycomb pattern that will shed muck and water just like a mud tire.

48 BUCK A LOG WITH AN AXE

You round a trail corner and groan: A fallen tree blocks the path. Your buddy's default response is to stomp to the back of the truck, pull out the chain saw, check the tension, futz around for fuel, find ear plugs, and look for safety glasses. By the time he walks back to the log, you have bucked the tree into pieces with little more than an axe and attitude. Smirking follows.

Bucking a log this way is not a beginner skill. It's best to have experience with an axe and to wear protective clothing. Stand on top of the log and chop a V-notch into the side, between your feet, using a six-stroke count: Make three swings angling in from the right—the first one high on the log, then low, and then in the middle. Next, repeat with swings angling in from the left—high, low, and middle. On that sixth and final stroke, flick your wrist slightly outward—an inch will do—the instant the bit bites wood. This will help toss the chips out of the notch and prevent the axe from sticking.

Cut halfway through one side of the log, then turn around and chop another V-notch through the other side. Plan the Vs so the tips of the two notches are slightly offset. This prevents the final stroke from over-traveling and sending the axe bit between your legs and the handle into your nuts at warp factor 9.

49 SPLIT CAMP WOOD WITH A TIRE

Old tires piled up in the garage? Don't think of them as eyesores. Those are handy wood-splitting devices that can save you time and trips to the chiropractor. Stack spare tires on top or around a chopping block, and those worn-out Goodyears hold wood rounds in place while you work axe magic. You can load the tire with multiple smaller pieces to split, or one large round to work into quarters. The wood stays inside the tire, so you can split smaller and smaller pieces without having to bend over and pick them up each time the axe falls. When the wood splits cleanly, the tire helps keep your axe from biting deeply into the block. Miss the round entirely—hey, it happens—and the tire catches the errant edge and guards your legs against a horrific gash.

There are a couple of variations, depending on the size of your chopping block. Just remember to drill holes or cut drainage slits into the lower sidewalls of the tires so they won't collect rainwater for breeding mosquitoes.

For larger chopping blocks (A), use a single tire. To hold the tire in place, use a heavy knife to create tabs along the sidewall on the side of the tire facing the ground. Cut through the rim bead and a couple of inches into the sidewall, depending on the diameter of your block. Slide the tire onto the top of the block, tabs facing the ground, leaving plenty of tire above the block surface to hold up the wood rounds. Nail these tabs into the side of the chopping block.

Use a smaller block (B) that will fit completely inside spare tires, and stack four tires with the block in the middle. The top tire needs to extend above the chopping block surface. Tie the tires together with parachute cord. This arrangement provides stability to smaller splitting blocks.

50 HAUL FIREWOOD WITH A WEB STRAP

To make a handy wood hauler, take a broken 1-inch ratchet strap, cut off the end with the hook, and tie a loop at that end. Lay the strap on the ground and pile sticks on it, then pull the male end through the female end and throw the bundle over your shoulder. You can carry twice as much wood in half the time.

51 ROLL A PAPER LOG

You can make a lightweight, compact fire log using just an old newspaper, water, and string. Take your paper and roll it into a tight cylinder and tie it with string. Next, soak it in water. After a couple of days of drying, the brittle paper will catch a flame quick, and the "log" will keep its form for a longer burn.

52 DIG A DAKOTA FIRE HOLE

Native Americans used a Dakota fire hole to hide cooking fires from their enemies. These small pits also excel in windy conditions and consume less wood while burning hotter than open fires. Plus, the layout provides a great platform for cooking. Here's how to channel your inner Sioux.

The fire hole works by sucking fresh air into the combustion chamber. Hot air rises from the hole, drawing air through the air vent and into the base of the fire. The cycle is self-sustaining, and digging the air vent on the upwind side of the fire hole helps capture the breeze like the air scoop on the Bandit's Trans Am.

Dig the fire chamber first. Excavate a pit 1 foot in diameter and 1 foot deep. Now widen the base of the chamber a few inches so it has a jug-like shape. This lets you burn slightly larger pieces of wood.

Dig the air tunnel next. Start about a foot away from the edge of the fire hole, on the upwind side, and carve out a mole-like tunnel 5 or 6 inches in diameter, angling down to the base of the fire chamber.

That's it. Top the fire hole with a grate or green saplings to hold a pot over the flames. When you break camp, refill the holes and leave no trace.

53 BURN YOUR GEAR INTO A HOT INFERNO

Marshmallows make awesome firestarters. What other odds and ends will burn long enough to catch a fire? Cheetos and greasy potato chips, for sure. Hand sanitizer. Plastic fishing baits. First aid bandages. Duct tape.

54 HANG A POT OVER A FIRE THREE WAYS

Forked sticks were the original duct tape—they could be used to make snares, make repairs, and hold down a buddy as you sawed off a gangrenous leg. (Maybe that last is a bit of a stretch.) But they do play a big role in one of the most basic of all outdoor skills: getting a pot boiling.

Technique A allows you to raise or lower the pot by adjusting the placement of the log.

Technique B is used on ground too hard to drive in a stick.

Technique C is downright futuristic: Unhook the stick from the short forked stick and you can swing the pot away from the fire.

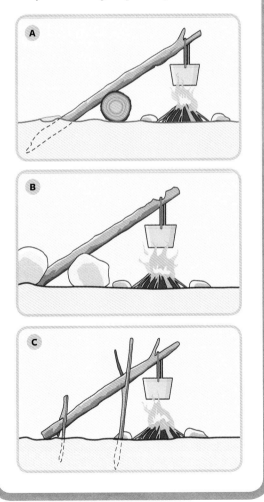

55 MAKE A SUMMER FIRE

The log cabin council fire is a great summer blaze: It puts out plenty of light with less heat than other campfire lays, and burns a long time with smaller pieces of fuel so you don't break a sweat hauling Yule logs back to camp. It's a bit of a pyro mash up. The outside is a log cabin fire built of slow-burning green wood, inside of which burns a teepee fire that throws out tall flames to light your way.

SHELL CONSTRUCTION First, build the outer shell of a log cabin fire. Start with two 6-inch-diameter logs about 24 inches long, and build a log cabin fire of 2 logs for each of 4 "stories," using smaller logs as you go up. Choose whole green logs or branches of a slow-burning wood that won't throw a lot of sparks, such as white oak, ash, birch, or ironwood. Keep these structural logs whole. Split wood burns more quickly, and you want this to burn very slowly. The log-cabin walls will hold the sticks of the teepee fire upright, and that's the next step.

STOKE THE FURNACE Inside the log cabin structure, build a teepee fire of dry sticks, branches, and split woods. Break some of these pieces into lengths 6 inches taller than the log cabin structure. When burning, they'll produce tall flames that give out plenty of light.

TURN ON THE LIGHT Inside the teepee, lay your tinder bundle and light it. Now use wood as a mood-setting dimmer switch: Feed the teepee fire from the top as the flames consume the wood. If the log cabin walls start to burn too quickly, dose with water to knock back the flames.

56 KNOW YOUR AXES & HATCHETS

At the turn of the 19th century, more than 200 different axe-head patterns were being manufactured in America. In 1925, long after the crosscut saw had largely replaced the axe as an industrial grade tree-feller, True Temper Kelly still offered no less than 28 axe head patterns. The choices are more limited today, but being able to swing an axe—or deftly work a hatchet—remains a core skill of the American outdoorsman. Here's what you need to know to match the edged tool for the woodsy job.

HEAD CASES: FIVE DESIGNS TO KNOW

1 FELLING AXE The classic American axe design, the felling axe evolved into dozens of regional variations such as the Dayton and Jersey axe. The thin, sharp bits excel at tasks that require cross-grain cutting, such as felling trees and removing limbs, but they are not the best choice for splitting wood.

2 BROADAX Designed to shape squared-off corners for timbers and railroad ties, or rounded poles for masts, the broadax was a fundamental tool in American history.

3 HUDSON'S BAY With a smaller handle and head, the Hudson's Bay design was favored by fur traders traveling long distances by canoe. Hefty enough to work through medium-size logs, it's light enough for limbing. Choking up on the slightly elongated beard increases control when shaping wood.

4 PULASKI Mostly used by firefighters and trail construction crews, the Pulaski boasts a traditional cutting bit on one side and a grubbing adze on the other.

5 SPLITTING MAUL The wedge-shaped head splits wood apart along the grain. A poor choice for anything else, splitting mauls are unsurpassed for chopping log rounds into fireplace-ready fuel. Small splitting hatchets bridge the gap between mauls and standard bits and excel around the campsite.

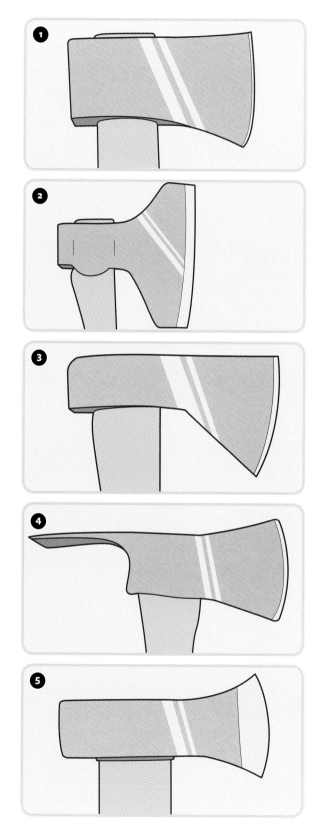

57 NAME THOSE PARTS

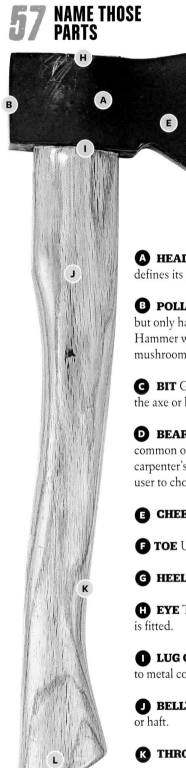

A **HEAD** The shape of an axe or hatchet head defines its primary use: cutting or splitting.

B **POLL** An extended poll helps balance the tool, but only hardened polls are designed for hammering. Hammer with an unhardened poll and you risk mushrooming the head.

C **BIT** General term for the cutting portion of the axe or hatchet head.

D **BEARD** A downward extension of the bit, common on tools designed for shaping wood, such as carpenter's axes and broadaxes. The beard allows the user to choke up the handle to control shaving.

E **CHEEK** Lies between the bit and the poll.

F **TOE** Upper corner of the bit.

G **HEEL** Lower corner of the bit.

H **EYE** The hole in the head where the handle is fitted.

I **LUG OR LIP** Metal protrusion gives more wood to metal contact and helps secure head to handle.

J **BELLY** The long midsection of the handle, or haft.

K **THROAT** The sweep of handle towards the grip.

L **KNOB OR SWELL KNOB** Prevents handle from slipping from sweaty hands.

58 CHOOSE YOUR WEAPON

BIT BY BIT The bit profile is the most important aspect of performance. A thin cutting profile works well when limbing felled trees or cutting campfire wood. A more wedge-shaped profile excels in splitting log rounds.

CONSIDER THE CURVE
A pronounced curve in the bit lessens bit-to-wood contact, allowing for deeper cuts. A flat bit cuts more evenly, but not as deeply.

GET A HANDLE ON IT
Proponents of curved handles consider them more efficient and easier on the hands. Straight-handle fans point out the strength inherent in wood grain running the length of the handle. Both camps claim greater accuracy. The best choice is the one that feels best in your hands.

SINGLE OR DOUBLE?
A double-bit axe can serve double duty. One blade is sharpened to a narrow felling edge for taking down trees. The other is ground to a more blunt edge for working through knots and cutting trees on the ground. The single-bit axe or hatchet has other advantages. The poll can be hardened for hammering, but even an unhardened poll can be pounded with a wood baton to boost the cutting power of hatchet-sized bits.

59 SHARPEN A MACHETE

For lane clearing, you'll want a 25- to 35-degree angle on a machete blade. Anything finer will roll and chip with heavy chopping. Clamp the blade in a vise, edge up, tip pointed toward you. Use a 12-inch bastard mill file, and wear heavy leather work gloves. Push the file into the blade at the proper angle: two 15-degree bevels create a 30-degree blade angle. With a correct angle on one side, turn the machete around and repeat. Finish the edge with a sharpening puck, which you'll carry into the field for touch-ups.

60 FINISH A BLADE WITH A LEATHER STROP

Using a leather strop to hone a blade to a whisker-shaving edge isn't just for small-town barbers. This final stage in the sharpening process removes the tiny burrs, nicks, and microscopic rolled edges left by even the finest-grit stones. To polish a knife edge with a leather strop, the knife must be quite keen in the first place. Then it's a simple matter of taking the edge to atom-splitting sharpness.

You can use a leather belt, but better results come from a bench strop, which is honing leather mounted to a block of wood. Charge the strop with a thin film of honing compound made from either chromium oxide or diamond paste. Chromium oxide is a favorite of many, but if the blade is made of the newer, harder stainless steels, diamond paste may be required.

Lay the knife on the leather nearly flat. Draw the edge backwards along the leather strop. The leather will conform to the profile of the knife edge. Start with very light pressure and increase if needed. Start with a dozen strokes to each side of the blade.

Once the knife, is shaving-sharp, wipe the blade clean with a few drops of honing oil.

61 | SHARPEN AN AXE

Before you begin, place your beat-up axe in a vise, with the head facing up. No vice? Use a stout C-clamp to secure it to the edge of a workbench with the edge just hanging over the table. Since you always push the file into the edge, never pulling it toward you, you'll need heavy gloves.

RESTORE THE PROFILE Hold the file and work it into the edge, maintaining the file at about 15 degrees. You want to work back into the axe head about 2 to 3 inches at the middle point of the bit, forming a clam-shaped effect on the cheek. When you can feel a burr on the backside of the blade, repeat the whole process on the other side.

SHARPEN IT Put a primary bevel into the first bevel by filing again, this time at a 10-degree angle on both sides. Hone with a whetstone, coarse side, then the fine, moving a honing puck in small, circular motions.

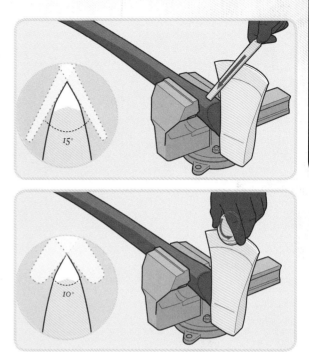

62 | GIVE YOUR KNIFE A SPA TREATMENT

Fixed-blades need only a quick wipe down with a damp cloth after each use and a light application of honing oil on the blade.

Folders and multitools collect blood and dirt at pivot points and locking mechanisms. If the tool has a plastic handle, immerse it in boiling water for one minute, then put it in a pot of warm water (so that quick cooling doesn't crack the handle). Scrub nooks and crannies with a toothbrush, working pivot points back and forth, then air-dry the knife before oiling. Use compressed air to blast out gunk.

Wipe away surface rust with an oily cloth or 0000 steel wool. Carbon blades naturally discolor with use. Bring them back to near original luster by rubbing with a cork dipped in cold wood ashes.

63 | SHARPEN USING A SHARPIE

When sharpening a knife (or axe or hatchet), it can be difficult to know for certain that you are maintaining the proper angle, and sharpening the exact edge and not the "shoulder" of the bevel. One way to tell is to "paint" the edge with a Sharpie or other marker. Look closely after each few strokes. If the ink is removed at the very edge of the knife, then you are sharpening the edge. If the ink comes off on the shoulder, leaving color on the edge, your angle is to shallow. If all the ink is being removed, you're re-profiling the edge to match the original angle. It's a great way to monitor your progress.

64 PREPACK FOR CAMPING

Organization wins the day. Buy three large plastic storage bins for the garage or basement and designate them for camping gear. In one, store sleeping pads, air mattresses, pumps, sleeping bags, cots, tents, and tarps. In another, pack up stoves, pots and pans, lanterns, hatchets, saws, and other camp tools. Keep the third bin stocked with items you'll need for camp and kitchen: a small bag of favorite spices, toilet paper and paper towels, camp soap, spare rope, first aid kit. Resist the temptation to raid the bins while you're at home and down to your last paper towel. Now all you have to do is load the bins into the truck, and half your work is done. At camp, the empty bins serve as great dirty laundry hampers and dry storage for firewood until it's time to pack up and head home.

No matter how you store and pack your gear, pack the tent and raincoats last, near the tailgate or on top of the trunk space, where you can retrieve them quickly without burrowing through a mountain of bins and bags.

65 ORGANIZE A GIANT DUFFEL

After a day or two at camp, a cavernous duffel bag devolves into a jumbled morass of clothes and equipment. Stop wasting your time rooting through this mess and get organized.

STEP 1 Buy some inexpensive stuff sacks in various colors and sizes, one for each different type of item you're packing: shirts, pants, rain gear, socks, underwear, and so on.

STEP 2 Roll clothing into tubes the length of the designated sack, and slide them in. Half a dozen shirts fit in a medium-size sack.

STEP 3 Your color-coded system helps you locate the item you want. Retrieving it is as simple as pulling the roll free while everything else stays in place—it's like removing a Vienna sausage from a can.

STEP 4 Pack spare gear such as headlamps, ammunition, and extra batteries in clear plastic resealable bags or small clear plastic dry bags.

STEP 5 Stuff your monstrous duffel with these smaller sacks, and you'll never spend another minute wondering where you put your favorite long underwear.

66 WHIP FINISH A ROPE

Certain details speak to the very soul of old-school outdoors. Think tattered chaps, cheap rubber hippers, and handlebar mustaches. Ropes tipped with a whip finish inhabit the same authentic terrain—that is, they look slicker than snot. And a rope with a whip finish can sometimes one-up the modern standby of holding the frizzled end to a fire, which can create a mushroom-like tip that is hard to work through a knot or may crack with hard use. Follow these illustrations for the basic whip-finish knot. One of the best things to use for whipping ropes: waxed dental floss. New-school twist: A few drops of superglue on the whip finish will lock the knot down even tighter.

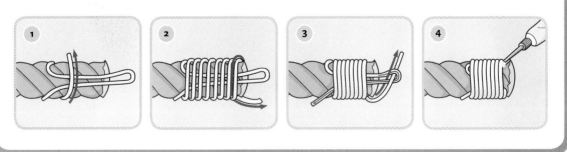

67 GO BEYOND DUCT TAPE

Duct tape is sent from heaven, no doubt. But here are 5 other sticky strips to have and to hold.

GORILLA TAPE Think duct tape 2.0, with a double-thick adhesive layer that grips surfaces as uneven as rusty metal, masonry, and lightly furrowed tree bark. The fabric itself is twice as thick as standard duct tape, with offset textile patterns that the manufacturer claims make it 145 percent stronger than duct tape 1.0. Its only shortcoming: Gorilla Tape doesn't stretch.

TENACIOUS TAPE Made from tough nylon tent fabric, this strong repair tape closes up rips in tents, tarps, sleeping bags, packs, and down jackets. Designed for field use, it lasts practically forever, and ratty strips on a scarred-up coat are badges of honor. Unlike off-the-shelf duct tape, it leaves no sticky residue when removed. Available in a half-dozen colors, plus clear.

RESCUE TAPE This self-fusing silicone tape chemically bonds to itself, creating an air-tight, waterproof seal almost instantly. It's perfect for field fixes of leaky hydraulic and radiator hoses on outboards and ATV fuel and water lines. It insulates 8,000 volts per layer and stretches easily, so it's a go-to tape for exposed metal connections and tool handle wraps.

TREAD TAPE Made with a textured, rubberized finish for ladder treads and outdoor steps, tread tape comes in rolls and strips. Use it to wrap climbing stand rails for a better grip, provide extra purchase on the bottom of a boat, and for a slip-resistant upgrade to ladder stand steps. Wrap handgun pistol grips and bow grips for a firm hold during warm weather seasons.

SINGLE-SIDED AUTOMOTIVE FOAM TAPE Cheap and easy to find, foam tape will soundproof climbing stands and metal shooting rails and protect rods from rubbing against boat seats and casting decks. Fold a small piece over metal zipper pulls and trim tightly for sound- and glint-proofing parkas and packs.

68 CARRY A TINY ROLL OF DUCT TAPE

Duct tape can be a lifesaver. But carrying an entire roll takes up valuable space inside a backpack—and you probably won't need that much tape. Instead, wrap a couple feet around a small lighter, or wrap longer lengths around a water bottle.

69 PROTECT LANTERN GLOBES WITH DUCT TAPE

If you're shipping a camping lantern on an airplane or just plan to haul the lantern over rough roads in your vehicle, protect the glass globe by wrapping with packing or duct tape before the trip.

70 SHOW A LANTERN SOME LOVE

Let a white gas-operated lantern sit around for months—or worse, years—and it may have trouble holding enough air pressure to work correctly. To recondition the pump assembly, remove the pump plunger. If the washerlike cup assembly is made of leather, work mink oil into the assembly. If it's neoprene, use light-duty oil, such as 3-in-One. The treatment allows it to expand for a tight, light-giving seal.

71 RIG A CANOE WITH PAINTER LINES

Buy a canoe and think it's ready for the water? Wrong. You need to spend an hour rigging that boat with painter lines fore and aft, and shock cord loops on the bow and stern plates for stowing those lines. Now you're able to pull your boat to shore, tug it off a rock, or line it up a rapid.

Painter lines are nothing more than ropes tied to a canoe's bow and stern. Lines 15 to 20 feet long work well, and use rope hefty enough that it is comfortable to pull. Never attach painter lines to handles, thwarts, or deck plates. You can pull them off under heavy loads. Instead, drill a hole through the hull 2 inches below the gunwales at bow and stern, and tie the lines with a bowline looped through the holes. To keep the lines out of the way, tuck coiled lines under a short length of bungee cord attached to holes drilled 6 inches apart through the deck plates.

If you don't want lines stacked on top of the deck plates, learn to tie a gasket coil to keep them ready and tangle free.

STEP 1 Coil the rope, leaving one end a few inches longer than the coil itself. Wrap the working end of the rope around the middle of the coil to form a half-dozen wraps.

STEP 2 Form a bight in the working end of the rope, and push it through the top loop formed in the coil.

STEP 3 Spread out the bight and pull it over the top end of the coil.

STEP 4 Snug this bight down to the existing wraps, and pull slack out of the working end.

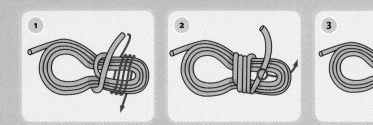

72 RIG A PACK ON THE SPOT WITH PARACORD

Need a pack in a jiffy? Use paracord and three branches to whip together a makeshift packboard and get hauling. Lash together a triangle of three stout sticks so that the width of the triangle is about the width of your waist. Make a shoulder harness with braided paracord, attached as shown. Lash duffel bags, bedrolls, tents, or a bear's hide to the packframe.

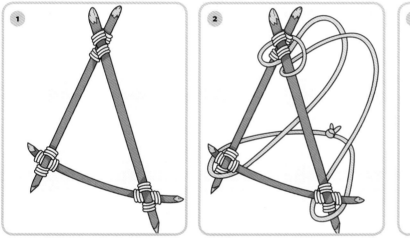

73 MAKE A CAMP TABLE WITH PARACORD

You can make a quick camp table with sticks, paracord, and the most basic of lashing techniques.

Drive a pair of sharpened sticks into the ground 2 to 4 feet from the trunk of tree. The diameter of the tree sets the distance between the sticks.

Lash 2 horizontal supports from the tree trunk to the top of each vertical stick.

Tie down a grillwork of cross sticks to the two horizontal supports. For an even quicker version, lash down cross sticks a few inches apart, and wedge other sticks between them.

THE CANOE BARREL

I'm a sucker for classic camping gear, from Duluth packs to Opinel knives to paper topographic maps. They have patina and class and hard-won authenticity.

None of this can be said of my most recent camping gear love: the canoe barrel. These hard-plastic containers are the best solution I've come across for packing food, cookware, and stoves for camping trips, whether I'm off for a week in a canoe or a weekend 20 feet from the truck tailgate. They are entirely waterproof, and tough enough to survive a swim through a Class V rapid. You can check them on an airplane. They make a nifty camp chair. The top doubles as a cutting and fish-cleaning board. Bread goes uncrushed for eternity. I can fit 10 days' of grub in a 60-liter canoe barrel, and still have room for the stove. They're not bear-proof by any means, but I've yet to meet the raccoon that can get inside one. They are ugly, available in a single shade of blue that is unknown in nature. But they bury the needle when it comes to usefulness.

Canoe barrels are the modern replacement for one of the most cherished pieces of canoe-tripping gear, the *wanigan*. Woven of ash or crafted of wood panels, wanigans were handed down from generation to generation. The very word wanigan is a honeyed term that comes from the Ojibway *wa·nikka·n*, meaning a pit in the ground for storage.

The canoe barrel is freighted with neither heritage nor charm. According to Kevin "The Happy Camper" Callan, one of Canada's most authoritative canoe trekkers, the canoe pack barrel has only been around since the 1980s, when a group of Ottawa canoe guides were casting about for better ways to protect food on long trips. They picked up a few old olive barrels from delicatessens and yard sales, and the rest is a story of function over form.

I ordered my canoe barrel from Recreational Barrel Works, of Peterborough, Ontario. I had a hard time finding a stateside distributor, although these days a few hardcore paddle shops in Wisconsin and Minnesota stock canoe barrels. I've gussied it up with a slick padded harness and a set of barrel bags that help organize gear, which I strongly endorse. Once a spice bottle or can opener finds its way into a canoe barrel's yawning maw, it will disappear into the abyss, as if swallowed by an enormous blue lava lamp. It might take years to find it, but rest assured: Once retrieved, it will be in perfect condition.

THE ART AND SCIENCE OF DIY

The Ozark Puffball was born on a picnic table in Missouri's Montauk State Park, where photographer Colby Lysne and I sat drinking beer and licking our wounds after an unimpressive show of fishing skill at one of the premier trout parks in the Show-Me state. All morning long, stocker trout had snubbed our dough baits, following them through slow riffles, eyeing them warily in the pools, but simply refusing to eat. We were stumped, but not yet beaten. It seemed that we needed some kind of hack for the lowly ball of scented dough, some trigger to turn the trout's obvious interest into a committed bite. The Puffball was Lysne's idea–I'll give him full credit–but it fell to me to field-engineer the innovation.

Our solution was to fasten a pea-sized glob of fluorescent orange PowerBait to a tiny #16 treble hook. Next, we smeared the glob with a skim of Secret Bait, a dough-and-glitter conglomeration made by some Ozark hillbilly and sold in every trout park for miles around. A split shot and split-second timing were the only other ingredients.

To work the Puffball's magic, I'd cast it downstream and watch the drift until a trout eyeballed the mutant wad but refused to eat. That's when I'd snap the rod tip, telegraphing a pulse of energy down the line, which jerked the Puffball just enough to release a brown smudge of atomized Secret Bait into the stream. Intrigued by the piquant fog, the fish would then spot the orange PowerBait emerging from the mist. It would be like waking up from a dream about Thanksgiving dinner to find a ham biscuit on your pillow. The wiliest trout couldn't resist.

Unorthodox? You betcha. But jerry-rigging a doughball is just par for the course for the avid angler. Fishing seems to bring out the shade-tree design engineer in outdoorsmen. With fishing, the margin between success and failure is often tippet-thin—and dependant on an angler's ability to innovate, modify, and adjust gear to specific conditions. Trim a spinnerbait's rubber skirt by a half-inch and you might double your rate of hook-ups. Upgrade a baitcaster's gears and you can rip lunker bass from the thickest weeds. Make your own fly rod and you can save hundreds of dollars.

And most fishing gear tweaks and hacks are cheap and easy. In fact, a lot of the tricks in this book require little more than odds and ends you likely have in your basement or garage right now. A small finishing nail to give a soft-plastic crayfish a more lifelike action. Leftover plywood for a worm box. An old coffee can to convert to a leech trap.

That's so much of the fun of fishing—figuring out how to use what's close at hand to better your odds at catching fish. After all, it's not enough to know where the fish are. It's not enough to be able to make the perfect cast or tie a gorgeous fly. You have to put a hook in the fish. You have to convince your quarry to eat whatever you've tied to the end of your line. Sometimes that's easy. Sometimes that's nearly impossible. You never know until you've done everything you can to stack the deck in your favor.

I learned that lesson down on Florida's Suwannee River, in a tip you can read about in this chapter. Sometimes the smallest tweaks can make a huge difference. During the spring spawn, the male redbreast sunfish, known in the South as a "robin," is a riot of crimson, green, and blue colors. Fishing for redbreast is a tradition so steeped in Southern culture that it's the subject of local festivals and highbrow doctoral dissertations. Jim Greek and Billy Cason, however, were less concerned about the

robin's role in the fabric of rural experience than in how to entice one onto a hook.

When I ran across this pair of anglers, they were each 64 years old and had forged a deep friendship based on a love of bream fishing. Thirteen years earlier, Cason was running a backhoe on his peanut farm when Greek, his neighbor-through-the-woods, dropped by to ask if he might have time to push dirt over his trash heap. Cason was there within 30 minutes. A couple of days later, they went fishing together for the first time. Ever since, they've fished two or three days a week. Every week. These boys know how to catch a robin, and they were happy to share their secrets.

"I think a worm's about the sorriest bait there is, at least for river fish," Greek told me matter-of-factly, as he threaded a cricket on a hook. Their go-to rig was a #6 extra-light wire hook topped with a small orange bead and a $1/16$-ounce bullet weight. But it was the bobber they fussed over most carefully. Each one was hacked very specifically.

I won't tell you how, not right here. Just turn to item #151 for the details. But I'll tell you this. Their change resulted in a cooler slam-full of robin, and a riverside fish fry I'll never forget. "It makes the line slide through the cork easier," Greek explained about their tweak. "It don't get hung up as bad, and drifts deeper. Sometimes those little changes make a difference."

As in all the difference.

74 SUPERCHARGE A LURE WITH A NAIL

With nothing more than a simple nail, you can make your softbait do all kinds of crazy moves. Here are a few.

A HANG YOUR HEAD Make a wacky-rigged worm or Senko even wackier by putting a small finishing nail into the head of the bait. The soft plastic will flail more erratically.

B MAKE A BACKDROP Push a nail into a soft-plastic shad's back just ahead of the tail and run a plain hook through the nose. The lure will drop back when you pause the retrieve.

C STICK IN THEIR CRAW Put a finishing nail into the tail of a soft-plastic crawfish and hook the bait through the head. The nail keeps bait and hook at a better fish-hooking angle.

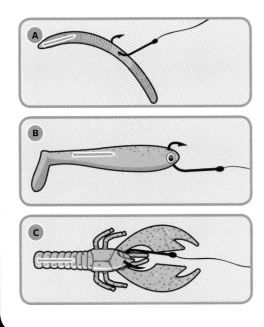

75 HACK YOUR PLASTICS

You don't have to fish with a standard lure. With a careful trim, your lures can take on new life.

A MAKE A MINISKIRT One solution to bass tapping at your spinnerbait without connecting is to add a trailer hook. That's fine for open water but can result in more snags around any structure. Instead, trim the skirt so it hangs evenly with the hook bend.

B SHAVE YOUR LEGS Sometimes bass grab the skirt legs of a hollow-body frog lure and miss the hook. Trimming legs back even ½ inch can reduce short strikes and actually give frogs a smoother side-to-side glide when "walking the dog."

C TAKE A BACK SEAT How many times have you reeled up a curly-tailed grub with no tail? Solve this by cutting away a portion of the front so the hook sits just in front of the tail. Cut back a soft-plastic shad for the same hook placement.

76 MAKE A WOODEN DOWEL POPPER

Making custom diving lures is a challenge. Lips, weights, balance, and buoyancy all factor in to getting one to swim properly. But making a popper is cheap and easy. All you need is a wooden dowel, some screw-in eyelets, hooks, split rings, and some simple tools, like a drill and sandpaper.

Cut the dowel to your desired length, taper one end of the cut piece with the sandpaper, drill out the mouth with a large bit, and screw an eyelet into the tail, the belly, and the mouth. How you decorate the popper is up to you, but it will float and it will pop, and you need not be an engineer to get it right.

77 AVOID TREBLE

I recently spent half an hour un-trebling a trio of snarled plugs and—more than once—I've had to extract trebles from human flesh. And they can rip fish mouths to pieces. If you're fishing with kids, especially, replace treble hooks.

Most spinner hooks aren't attached with a split ring, so use side-cutting wire snips to remove the trebles. If the hook eye is particularly stout, clip it in two places to create a gap, and slip it off the body wire. Replace with open-eye hooks.

Before replacing trebles, evaluate the track of topwater and diving lures so you can compare their performance with single hooks. Most will do fine. For many largemouth baits, replace the hooks with some 1/0 or 2/0 ringed live-bait hooks. Remove the belly treble entirely, or just replace it with a ringed live-bait hook with its point facing forward. The point on your trailing hook should face up.

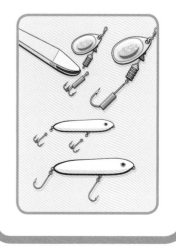

Working just an hour or two a night, you can build a fly rod in less than a week, and fish with your handmade custom beauty for the rest of your life. Rod kits contain all the components and instructions, and you can use rod blanks that vary from basic to cutting-edge.

→ **SEAT THE REEL** Find the hood recess at the base of the handle. You'll probably need to enlarge it slightly to fit the reel seat hood. A rotary tool works well. Set the handle aside.

Use $\frac{1}{2}$-inch-wide masking tape to create two bushings under the place where you'll glue the reel seat, just thick enough so that the reel seat fits snugly over the bushings. Spread waterproof two-part epoxy over these bushings, then slowly slide the reel seat into place. As you slide the reel seat down, fill all gaps with epoxy. Attach the butt cap with epoxy.

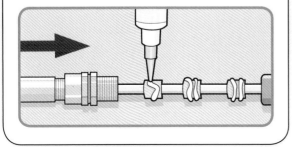

→ **TOP IT OFF** Use epoxy to glue the tip top in place.

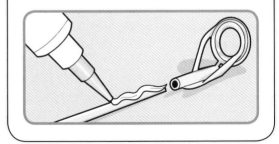

→ **HANDLE IT** The rod channel needs to be custom fitted to your blank, so use a tapered rat-tail file to create a good fit. Go easy and check the fit frequently. You should have to use gentle pressure to fit the handle into place. Once you have it right, prepare the blank by gently sanding under the handle with 200-grit sandpaper. Spread more epoxy at the location of the handle, and slide the cork into place. If your kit has a winding check, glue it into place now.

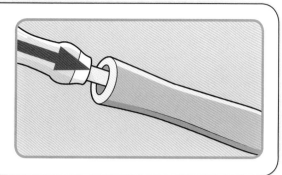

→ **GET GUIDANCE** Taper the end of each guide foot with a fine-metal file. Rod-building kits will come with a spacing chart. Hold guides in place with thin strips of masking tape. For a consistent width, mark up a business card with the desired width of the wrap, and use it as a template to mark the beginning and ending points of each guide wrap with a grease pencil.

Begin by wrapping the rod blank with a half-dozen tight wraps over the tag end of the thread. Snip off the tag and continue. As you spin the rod, angle the thread from the spool slightly so that each wrap is snug against the previous one. To finish a guide wrap, stop when the wrap is $^1/_8$ inch shorter than the planned finished length. Form a loop of monofilament with an overhand knot, pinch it so that the closed end is narrowed, and place this closed end on top of the wraps so that the pinched end sticks out just a bit. Wrap over this loop to the end of your wrap marks and cut the winding thread with a 3-inch tail. Thread this through the exposed end of the loop, then pull back toward the wrap. This will pull the loop and the tag end under the wraps. Trim the excess with an X-Acto knife.

To hold the rod in place and provide thread tension while wrapping the guides, make a rod wrapper: Cut notches in a cardboard box to hold the rod blank horizontal. Run thread under a book and through a small hole punched through the box.

Last, wrap the female end of the ferrule with a $^3/_4$-inch wrap to give it added strength.

Apply rod finish to all the windings. To prevent the finish from running, support the rod in a horizontal position and rotate 90 degrees every minute for 15 minutes.

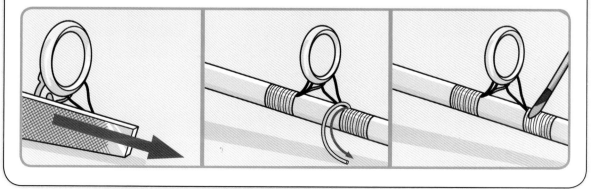

79 MARK FLY LINES

I had wads and wads of mystery fly lines until I started marking each new fly line with a permanent marker: eight tiny little hatch-marks at the end of the fly line for an 8-weight, seven hatch-marks for a 7-weight, etc. Simplified my life and saved money.

80 FLOAT A LINE WITH AN EARPLUG

For a cheap yet effective bobber for light-tackle fishing, use a foam earplug. Just thread the hook through and slide it to the desired position on the line. You can make it a slip bobber by inserting a length of plastic coffee stirrer.

82 DAMPEN LINE TWIST

A big problem for spinning anglers, whether using live bait or lures, is dealing effectively with line twist. This can cause tangles or affect the action of a lure to the point where it won't attract fish. Here's how to keep the line running straight and true.

STEP 1 Close the bail with your hand, not the reel handle. When you turn the handle, the spool also turns slightly before the bail snaps shut, which causes the line to twist.

STEP 2 Set the drag properly. If the line slips too much while you're playing a big fish, you'll end up with line twist.

STEP 3 Let the rod fight the fish. Spooling line under tension creates line twist. When you have a big fish on the line, raise the rod. Reel in line only while lowering the rod (when the line is no longer under tension).

81 FISH A GREASED LEADER

Before strike indicators, fly casters greased leaders to provide bobber action and fly suspension. It's still a great tactic. Fishing with a greased leader suspends pupae and midges at predetermined depths and makes it easier to track the path of a fly by keeping an eye on the floating leader. But there's a cost. A leader floating in the film is more visible to trout. Beware.

Use a thick silicone paste, and smear the goo on your thumb and forefinger. Pinch the leader butt with these fingers, and pull the leader through. Stop a few inches farther from the end of the tippet than the depth you want to suspend the fly.

83 SEE RED (OR NOT)

There are line companies that sell red line because it's supposed to disappear underwater, and lure companies selling red lures and hooks that they say make a lure look like a bleeding baitfish. Confused?

Fish can see color and lots of different hues as it turns out. You get a thumbs-up, then, on adding crimson hooks and those cutting-edge realistic colors to your tacklebox—as long as you're not fishing too deep. Here's why: Red is produced by some of the longest wavelengths in the visible spectrum, and these longer wavelengths are the first to be absorbed by water. That means that the color red nearly disappears in water below, say, 12 or 15 feet. Next to go are oranges, yellows, and greens.

Which is where those red lines are a factor. The deeper you go, the less distinguishable red objects will appear. If you want to fish with red line in shallower water, use a fluorocarbon leader.

84 KNOW YOUR CANOE

The right canoe is the one that can handle the conditions you'll most likely encounter and haul your stuff while allowing you to cast, plunge over a 3-foot ledge, or stay straight out on open water. Here's a guide to features to consider in a fishing canoe.

→ **HULL MATERIAL** Forget aluminum. For a tough, sturdy, maintenance-free craft, there are two choices: cheaper (and heavier and also more susceptible to sun damage) rotomolded polyethylene or the old proven Royalex laminate. If you want to get to where you want to be fast, and there are no rocks in the way, consider a fiberglass hull or a more modern composite such as those including Kevlar. These are the lightest canoes ever made—a 16-footer can tip the scales at less than 45 pounds—but they are expensive.

→ **GUNWALES** The top rails of a canoe, which provide support and rigidity.

→ **BOW FLARE** The outward-sloping sides at the bow of the canoe. Will turn away chop for a drier ride— good for big expanses of whitewater.

→ **BEAM** The boat's maximum width.

→ **TUMBLEHOME** The inward slope of the side as it approaches the gunwale. This helps keep your hands closer to the gunwale as you paddle more easily.

→ **HULL STYLE** A canoe with a traditional style (as shown here) is built with a stern and bow that are similarly shaped, tapering to points at each end. An asymmetric hull is more pointed at the bow than at the stern, which lets the canoe glide more efficiently.

→ **ROCKER** A lift of the canoe bottom at the bow and stern. Rockered boats turn more easily.

THE BOTTOM LINE If you're canoeing out in quiet waters, beamy, rockerless boats are stable enough so you can stand up and cast, and they swallow minnow buckets, tackleboxes, spare rods, and a couple of kids with ease. Crank up the paddling conditions, however, and you'll need more technical goodies. For big-lake fishing with wind and waves, a deeper bow and a more pronounced bow flare will turn away wind-blown chop. If getting to big fish requires finessing through Class III whitewater, you'll definitely want a boat with rocker and a good Royalex layup. No matter the water, a bit of tumblehome makes it easier to land fish over the side.

85 PULL OFF A CHEAP CANOE-CAMP TRIP

It's late spring and the dogwoods have bloomed. The first quail chicks are in the nest. Nothing could be finer. The water is warm enough for a quick dip, the nights still cool enough for a fire. Every element of the natural world is begging with you, pleading with you: Put a paddle in your hand, now.

You're not going to find an easier getaway. In a three-day canoe-camping trip, you might spend 75 bucks if you really try. There's a 90 percent chance that you'll find a canoe-camping river within 20 miles of your garage, and it's a good bet that the gear and food you need are in your gear closet and refrigerator right this very minute.

KEEP IT SIMPLE Grab twenty bucks for gas (maybe $25 tops), another $10 for live bait from the gas station. Pack half the clothes you think you should, because you'll only wear shorts. Bring two rods: a good spinning outfit and a 7-weight fly rod that's light enough to make panfishing fun and heavy enough to handle a middling-size river monster. You'll want simple lures that you can lose in heavy timber—in-line spinners are a good bet—and hooks and sinkers for live-bait rigs. River fish are willing, so pack half the food you think you'll need, and eat what you catch. (Don't scrimp on the frying pan, though. Bring the big one.) Pack a tarp and leave the tent. Stow an extra paddle. Drag live baits along the bottom of the deep scour holes you find on the outside of river bends, and fire those spinners at every blowdown, rock pile, and current seam you pass.

SET ASIDE $40 FOR GROCERIES Make a list on the fingers of one hand. Eggs, bacon, oil, fish batter, and beer. Grab a loaf of bread from the cupboard and rake all the leftover lunch meat into a cooler. Fill some jugs with water. Leave a note for your spouse and food for the dog. Cut the grass so the neighbors won't talk. Go now, right now, before the phone has a chance to ring.

Pared down to the basics, every moment on a river is seasoned with the memory of the moment just before, and the promise of the next river bend, and the next cast, the next shooting star that streaks across the sky and brings a grin to your face when you think of your best wish ever: next weekend, spent just like this.

86 MASTER THE BIMINI TWIST

Tying the Bimini twist seems to be every angler's nightmare—at least among those who haven't tried it. Although it can look intimidating, it isn't all that difficult. After 30 minutes of practice, you should be able to tie this important knot easily. The Bimini creates a doubled line ending in a loop. The doubled line can then be tied directly to a lure, swivel, or hook. Often, a Bimini is tied in a light running line or leader, and the loop is then tied to a heavier shock leader. That's standard procedure in flyfishing for bigger fish like stripers, tarpon, marlin, and tuna.

STEP 1 Start by doubling about 3 feet of line. Hold the tag end and standing line together in your left hand. Put your right hand into the loop at the end. Rotate your right hand clockwise 20 times to make a series of spread-out twists in the doubled line.

STEP 2 While seated with your knees together, use your right hand to spread the end loop over both of your knees. Keep holding the tag end and standing line with your left hand so the twists don't unwind. Now grab the tag end with your right hand, still holding the standing line with your left.

STEP 3 Pull on the line with your hands upward and slightly apart. At the same time, spread your knees to put tension on the loop. This will make the twists pack closer together.

STEP 4 Now move your right hand (tag end of line) downward so the line is roughly perpendicular to the twists, and slightly relax the tension from your right hand. Maintain tension on the loop with your knees and on the standing line with your left hand. You'll feel the tag end start to wrap itself around the twists. Keep loosening tension with only your right hand as the tag end wraps downward, over the twists and to the beginning of the loop over your knees.

STEP 5 Anchor the resulting wraps by making a half hitch with the tag end wrapped around one side of the loop. Then make three half hitches around both loop strands, pulling the hitches up tightly against the base of the wraps. Trim the tag end, breathe a sigh of relief, and try it again.

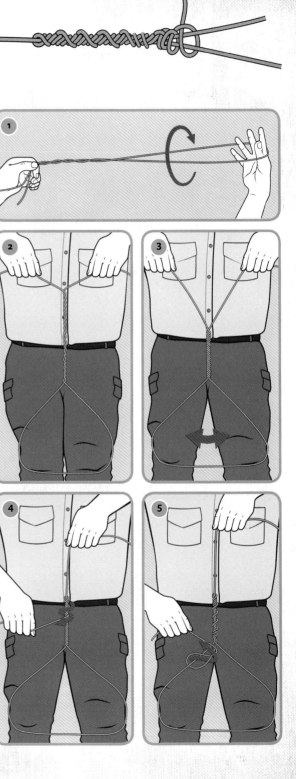

87 RIG A KILLER CANE POLE

The simplest pursuits—such as attempting to catch every panfish in the pond with a cane pole—still benefit from careful attention to detail. Here's how to rig cane the right way.

STEP 1 To keep line kinks to a minimum, use Dacron line and tip it with 2 feet of monofilament leader. You'll need a working line the length of the rod, plus 4 feet.

STEP 2 Tie the line off at the midpoint of the cane pole. Spiral-wrap the line to the tip, and tie it to the pole with a half hitch. If a cruising hawg bass crashes your crappie party and breaks the pole, you'll still be able to fight it to the finish.

STEP 3 Rig the line with a slip bobber that you can peg for varying depths, pinchback split shot, and a longshanked Aberdeen hook to make it easier to slip the point from a fish's mouth.

89 ORGANIZE HOOKS WITH SAFETY PINS

Tired of getting varying styles and sizes of hooks mixed up in your tacklebox? Use safety pins to keep them organized. Simply feed the pin's point through the eyes of the hooks and clip the pin shut. A load of hooks can fit onto one pin, and it's an easy way to keep the different kinds sorted.

88 PATCH GRIP POTHOLES

Favorite rods get used hard and can develop nicks, dents, pits, and cracks in the cork handle that might lead to total breakdown if not patched. Smoothing out a grip is a snap. First, create a few tablespoons of cork dust by sanding an old grip or even wine cork with 60-grit sandpaper. Mix in carpenter's glue in about a 50-50 ratio, and stir to create a thick paste. Next, pick out any loose shreds and pieces of cork in the grip's damage zone, then pack in the cork paste. Use a bit of excess, as the paste will shrink while it dries. Once dry, shape and smooth with 220-grit sandpaper, and you're ready to go.

90 HAVE A MIDDAY QUICKIE

Most family therapists agree that an occasional midday quickie results in greater concentration on work tasks and overall happier relationships. But pulling off a successful lunch-break mini-fishing trip requires a bit of logistical foreplay and the proper tools. Here's the drill.

PLAN IN ADVANCE In addition to your rod and tackle, stash a few specific items in the backseat. Hip boots will pull up and over your chinos, keeping mud off your work pants. Waterless hand sanitizer is great for a quick cleanup behind the wheel during the frantic drive back to the office. A small pump bottle of spray fabric freshener will knock the fish-slime funk from your French cuffs, but a clean dress shirt could come in handy, as well.

BE EFFICIENT Know where you're headed as soon as your butt hits the car seat. A 20-minute drive to a bass pond still gives you 50 minutes of fishing time during a 90-minute lunch break, which you should be able to pull off every now and then. Figure on high-percentage casts: frothy buzzbaits that get a bass's attention, or weedless worms that won't hang up in brush.

STAY SUBTLE Keep your itinerary on the down low. Bosses that look the other way at a three-pint lunch might go ballistic if they knew you'd punched out for the perch pond.

91 MASTER THE PALOMAR KNOT

The Palomar is crazy strong and a cinch to tie in the dark. Thread a 6-inch loop of line through the hook eye (1), and tie a loose overhand knot so the hook dangles down from the middle (2). Slip the loop formed by this overhand knot over the hook (3). Moisten loops and pull both the tag and standing ends together, making sure that the finished knot rests against the hook eye.

92 BE A 21ST-CENTURY ANGLER

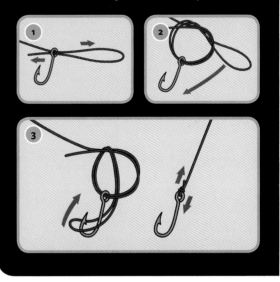

When buying a fishing vest, I would caution you against buying one with too many pockets. I've seen some anglers wearing one of the modern vests that have so many pockets that I'm afraid if they fell down, they would be unable to get up without assistance. The more pockets you have, the more you are tempted to fill them up. Soon you have enough fly boxes and other equipment slung on your upper body that you could open a fly shop right on the stream. In addition, at the end of the day, carrying all that stuff, most of which you did not need, will add to your fatigue.

93 HIT NOTHING BUT NET

Many anglers lose a big fish while they're attempting to net it. That's why it's important to make sure you have the right net for the job and know how to use it. These tips will get more fish in the bag.

GO BIG A common netting foible is using a hoop that's too small. Always choose a hoop two sizes larger than you think you need. A hoop that's too big is not often an issue, but trying to catch a muskie in a net intended for bass is a recipe for heartache.

GO LONG Having the extra reach that a long-handled net provides is definitely worth the effort when a big brown is thrashing on the surface. Having to reach too far out forces an angler to put more strain on the line in those last critical moments. It can also throw a net man off balance as he's stretching out over the gunwale of a boat.

SCOOP SMART If you're wading in moving water, get downstream of the fish, then lift its head slightly out of the water while scooping at the same time. From a boat, you should always net a fish head first. The rod man should also make an effort to guide a fish's head into the net that's already submerged. Any misses or tail bumps can spook fish, causing them to surge and pull the hook or break the line.

94 SKIN A CAT WITH YOUR TOOLBOX

Back in your grandpa's day, skinning a catfish meant nailing the sucker to a backyard pine tree and stripping the skin with pliers. It doesn't take much to bring the old-timers' technique into the 21st century for the same results. Here's how.

SCORE IT Place a 3-foot-long 2x6 board on a level, waist-high surface (a truck tailgate works well). Using a knife, score the skin all the way around the head, just in front of the cat's gill plates. Make another slit down the length of the fish's back.

NAIL IT Drive a 16-penny nail through the fish's skull in order to secure it to the board. Cut off its dorsal fin. Brace the board against your waist, with the tail pointing toward you. Grasp the skin with fish-skinning pliers or whatever is handy from the toolbox, and pull it down to the tail and off.

GUT IT Remove the fish from the board. Grasping the head in one hand and the body in the other, bend the head sharply downward, breaking the spine. Now bend the body up and twist to separate head from body. Open the belly with your knife, remove the remaining viscera from the body cavity, and rinse thoroughly. These instructions are for eating-size cats—say, 4 pounds or less. Anything larger, and you'll have to whack the head off with a cleaver.

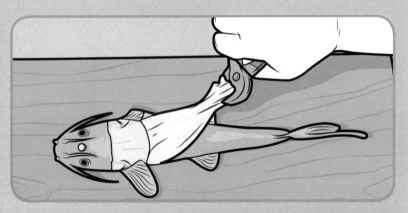

96 CLEAN FISH IN 40 SECONDS

To clean a fish, many anglers remove the head, slice open the belly, and scoop out the guts. This is an easier and faster method, especially for any smaller catches, such as panfish. Place the fish on its back, then slide the point of your knife in the skin below the lower jaw (A). Holding the blade parallel to the jaw, cut away the jaw's under section. With the fish still on its back, detach the top of the gills from the backbone. Grab the cut-away jaw and slowly pull toward the tail (B). Everything, including gills and entrails, will come free.

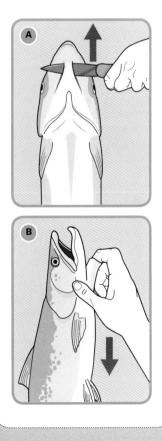

95 MEASURE FISH WITH YOUR WALLET

If you've landed a great fish but there is no measuring tape to be found, pull out your wallet and grab a bill. A dollar bill is 6 1/8 inches long. Fold it in half and it's just a smidge over 3 inches long. Two bills laid alongside your fish will mark a fish that's 12 1/4 inches long. Take a quick photo with a couple George Washingtons smirking beneath a trout or panfish and you'll have positive proof of your prowess.

97 RUBBERIZE YOUR REEL HANDLE

You've probably walked by Plasti Dip in the hardware store a hundred times without giving it a second look, but the liquid rubber can provide great tackle applications. Use it to coat the end of your reel handle for added grip when burning spinnerbaits or aggressively twitching jerkbaits. Your fingers won't slip off from rain, sweat, or fish slime. You can also rubberize the front of your spinning reel's drag cap to allow easier adjustment. To increase the grip even more, pour the amount you need for coverage into a separate container and mix in some fine sand.

98 REPLACE DRAG WASHERS

If you've noticed your drag getting a little sticky lately, or want top-shelf drag from a mid-shelf reel, upgrade the reel's drag washers. Several companies, including Smooth Drag and Australia's Jack Erskine Precision Reel Engineering, machine custom drag washers for myriad reel models. Many aftermarket washers are carbon fiber, which is lighter, stronger, smoother, and more heat resistant than that used in most stock washer materials.

Reel companies such as Daiwa, Shimano, Penn, and Abu Garcia also offer drag upgrade kits for many models. Kits often include drag components from their high-end reels that will also fit on their less expensive models.

99 ROPE-TAPE YOUR GRIP

Having a good grip on your rod can make or break a fish fight, especially when you're fishing for big species like salmon or muskies. Even if the rod's handle is tucked under your arm, the less it slips and moves, the more control you maintain.

To increase that grip, try wrapping your handle hockey stick–style. Start with a spool of cloth stick tape; you'll find it at sporting-goods stores. Make a few wraps around the butt of the rod, unwind about a foot of tape, and spin the spool to create a thin tape rope. Wrap that rope in inch-wide spirals around the handle toward the reel. Next, wrap the tape flat down the handle toward the butt, covering the thin rope. Not only does this wrapping style boost your grip as you hold the rod, it's extra protection against the rod's slipping out of a holder on the troll.

100 CHANGE BEARINGS

Tournament distance casters need skill to send weights out hundreds of yards with a bait-casting reel—but gear factors in, too. Many of the casters replace the reel bearings with custom upgrades.

Even if you don't need to cast a lure up over the moon, extra distance is always useful.

Companies like Boca Bearing and Big Green Fish produce custom ceramic and ceramic-metal hybrid reel bearings for many models that won't corrode, are much lighter than stock metal bearings, and spin more freely than many factory bearings. Working on the guts of a round-profile baitcaster takes patience and focus (reading the manual helps), but new bearings can extend a reel's life and can get a muskie spinner, striper plug, or a big chunk of catfish bait into distant honey holes much more frequently. And that equals more fish.

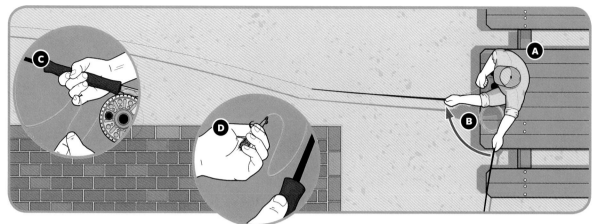

101 FLY-CAST TO A MOVING TARGET

Got that double-haul down pat? Then you'll need it for this challenge: Drop a fly in front of a moving gamefish, at 60 feet, with no more than two false-casts—all while you're standing up on the bow of a boat with your guide shouting, "Two o'clock! Now! Now!" Here's a backyard drill for the redfish marshes, the bonefish flats, and the stripers grounds.

STEP RIGHT UP Stand on a picnic table (A). It's about the size of the casting deck on a flats boat and will give you a sense of being out on the edge where the action happens.

DOUBLE STACK Strip 50 feet of shooting line from the reel and stack it in large loose coils in front of your left foot (B). If you shoot that line now, it will be pulled from the bottom of the stack, all but guaranteeing an

unrighteous tangle. You can avoid this problem, though: Grasp the line where it exits the reel in the crook of the pinky on your rod hand (C). Now, with your free hand, grab the fly line and pull all of it through your pinky, essentially re-stacking the line so it will shoot tangle-free.

FIRE WHEN READY Pull 10 to 12 feet of the stacked line through the rod tip. Hold the fly at the bend of the hook in your reel hand (D) and point your rod tip up. This is the ready position.

GET ON A ROLL Begin with an aggressive roll cast to load the rod, and let go of the fly as you snap the rod forward. Back-cast with a haul, then shoot the line with a forward cast with another haul. If you need some more distance, false cast one more time.

102 GET A FLY TO THE BOTTOM OF THINGS

There was a time when my buddies and I set out to catch every fish possible on a fly rod. When the fish is an amberjack, skulking in 60 feet of water, that presents a difficulty. To sink the flies, we tied a small dropper line of light trout tippet from the hook bend in a big nasty fly to a 3-ounce surf sinker. We marked wrecks with the bottomfinder, then we dropped our weighted fly rigs overboard. When the sinkers hit bottom, we hauled hard on the lines to snap the mono, freeing the flies to flitter seductively in front of bottom-dwelling predators. Now, that was a fight.

103 DO THE CHUCK 'N' DUCK

Adding on four big split shot ahead of a nymph can take the sexy out of fly casting in zero time flat. But when faced with a deep, dark hole that might just be a home for a massive brown trout or a big steelhead, there are times you have to suck it up and dredge. Getting that much lead out to the top of the pool without smacking yourself in the back of the noggin takes skill. Master the chuck-'n'-duck cast, and you'll score more fish and suffer fewer welts.

STEP 1 You have to avoid false casting, so start out by feeding line straight downstream with the rod tip held high to stop the weights from snagging on the bottom until you have enough length to reach the top of the hole you're trying to fish.

STEP 2 In one smooth motion, swing the rod up and over your downstream shoulder, getting the line swinging in an arc over the water behind you. Keep the line tight so that it stays straight and extended. If the line should collapse, get ready for a thump to the cranium.

STEP 3 When your line gets to the 1 o'clock position, get down, bow your head, and then bring the rod straight over your body, pointing the tip exactly where you want the rig to land.

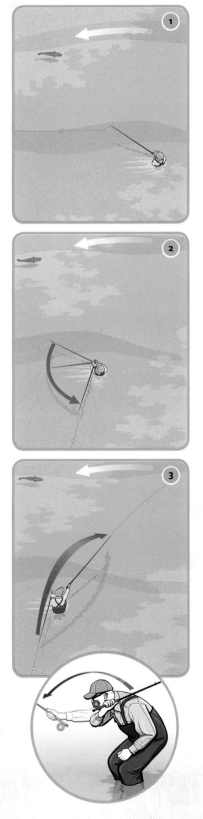

104

MAKE A SPIN-FLY MASH-UP OUTFIT

Putting a spinning reel on a fly rod might not seem to make much sense unless you understand all the intricacies of presenting various tiny jigs and spinners on small streams full of easily spooked trout. The whippy tip makes it possible to toss light lures farther and with more accuracy than a shorter spinning rod. Likewise, the rod length allows you to fish into tight seams and eddies without casting at all. When a trout strikes, the longer, softer rod will let you maneuver it around rocks and overhanging limbs more delicately. Some steelhead anglers customize such outfits further by fitting fly rods with large gathering guides and spinning-reel seats; for small streams, those tweaks aren't necessary. Ultralight or ice-fishing reels will fit the seats of most 3- to 5-weight fly rods. If you prefer a longer grip, tape your reel into place farther up on the rod's handle.

105 STROKE LIKE A PRO

These four paddle strokes will get you there and back with efficient style, whether you are headed to fish camp or trying to line up the perfect cast.

J-STROKE	DRAW	PRY	LOW BRACE
WHY To keep the canoe moving in a straight line.	To move the canoe toward the paddler.	To move the canoe away from the paddler.	To stabilize a tilting boat.
HOW As the paddle approaches your seat, turn the thumb of your top hand away from your body. At the end of the stroke, point your thumb straight down, and pry the blade slightly.	Keeping your top hand as high as possible, extend the blade as far from the canoe as you can. Draw the blade through the water in a short, powerful, inward stroke.	Turn the blade parallel to the gunwale and slide it into the water so that the blade is under the canoe. Pry the paddle blade at an angle perpendicular to the boat.	Reach out with the paddle horizontal and perpendicular to the water, both hands below your chest. Smack the water and push down quickly and powerfully.

106 USE THE MIRACLE OF MINICELL FOAM

Everyone knows about the multiple and miraculous uses of duct tape. Fewer know about an equally useful material: minicell foam. Used by experienced canoers and kayakers to build pedestal seats and pad brace points for their knees and thighs, minicell foam is inexpensive, incredibly lightweight, absorbs little water, and glues well in both wet and dry applications. Available at specialty paddling shops, it comes in sheets from $1/4$ to 2 inches thick. I go through the stuff like water.

- Line boat rod tubes with a cylinder of foam to protect guides and graphite.
- Keep a square in your truck for a dry, cushy surface to stand on while changing into waders or hippers.
- Carry a square for a quiet, dry seat at the base of a tree.
- Cut out insulating boot insoles.
- Wrap vacuum bottles for better insulation.
- Make handy fly patches by wrapping boat rails with strips of foam, or glue small squares to boat sides or consoles.
- Pad boat seats.
- Cut a sheet of minicell the size and shape of a cooler, and place it on top of the cooler's contents before shutting the top. The "cooler gasket" will dramatically lengthen the life of the ice.
- Glue together a cylinder and bottom for an inexpensive, lightweight case for electronics you stash in a tackle bag.

107 WEAVE A CANOE SEAT WITH DUCT TAPE

I blew out the cane seat on my canoe 8 years ago and put together a duct-tape field fix that I figured would hold up till I got home . . . did I mention that was 8 years ago? The seat is still as comfortable as ever, drains rain and splash, and scores admiring looks from other duct-tape junkies. I know you can also do this with nylon webbing and a staple gun. But why would you?

STEP 1 Remove the old cane or nylon webbing. Nylon webbing is held in place with removable screws. Cane is most commonly held in a groove cut into the frame and pinned with a wood strip, much like a door screen. To remove cane, pry the strip out. Clean the seat frame with warm water and a mild detergent, and let dry.

STEP 2 Run a band of duct tape four layers thick vertically across each end of the seat frame. Take care to avoid wrinkles.

STEP 3 Wrap a four-layer-thick duct tape band horizontally around the bottom of the seat frame, leaving a half-inch gap between the tape and the frame edge. Next, alternate with vertical and horizontal bands until the seat frame is filled.

STEP 4 Maintenance is critical. Apply sunlight, butt sweat, and fish slime regularly.

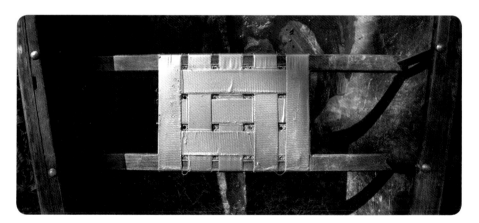

108 ROCK A BENT-SHAFT PADDLE

At first I felt a bit dorky using a bent-shaft canoe paddle, like I came off as some efficiency freak who analyzes mathematical power functions for fun. But a bendy lets me paddle farther, faster, and easier, and also saves my shoulders for tasks like pounding bass bugs into a summer breeze hour after hour. Now I won't paddle without a bent-shaft paddle, and I've shipped my favorite paddles to waters as distant as Alaska and Labrador.

There's no denying the oomph it puts in my stroke, especially in slack water. A bent-shaft paddle gives you a longer sweet spot at the peak place for energy transfer—right as you muscle the blade past your hip. And a bendy won't push as much water upward as you sweep it out of the river.

109 DRY WET WADERS

The only thing worse than going overboard in your chest waders is that sickening squishy sensation the next time you stick your tootsies into those cold, wet boots. Drying out chest waders can take forever, unless you speed up the process with a few common household items.

FISH WRAPPER Wad up newspaper and stuff it into the boots. Replace frequently. Newsprint will soak up a lot of moisture and is much less expensive than paper towels.

HANG 'EM HIGH Fold the chest part of the waders down several times to expose the boots. Hang upside down in a closet or from a wall hook. Place a box fan on a chair under the boots so the breeze blows into them.

DIY BOOT DRYER Cut a 6-foot length of spare PVC pipe into two 3-foot pieces, using a diagonal cut. (You'll want pipe at least 2 inches in diameter.) Roll the chest part of the waders down over the boots. Insert the pointed end of a PVC pipe into each boot so that the open part of the pointed end faces the toes. Now turn the waders over and stand them up on a heat register.

110 PATCH WADERS ON THE STREAM

At best, leaky waders can turn a fishing trip into a bone-chilled, shivering torture test. At worst, they sink your trip completely. The patch kits for non-neoprene waders made of rubber, canvas, or breathable membranes will often require a full day to cure, but you can make your own on-the-stream emergency patch job with a piece of women's nylon hose and fancy adhesives. Here's your emergency patch kit.

YOU'LL NEED

aquaseal • cotol-240 cure accelerator • small piece of nylon hose • duct tape

STEP 1 Use the Cotol-240 to clean around the tear. Rub with a clean cloth to dry. Close the tear with duct tape on the inside of the material.

STEP 2 Cut a patch from the hose large enough to cover the rip plus 1/2 inch on all sides.

STEP 3 Mix 3 to 4 parts Aquaseal to 1 part cure accelerator. Stir with a clean stick.

STEP 4 Soak your patch in the Aquaseal, then place over the rip. Let the patch dry for 1 to 2 hours.

111 FISH A BUSH HOOK

In many parts of the country, bush hooking is a revered tradition. Using small boats and canoes, anglers rig set lines to limbs overhanging the stream, then while away the hours working one line after another. For hunters and anglers camping on or near moving water, it's a fine way to fill a frying pan while attending to camp chores or chasing other fish and game.

To fish a bush hook, find a stout sapling or limb that extends over the water a few feet upstream of a desired fishing location. Your best bets are strong eddy lines, tributary outfalls, and any deep holes beneath undercut banks. To tie the bush hook, attach a three-way swivel to 30- to 50-pound monofilament line. Tie one dropper line to an egg sinker, and another to the hook. Tie the bush hook to the sapling or branch, load the hook with a bait that will hold up to strong current—cut bait, live shiners, shrimp—and drop it into the water. You'll want to check it every couple of hours.

And check your local laws. Some states consider bush hooks as commercial gear, and may require the use of a cotton line or other specifics. Other states don't consider bush hooks as "sporting tackle." But to hungry hunters or drift fishermen, such distinctions fade away once you sink your teeth into a freshly caught catfish filet.

112 HOLD ON TIGHTLY

Inshore and surf anglers know to match the sinker to the fishing conditions.

PYRAMID SINKERS Perfect for holding a bottom rig in sand, these sinkers can get hung up in rock jetties.

SPUTNIK SINKERS These sinkers have wires that dig into the bottom for rough-weather holding power and release and fold against the sinker for an easy retrieve.

BANK SINKERS These sinkers, which are easier to retrieve than pyramids, have a bit of bottom hold, so they are good in calm-water but will move around in currents.

HATTERAS OR STORM SINKERS These sinkers will hang tight in swirling bottom currents.

Sputnik Sinker

113 TAKE JAW-DROPPING FISH VIDS

That perfectly lit hero shot with water dripping from the fish and the stream glittering in the background is so . . . okay. Taking your fish photography to the next level will mean taking it underwater with a point-of-view camera like the GoPro.

SLOW DOWN Use a lower frame rate, such as 24 frames per second. You'll need the added boost in light gathering underwater, and this will also reduce visual "noise" in the video. If possible, choose the 4:3 format to take advantage of a slightly taller and wider frame.

FIGHT FOG Some manufacturers offer antifog inserts, which work great. Another trick: Open up your camera's housing and hold the camera near the car air conditioning vent for a few minutes before you get out of your vehicle. Then close up the camera, thus trapping the superdry air inside.

CONTROL THE POLE Whether you're in a boat or wading, dedicate a pole or stick for the camera. Net and gaff handles, broomsticks, and tree branches all work. A pole helps hold the camera steady, and enables you to get it into position for hero shots. Speaking of which . . .

MAKE LIKE HITCHCOCK Experiment with camera angles. With the camera on a pole, capture the trolling motor propeller or your wading boots moving along the stream bottom. Film a lure or fly as it's worked through the water. Then take some time to dial in these two shots.

Mount the camera to a fixed stake in the water, a few inches above the surface, back off, and cast toward the camera. With a dry fly, you can cast as close as you want to get, or plop the fly slightly upstream and let it drift into the shot. With a bass plug, better aim a foot or two in front.

One of the coolest videos is a release shot taken from slightly below the fish, showing it being held underwater with the angler's grinning face above. Be sure the sun is to the side or in front of the angler to avoid a dark silhouette. Move the camera into position with a pole, guided by verbal instructions from the angler. Get the camera close to the fish, maybe a foot or so. Basically, if the angler can't see the camera, the camera can't see the angler.

114 KEEP A WORM BOX

Nursing a summer-long batch of red wigglers is as easy as hammering a few nails and remembering to save banana peels from the trash can. Also, raising your own bait means you can slip out of the house and hit the pond well before Mama comes home. Just like in the old days.

NEW-SCHOOL TWIST If the summer heat becomes a concern, fill up a milk carton with ice and push it into the middle of the bed.

BUILD IT Cut a sheet of CDX-grade plywood, which is made with water-resistant glues, to your box dimensions. Nail it together and drill a dozen $1/2$-inch holes in the bottom for drainage.

FILL IT Dig a hole in a shady spot and sink the box, leaving a few inches of board free. Fill it with some shredded newspaper, leaves, peat moss, and soil. Moisten lightly. Cover and let sit for a week.

FEED IT Add a few hundred worms and feed them two times a week. Keep the bedding moist but not wet. On the menu: lettuce, fruit and vegetable waste, and the occasional nongreasy leftover.

115 CATCH BAIT WITH A BLADE OF GRASS

Catching a tiger beetle larva is almost as much fun as using one to catch a panfish. Look for a hole in the ground about as big around as a pencil. Likely spots are bare patches in a sunny backyard, a local park field, just about anywhere you can find hard-packed soil or sand. Break off a tall reed, like broomsedge, about a foot long. Insert it gently into the hole, lifting and dropping until it finds the bottom—which isn't really the bottom, but the top of the larva's hard flat head. When the grub uses its pincers to move the offending stem, you'll see the reed start to jiggle. Quick as you can, snatch the grass straight out of the hole. If you're lucky, or just plain good, an inch or so of creamy grub is yours for the taking.

116 MAKE A PLYWOOD BAIT FARM

There's a quick, inexpensive, and easy way to ensure a steady supply of live bait for a quick trip out to the panfish pond and, at the same time, provide salamanders, lizards, and snakes a safe place to live. Herpetologists have long used coverboard surveys to track the populations of amphibians and reptiles. Coverboards are simply large pieces of untreated plywood that are placed on the ground and later lifted and searched under for a wide array of creatures. (Chemicals found in treated woods can leach into the ground below.) One coverboard project has tallied 27 species of salamanders, frogs, snakes, and turtles hunkered down under these makeshift shelters. The plywood rooftops provide security, moist soils, and protection from predators. All that is equally attractive to earthworms, crickets, and beetle grubs—the Holy Trinity of live bait for panfish.

Coverboard sizes are dictated by how much ground you want to cover. A dinner-plate-size coverboard set in a shady corner of your backyard should shelter enough crickets and worms for a quick after-work trip out to the local pond. A full 4-foot by 8-foot plywood sheet might end up home to half a day's worth of serious bait dunking. All you need to do is put down the plywood in a shady spot and give it a few weeks to work its magic. Use a short stick with a protruding branch to lift up the edge of the coverboard—never put your hands and fingers under the edge of a device that's designed to attract reptiles—and remember to lower the coverboard gently back down to the ground to prevent damage to the creatures you've attracted.

118 MAKE A KICK SEINE

Seining up a mess of local live bait is the old-school match-the-hatch strategy. This DIY seine folds up small enough to stow in a vest pocket.

STITCH IT Hem a tube sleeve into the short sides of a 30-by-12-inch piece of white flexible nylon netting. Use some nylon thread instead of cotton. Fold over a protective layer of duct tape along the seine's bottom edge.

USE IT Insert a pair of sticks into the hemmed sides, wade out into the stream, plant the bottom of your seine firmly into the creek bed, and have a buddy kick around on the bottom a few feet upstream. (Check local regulations, and only use bait native to the waters you fish.)

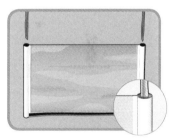

117 CATCH BAIT LEECHES WITH A COFFEE CAN

Ribbon leeches are irresistible to fish and a snap to catch. And unlike the decidedly nasty horse leech, ribbon leeches aren't bloodsuckers, but tiny predators and scavengers. So, no worries about them cozying up to your nether parts. To load up, punch or drill a bunch of 3/8-inch holes in the sides of a coffee can, and bait it with hunks of bloody beef or fish heads. Smash the can shut with your boot, tie a length of box twine to the can, and place it in a few feet of water. Be sure to look into the trap by sunrise. Leeches are nocturnal, and they'll check out of your coffee-can diner not long after daylight.

119 RIG A PORK RIND

Tipping your lure with a pork rind may feel a bit like pulling on a pair of old scratchy wool pants, but a little BBQ on a bass bait can transform a slow day on the water to epic status.

To attach a commercial pork-rind trailer, find the small slit on the front end of the chunk. Insert the hook through the fat side first, and out the skin side. That's it. Pork rinds dry out quickly and will lose their wiggle, so drop your bait into a small water bucket whenever you're motoring to a new spot. To make hook removal easy, snip a coffee straw into half-inch lengths, slide one over the hook tip and barb (A), and slip the pork off the hook.

NEW-SCHOOL TWIST Dial up a triple threat for a jig-and-pig by adding a glass rattle. Or add a strip of colored yarn (B) to a spoon tipped with a pork rind.

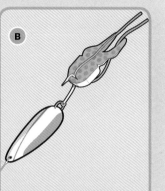

121 BAIL A BOAT WITH A JUG

Cut the bottom 2 inches off a 1-gallon plastic milk jug and you'll have the best boat bailer on the planet. The squared-off profile swallows a load of water in a single swipe, or turn it so that a corner of the jug fits into canoe ends or hard-to-reach bilges. The thin sides have the perfect amount of give to match the shape of boat hulls.

120 MASTER THE ARBOR KNOT

The best way to connect line to a reel is also the simplest. The arbor knot works with any type of reel and line (although superbraids require about 10 yards of mono added to the spool first to prevent slipping.)

STEP 1 Pass the line around the reel spool and back out again the same way the line entered. For example, on a baitcasting reel, pass the line through the levelwind eye, around the spool, and back through the levelwind eye.

STEP 2 Use the tag end to tie a simple overhand knot around the standing line. Tighten that knot.

STEP 3 Tie an overhand knot in the tag end, then tighten and trim. This will keep the first knot from slipping free.

STEP 4 Pull on the standing line until it tightens on the spool with the two knots binding securely against each other. Now you can spool the reel.

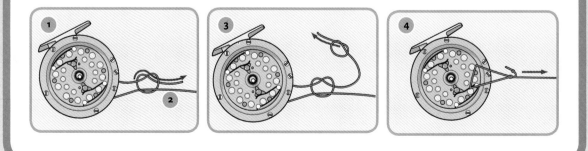

124 UPGRADE YOUR LIVE BAITS

Still globbing your worm on an Aberdeen hook? Seriously? Here are three smart bait-rig tweaks to help you catch more fish.

KEEP AN EYE OUT Pinch one eye from large baitfish such as a shad or bluegill. The bait will struggle in the water, attracting predators.

GET A DYE JOB Clean dirt from a dozen nightcrawlers and put them in a bowl. Add 1 tbsp. food coloring (green is great) and stir. Cover and refrigerate for at least three hours and as long as overnight.

PLAY SHELL GAMES Add crushed eggshells to catfish dough. The fragments catch light, adding a bit of sparkle to dull dough baits.

122 FISH A CRICKET ANYWHERE, ANY TIME

Loads of fish go wild for crickets, and if you fish with a cricket bait, make sure you give it a little lively action to draw the fish's attention.

SWIPE THE PLASTIC A black Rebel Crickhopper crankbait is the best light-tackle cricket lure you'll find. But don't simply cast and retrieve. Let this lure sit on the surface, then give the rod a sharp, short sideswipe. The Crickhopper will duck under and wobble like a struggling cricket. Let it float back up and sit again for a few seconds. Repeat until a trout or crappie sucks it down.

LAY THE SMACKDOWN Big streamers are usually associated with nighttime flyfishing for trout, but a black foam cricket can do equal damage. Foam is a loud fly material and makes a harder slap when it hits the water. Lay the fly down aggressively to enhance the pop. Then just let it drift through dark eddies or seams until you hear the louder pop of a striking brown trout.

GO ON A WEIGHT-LOSS PLAN Live crickets are often fished under a bobber with a split shot, but they don't live long. Instead, rig the bait on a bare dry-fly hook to reduce the weight and coat the first foot of your line with dry-fly floatant. The bobber will still give you casting distance, but the cricket will squirm on the surface, drawing up big bluegills for exciting strikes.

123 USE SALT TO KEEP EGGS ON A HOOK

Have you ever wondered how to keep from losing your fresh salmon-egg bait to a strong current? Simply empty your jar of eggs on a saucer and sprinkle lightly with table salt. Return them to the jar and go fishing immediately. Your eggs will seem to have become "rubberized" and will stay on the hook.

125 TROLL THE BACKCOUNTRY DOWNRIGGER

Thanks to fishing kayaks and easier access to remote wilderness, going deep in backcountry lakes is a great way to reach walleyes and trout. To target fish at 40 to 60 feet deep, use light lines to slice through the water column and a weight to pull your lure into the depths.

MAKE A TRIPLE PLAY Spool a reel with dark green 6-pound mono or 8-pound braid. Tie on a 3-way swivel. To another eye, tie 4 feet of mono, and to this tie a 1- to 3-ounce bell sinker. Tie 3 feet of mono to the other eye, and attach a light lure like a small spoon.

GO OVER EASY The trick is to get deep without tangles. Paddle forward and ease the rig overboard. Let line out a few feet at a time, occasionally pinching line so it goes taut behind the boat. As forward momentum slows, set the reel bail, get up a bit more speed, then flip the bail and let more line out. Once you hit bottom, crank the weight up a foot and paddle in a zigzag line.

126 TROLL AT A SNAIL'S PACE

Before the advent of bow-mounted trolling motors, old-schoolers devised a way to maneuver a boat ever so slowly, and ever so precisely, over tightly holding fish in rough water. Backtrolling is basically trolling in reverse, and it still works wonders on walleye, shad, steelhead, stripers, and any other fish holed up in current or windy conditions. Old-fashioned tiller motors work best.

SET IT UP Set rods in the downstream facing rod holders, or hand-hold them. With most fishing almost directly under the transducer, you can bounce a bait on a fish's head.

BACK IT UP With fish marked or a desirable bottom contour identified, knock the motor in and out of reverse to slow the boat or hover it in position. Set your mind on s-l-o-w and crawl baits through the strike zone. Don't be hesitant to make minor course adjustments.

STAY DRY Using a breeze-blown chop to brake your boat is a wet undertaking as waves slop over the transom. Take too much water over the stern and safety becomes an issue. You can buy custom-fitted splash guards, although you definitely win old-school style points for making your own out of Plexiglas and old rubber auto floor mats.

128 TROLL A FLY

Trolling a streamer pattern is a deadly way to fish. Many times, all it takes is to long-line your fly line, leader, and fly behind the boat. To go deep, however, tie up a selection of lead-core trolling sections from 5 feet to 25 feet long, using nail knots to create loops on each end. Use these ahead of your leader to get flies deep, deeper, and right on the bottom.

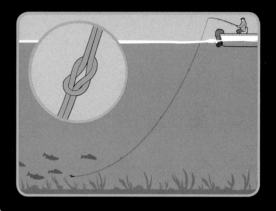

129 KEEP MUCK OUT OF YOUR TRUCK

A 2-by-3-foot piece of indoor-outdoor carpet is a great wader changing mat. It rolls up small enough to stash under car seats and dries fast.

127 FIX ANY FLAT

I've used a Springfield Quick-Change Trailer Jack to change tires on everything from a utility trailer to a small johnboat trailer to a double-axle saltwater boat trailer. It's the size of a Frisbee, and you can stow it anywhere, so I take it everywhere. One of my best $40 investments, it also makes greasing bearings easier.

130 PACK A FLY VEST THREE WAYS

All those pockets! All those gadget holders! All those gizmo attach points! Here's what to load into a fly vest, tailored to the conditions you're likely to face.

LIGHT & FAST You're hoofing it past the yahoos for a surgical strike in the headwaters. You need a stripped-down tool kit.

- Flybox
- Nylon leaders and tippet material
- Fluorocarbon leaders and tippet material
- Fly floatant
- Split shot
- Strike indicators
- Line nippers
- Hemostats
- Duct tape
- Small flashlight

TACTICAL TECHNICIAN

You're taking your time on tough trout with discerning palates. Add these items to the Light & Fast list.

- Another flybox or 3
- Fly desiccant
- Sink tips
- Fly line cleaner
- Thermometer
- Small kick seine
- Hook file
- Wading staff
- Blood knot/nail knot tool
- Multitool
- Superglue
- Net
- Rain jacket
- Bug dope
- Sunscreen

ALL DAY & THEN SOME

You're not stopping till it's dark-thirty, and maybe not even then. Add these items to the Tactical Technician list to tide you over till dawn.

- Knife
- Emergency space blanket
- Whistle
- Toilet paper
- Lighter
- Strike-anywhere matches
- Beef jerky
- Water treatment tablets

Since heat and sunlight are hard on fishing line, you need to be careful when storing spare monofilament and fluorocarbon line. Most manufacturers will tell you that storing line for up to a year is no problem, but there are some significant caveats. First, always use bulk spools for long-term storage. The larger diameter of bulk spools will cut down on the problem of line memory, in which the coiled line retains loops that will snarl your casts come springtime. Equally important to line stability is a relatively constant environment without large temperature fluctuations. A simple solution: Stack bulk spools in a couple of shoeboxes and jam them up on the highest shelf in the hall closet.

132 RIG AN ON-THE-STREAM FISH STRINGER

If you find yourself without a fish stringer, here's an easy way to keep your catch. Cut a 2- to 3-foot vine—muscadine, greenbrier, you name it. Strip off the leaves and sharpen one end. Now thread the sharp end through the fish's gills and mouth, and wrap the vine ends around themselves a half dozen times to form a hoop. Anchor it in the water with a stick driven into the mud.

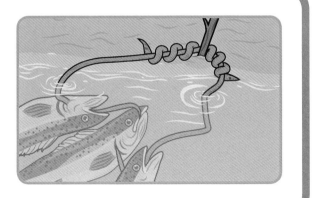

133 FEATHER A SPINNING REEL 50 FEET

An open-face spinning reel may not have a baitcaster's reputation for minute-of-angle accuracy, but you can still cast lures into tight spots from a decent distance with these popular rigs.

The secret is to feather the outgoing line against the lip of the spool, much as you slow the revolution of a baitcasting spool with your thumb. It feels a little goofy at first, especially since you have to cast with both hands near the reel. But then you get used to the technique, and you start dropping lures into lily pad openings the size of a cheeseburger bun, and you'll remember that disentangling your spinnerbaits from low bushes felt a lot goofier. Here's the drill for right-handed casters.

WIND UP Start with the reel handle pointing up (A). This will ensure enough clearance so you can . . .

BAIL OUT Place your left hand under the handle and cup the spool in your palm (B). Open the bail with your left thumb or the fingers of your right hand. With your left hand, reach around the bottom of the spool, and extend your left index finger so you can . . .

HOLD THE LINE Trap the outgoing line against the spool rim with the tip of your left index finger. Now comes the goofy part: Make a standard cast, while keeping the outgoing line pressed against the spool rim (C). Your left hand will travel with the spinning reel. Keep holding the lines with your left index finger so you can . . .

CONTROL THE CAST Release the line to send the lure toward the target. Use slight finger pressure against the spool lip to slow the line (D), then stop the at the precise moment so you can . . .

HOOK A BASS Drop it so close to bass cover that a fish will strike out of sheer admiration for your marksmanship.

134 CONVERT TO MANUAL SHIFT

Pro bass anglers rarely, if ever, trip the bail on their spinning reels by turning the handle. That's because closing the bail with the handle can spin a little slack line onto the spool, which can lead to twisting. The bail is also the part of a spinning reel that fails most often. To prevent knots and malfunction, unscrew the side plate that houses the internal bail gears and remove the spring. Some reels require the removal of small bail-tripping mechanisms as well, but on many models, ditching the spring will suffice. A manual bail forces you to close it by hand, letting you keep tension on the line by flipping it as soon as your bait or lure splashes down. Look online for free reel schematics that can help you remove the correct parts.

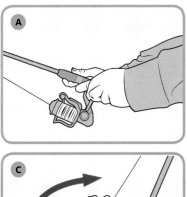

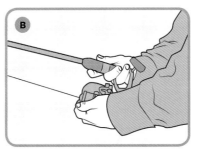

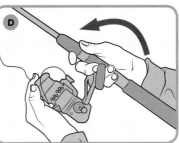

135 MAKE YOUR OWN IN-LINE SPINNERS

Building a spinner takes all of two minutes, and the only tool you need is a pair of needle-nose pliers. You can buy kits at the big sporting goods shops that include a range of bodies, blades, and beads, or order parts individually for more customization. Here's how you can create your own inexhaustible supply of deadly fishing lures.

Before you begin assembling the spinner, add desired details to components, such as paint or flash tape to blades, and squirrel-tail hair or colored tubing to treble hooks.

STEP 1 Thread a treble hook onto an open-eye wire shaft.

STEP 2 Pinch the ends of the shaft together and slide a spinner body over the top. Solid brass bodies add heft for deeper-running lures and greater castability. Trim any excess wire and add beads.

STEP 3 Thread the blade onto the clevis, and slide the clevis onto the shaft. The blade's concave side should face the body.

STEP 4 Using your pliers, grasp the shaft firmly about ³⁄₁₆ to ½ inch above the clevis or terminal bead. Hold the pliers steady and slowly bend the shaft three-quarters of the way around the nose of the pliers and under the main shaft until you have formed a loop.

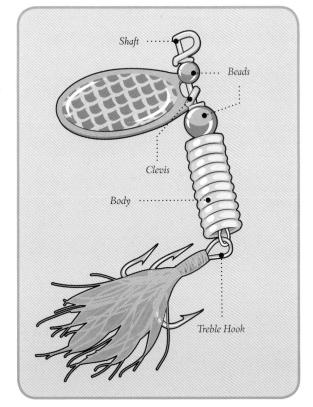

Shaft

Beads

Clevis

Body

Treble Hook

STEP 5 Wrap the tag end of this loop tightly around the shaft twice, as close to the pliers as possible. Trim the end with wire cutters.

136 WIDEN YOUR GATHERING GUIDE

Ask a custom rod builder about common requests they receive, and one will invariably be using a gathering guide wider than what is typically used on stock rods. The gathering guide—the guide closest to the reel on a spinning rod—allows line to peel off the reel smoothly during the cast and feed back on the spool evenly during the retrieve.

A wide gathering guide increases both casting accuracy and distance by giving the line more freedom of flow during the cast and will let you feather the line more effectively when you need to put a frog between two pads. During the retrieve, it can reduce kinking and memory by adding more tension to the line as it winds back onto the reel. You will also be able to use a reel with a wider spool on a lighter rod. That means you can increase your line capacity without the need to downsize line strength and lure weight. And you'll be able to use a lighter outfit for bigger fish.

137 MASTER THE WORLD'S FAIR KNOT

This easy knot was the winner of a Great Knot Search event sponsored by DuPont (Stren fishing line) at the 1982 World's Fair. Use it for tying on hooks, lures, or swivels with nylon monofilaments. It's almost like the Palomar knot because you place a doubled line around the hook's eye, but this knot does not require you to pass the hook or lure through a large loop of line.

STEP 1 Insert a doubled line loop about ¹/₂ inch through the hook eye.

STEP 2 Fold the loop back on itself as shown, keeping it in position by pinching with your left thumb and index finger at the hook eye.

STEP 3 Feed the tag end downward through the loop, under the doubled line in front of the hook eye, then go back up through the loop.

STEP 4 Next, run the line's tag end through the loop that was formed in the previous step.

STEP 5 Pull steadily and firmly on both the standing line and the tag end to tighten.

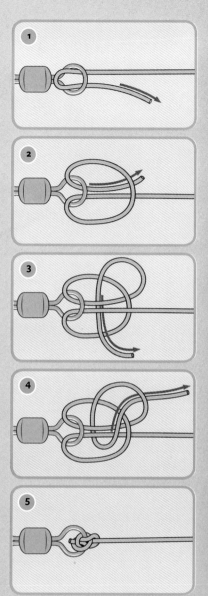

139 BUILD A PREDATOR RIG

Gather up all your tired, your lipless, your scarred and rusty Rapalas, the wretched refuse of your ancient tacklebox . . . And make from them a truly awesome predator rig.

Remove the hooks from a plug. Tie it to your line, and then tie a short stout dropper between the trailing eye and a big in-line spinner or spoon, such as a Dardevle. (If fishing for toothy predators like muskies, use wire.) Now you have a rig that looks like a fish that's chasing after a smaller fish, which can trigger a bite like nobody's business.

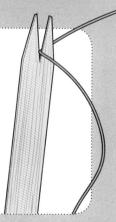

138 REMOVE HOOKS WITH A POPSICLE STICK

Traditional hook disgorgers, such as hemostats and needle-nose pliers, can tear up popper bodies and wings, damage hooks, and nick tippets and knots. The best hook removal tool for smallmouthed bream is a simple wooden Popsicle stick. Whittle one end of the stick to a width of ¹/₄ inch. Place the stick on a hard wooden surface, such as a picnic table. Use a knife blade to cut a V-notch into the narrowed end of the stick. Now just slide the V-notch down the line to the hook eye, and pop the popper free.

The trout stream is transparent and the hatch consists of super small bugs, so you've tied on a hair-thin 7X tippet. You're landing plenty of small trout, but suddenly a 22-incher sips the fly. How do you keep it on and get it to the net?

"Nothing can be sudden," says Joe DeMalderis, a trophy trout hunter who guides from the upper Delaware River in New York to Patagonia in South America. "Everything has to be done easy, starting with the hookset. You want to gently lift to set. If you swing hard, it's already over. The whole key is managing your line and keeping pressure on without doing anything jarring. When the fish gets on the reel, loosen your drag and keep your hands off. If the fish wants to take line, let it go.

Whether you're wading or in a drift boat, chasing the fish is a must. When it's time to net, try to gently lead the fish into a bag that's already submerged. Don't take a sudden swipe, because if you hit the tippet, it'll break.

"If you panic, you don't have a chance. People are afraid of light tippets, but 7X is a lot stronger than you think. I tell clients to tie their 7X to a bush and slowly bend the rod. They'll bend it almost in half. But if you whip the rod fast, the tippet will snap. As soon as you try to stop the fish by choking off the line or changing directions too suddenly, it's over. It's a balancing act, and if you do one tiny thing wrong, you risk losing the trout. Most mistakes happen because the angler is panicked and does something too abruptly."

141 SET A SPOOL BRAKE

Calibrating a baitcasting reel is one of those skills it behooves the total outdoorsman to develop. Do it correctly and you'll head off those annoying bird's nests that result from an over-running spool. Follow the steps below if you're a right-handed angler. The adjustments will be opposite for southpaws. Recalibrate each time you change lures.

STEP 1 Hold the rod in your left hand at a 45-degree angle, with the lure attached to the line and about 4 inches of line out from the tip top.

STEP 2 The clutch knob should be on the handle side of the reel. Turn it clockwise a few turns to overtighten. Rest your left thumb on the reel spool.

STEP 3 Push the thumb bar with your right thumb. Remove your left thumb from the spool. The lure shouldn't drop; if it does, tighten the clutch knob.

STEP 4 Slowly turn the clutch knob counterclockwise until the lure begins to descend from its own weight.

STEP 5 Give it a cast. If it feels like the brake is too tight for the distance you want, loosen the clutch knob. If the spool backlashes, tighten it slightly.

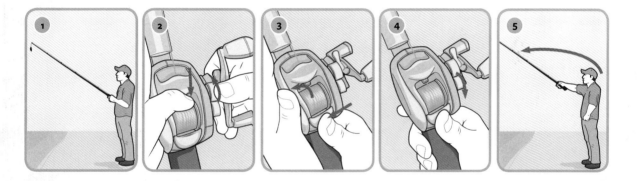

142 STRIP INTO A HAMPER

Collapsible laundry hampers make a fine stripping basket for fly anglers casting from an open boat. They collapse down to an easily storable disk shape, weigh little, and will keep fly line from blowing around the boat and catching on everything. To customize, cut a circle of plywood to match the bottom of the hamper and glue egg crate foam to the top of the plywood. The weight of the plywood keeps the hamper from turning over, while the egg crate foam will help keep the line from tangling as you double-haul towards the horizon.

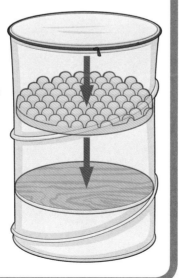

143 IMPROVE FLY LINE MEMORY

If you know you won't get a chance to flyfish for a while, keep your fly line from developing a curl memory by wrapping the first 50 feet around a large cylindrical object. Coffee cans work great, as do boat bumpers, large dog training dummies, and empty 2-liter bottles. Once your dark hiatus is over, your line will cast farther and lie straight on the water.

Nothing beats the heat like wet-wading a smallie stream. Here are all the lures you'll need for a great day on the water.

1 CABELA'S FISHERMAN SERIES WALKING DOG The scooped mouth on this 3½-inch walker throws a bit more water than a classic Spook.

2 ARBOGAST HULA POPPER When smallmouths get more dialed in to sipping bugs than chasing baitfish, break out a 1¾-inch black Hula Popper.

3 JIGHEADS Whether for stuffing a tube or jigging a Fluke in a hole, a small assortment of plain round and tube jigheads is a must. Pack ⅟₁₆- through ¼-ounce weights.

4 ZOOM FLUKE A Fluke shines when a subtle presentation is in order. Rig a pearl-white 4-inch bait on a weedless hook, cast upstream of the zone, and let it flutter down with the current like a dying baitfish.

5 STRIKE KING BITSY TUBE These 2¾-inch baits imitate everything from darters to crayfish to hellgrammites. Let them tumble over the bottom or jig them hard.

6 PANTHER MARTIN SPINNERS Panther Martins get down fast in strong current, and a single-hook model tipped with a grub kills on the swing.

7 MATZUO NANO POPPER This 2-inch bait is a go-to popper on smallmouth streams. It splashes down softly and can be worked subtly on light gear.

8 RAT-L-TRAP When you come across a deep hole and can't turn a fish in the middle of the column, a 'Trap ripped tight to the bottom often scores.

9 HOOKS Wide-gap worm hooks in size 2/0 come in handy for rigging baits weedless. Carry some size-4 finesse hooks for wacky-rigging soft plastics or in case you happen to find a live crayfish scurrying around the rocks.

10 RAPALA JOINTED ORIGINAL FLOATER
Sometimes a joint can make all the difference in drawing strikes, especially in broken water where the current helps impart the action.

11 RAPALA X-RAP This stickbait on steroids is a hands-down favorite small-stream hard bait. It shines in faster water where a few forceful jerks make it slash violently.

12 RAPALA ORIGINAL FLOATER In slow stretches, where you want to work a stickbait with a little more finesse, it's tough to top an Original Floater.

13 YAMAMOTO SENKO Wacky-rig a 4-inch Senko and drift it, weightless, through seams and eddies with your rod held high and a finger on the line.

145 SURVIVE THE FROG CHOMP

Hollow-body topwater frogs are deadly on big bass in the pads, but if you watch a pro work one, you'll notice there's some finesse to the hookset. Most baits of this style feature two stationary single hooks on the back instead of treble hooks that dangle and pivot. By swinging the instant a bass crushes the frog, you are likely to score nothing more than a lure flying at your face. Giving bass time to eat a hollow-body frog is critical. It might take serious willpower to resist the set, but if you let the bass take the frog under and wait for the rod to load before you swing, you'll land more hawgs.

146 TIE THE NICKENS KNOW-NOTHING

I've been told that fish strike my Know-Nothing Shad Ball because they are insulted by such a simplistic offering. Whatever. I can tell you that it requires only four materials, and you have to know nearly nothing to tie it. It has caught hickory and American shad, stripers, bluegills, crappies, bass, and with the addition of a Mylar tail, Spanish mackerel, bluefish, and false albacore. What it lacks in fancy it makes up for in flash. Tie it with heavy eyes and fish it with a weighted line.

YOU'LL NEED

size-4 streamer hook • 6/0 white thread • dumbbell, nickel-plated eyes • krystal flash chenille body, medium

STEP 1 Secure the thread just behind the hook eye and wrap a thread base one-quarter the length of the hook. Tie dumbbell eyes on top of this base with crisscross windings. Don't crowd the hook eye; you'll need space to anchor the chenille. Add a drop of head cement to the dumbbell eye wrappings. Now run the thread wrap down the shank to just before the hook bend.

STEP 2 Tie in chenille at the hook bend, then wrap the thread back to the eye of the hook. Wrap the chenille forward up the hook shank. Wrap one winding in front of the other for a slimmer, faster-sinking profile, or double up the wraps to build a bulky body. Form a head by wrapping the chenille over the dumbbell eyes, using crisscross windings.

STEP 3 Secure the chenille to the hook in front of the eyes with a few wraps of thread. Build up a thread head, then whip finish the thread and dab with head cement.

In an anchored boat on moving water, cast the fly straight across the current, then feed line and sweep the rod tip downstream as the fly sinks. Strip with short jerks all the way to the boat.

147 DYE BUCKTAIL LURES & FLIES

The most common natural material for lures and many flies is the tail of a white-tailed deer. Those long hairs are found in bucktail jigs, bass bugs, Clouser Deep Minnows, and many other fish catchers. Here's the 4-1-1 on preparation.

STEP 1 To skin the tail, split the underside with a fillet knife to within a few inches of the tip. Peel back the skin, wrap the tailbone with burlap, grasp it firmly, and pull the bone free. Continue the incision to the tip of the tail and scrape away all flesh and fat. Rub with salt or Borax and freeze.

STEP 2 To dye the hairs, soak the tail overnight in water and dishwashing detergent, rinse, and dry completely. Mix a solution of sugar-free Kool-Aid, water, and vinegar at a ratio of 2 ounces vinegar to 1 cup water. Pour this into a glass jar and submerge the tail. Place the jar in a larger pot of gently boiling water for 20 minutes to an hour or more. Check often for color. Remove the tail, blot, and tack to a piece of plywood to dry.

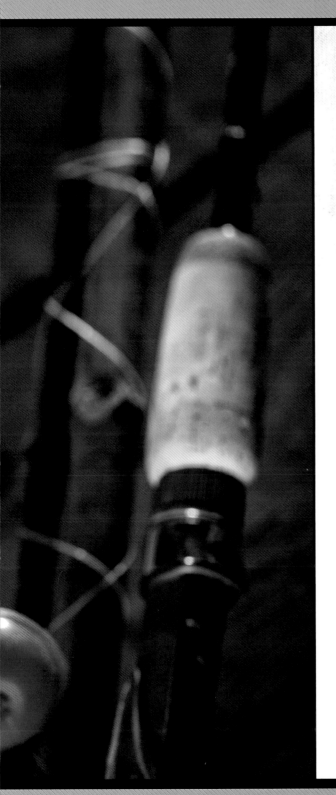

I can't recall the first time I fished with a Zebco 33 spincasting reel. When was the first time I saw the sun rise? How long have I been wearing pants? Hasn't the 33 been around since forever?

Almost. In the 1940s, a Texas watchmaker, barber, and inventor named R. D. Hull created a new kind of fishing reel inspired by a string reel he saw in a grocery store. The fixed spool allowed butcher twine to feed off the end with few instances of backlash, the bane of baitcasting reels of the period. Hull pieced together a prototype with, depending on which account you read, a Folger's Coffee can lid or a beer can. He took the contraption to a few investors he knew, but they weren't impressed. These were the same men who years earlier had kicked in $7,500 each to bankroll Hull's first rodeo with fishing reels, a design he called the "Lashmaster." That company went belly-up.

Undaunted, Hull continued the hunt for more amenable investors, and in 1947, stumbled across the Zero Hour Bomb Company of Tulsa, Oklahoma. Zero Hour made electrical time bombs for the oil-drilling business. Its patents were about to expire, and it was looking for new items to manufacture. A single employee—an ardent angler—convinced his bosses that Hull's new fishing reel was the next big thing. The Zero Hour Bomb Company started production of Hull's "Standard" reel in 1949. In 1952, the Model 22 hit the market. Two years later, Zero Hour debuted the Model 33. The reel flew off store shelves; it was so successful that in 1956 the company changed its name to reflect a shift away from the time-bomb trade. The name "Zebco" has been one of the most recognizable brands in fishing ever since.

Perhaps the most famous fishing reel ever invented, the Zebco 33 is as utilitarian as it gets. Its predecessors were dubbed "a beer can with a hole in each end," but the 33 was chromed up like a classic Cadillac bumper, with a push-button action and a fish-face bell that kept line unspooling free and true. It was marketed as a revolution, a reel so easy to use and cast that, literally, a monkey could fish with it. For a while, a Zebco "Fishing Chimpanzee" proved the point, traveling the sports show circuit, clad in overalls and a porkpie hat.

To date, Zebco has sold more than 40 million Model 33s. I have owned at least three over the years, and one still has a place in my fishing quiver. Over the last few decades, Zebco has been bought and sold, and the company moved its manufacturing overseas in the late 1990s. But Tulsa remains the worldwide Zebco HQ, just as the venerable 33 remains the defining fishing icon of generations of anglers.

148 FISH LIKE A JAPANESE STREAM WARRIOR

Developed in Japan 200 years ago, tenkara fishing was introduced to American anglers in 2009. It involves using a very long fly rod with no reel; the line is tied directly to the tip. Using a truncated style of short-distance casting, anglers can use these rods to reach across conflicting currents and prevent a faster (or slower) current from pulling the fly and causing drag. Adherents are nearly worshipful of tenkara, which they say puts more emphasis on skill and less on gear.

Tenkara rods telescope, and some can extend to nearly 15 feet. With a base length of less than 2 feet, they're great for packing into tight headwaters. Use the longest rod you can. The limiting factor is how much canopy might impede the cast, not overall length. You'll quickly get used to the length, and you'll want the line control.

Lines are about the length of the rod and attach to the rod tip. There are two broad types: More traditional tapered lines afford a super-delicate fly presentation. Newer level lines are more easily altered on the stream but harder to cast. Lines are tipped with a short 3- to 4-foot tippet.

Most tenkara flies feature a reverse hackle in which the feather is brushed forward towards the hook eye. This gives the fly a pulsing, bloomlike profile, like a jellyfish opening and closing. Unlike traditional western flyfishing, tenkara places little emphasis on fly selection, and more on manipulating the fly to entice a strike.

149 CATCH A DINOSAUR WITH A ROPE

Longnose gar have been around for about 100 million years, skulking in freshwater with few predators. You can change that with a simple homemade rig. Cut 6 inches of yellow braided nylon rope and melt one end with a lighter or match. Unbraid the strands from the other end for two-thirds the length of the rope. That's your lure: a tooth-snaring garish yellow plug with no hook. Attach it to a stout leader with a slip knot and chuck it into gar water. When the fish strikes, give it slack so it works those fine teeth into the rope, shaking its head to snare it even more firmly. Only then should you apply pressure and bring the prehistoric beast all the way to the boat.

150 SHOOT DOCKS FOR CRAPPIE

Docks provide shade, baitfish, ambush cover, and even a little night mood-lighting, at times. It all comes together as super crappie cover—except for those pesky docks. There's no way to get a traditional cast in between all those boat lifts, finger piers, pilings, and gangways. You'll need to shoot your way in.

Shooting docks for crappie is where fishing meets bowhunting. You turn your rod into a bow and your grub into an arrow, shooting a jig deep into shady haunts beneath a dock. Look for old docks with wooden posts. Spool an open-face spinning reel with high-visibility monofilament in 4- to 6-pound test. Use a medium-light or even ultralight rod in the 5- to 7-foot range. Arm it with a soft-bodied crappie jig. You are locked and loaded.

STEP 1 Point the rod tip up and open the bail. Release enough line so the lure falls to the bottom rod guide. Trap the line against the rod with the trigger finger of your rod hand. With your free hand, grasp the jighead between your thumb and your forefinger and middle finger with the hook point up and the rest of your fingers extended out of the hook's way. Holding the jig to your side, extend the rod tip toward your target zone. This creates a bend in the rod.

STEP 2 Keep the drawn line between the rod tip and the jig low and parallel to the water. You may need to crouch. The lure should start skipping just before the dock.

STEP 3 Let go of the jighead first, and in the next instant, release your trigger finger to allow the line to play out. To keep the lure from hitting the rod tip, pop the rod tip upward upon the release.

151 GIVE REDBREAST SUNNIES THE SLIP

One of the downsides of trying to fish and hunt for everything is that I miss being consumed by a single passion. On a trip to Florida's Suwannee River, I ran into a couple of codgers who fished for redbreast sunfish an incredible 75 days a year. They deep-drifted crickets with 1/16-ounce bullet weights, but it was the bobbers they fussed over like kids with a puppy. They modified off-the-shelf 2-inch slip corks by removing the hollow inserts and pushing inserts from the next size up into the line channels. Monofilament slid twice as easily in those larger channels, allowing the crickets to attain deeper depths.

152 MAKE YOUR OWN SAND SPIKES

There's nothing to making your own beach sand spikes, which make running multiple rods an easy task. Try it with schedule 40 PVC, which is a heavier, more impact-resistant pipe than standard lightweight PVC.

STEP 1 Cut one 6-foot length of 1 1/2-inch-diameter PVC pipe into two sections, using a sharp 30-degree angle. Sand both ends of the pipe to smooth rough edges. You can stop here or continue on for an upgrade.

STEP 2 On the flat end, mark a hole 12 inches from the end and drill a 1/4-inch hole through both walls of the pipe. Thread a 2 1/2-inch galvanized bolt through the hole, and fashion with a lock washer and nut. The butt of a surf rod will rest against this bolt, keeping the reel away from the lip of the pipe.

STEP 3 If you're really feeling fancy, add an S-hook. Use pliers to crimp one end of the hook down to about 1/4-inch diameter, and bend the hook in the middle so that the two ends are perpendicular. Thread this onto the bolt before attaching the lock washer and nut, and you'll have a handy hook on which to hang fishing towels, sunglasses, or a small tackle bag.

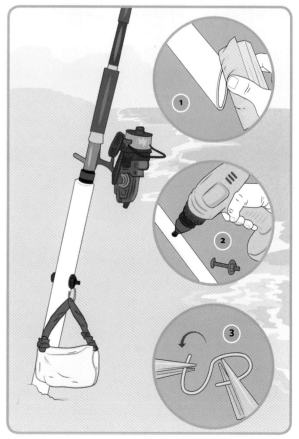

153 THROW A ONE-TWO PUNCH FOR SMALLIES

Wading a small stream for smallmouth bass is a fun way to spend a spring or summer day, but scoring big fish in this kind of water can be far more challenging than hooking up on a mighty river or deep lake. While small bass in streams might be ravenous, large bronzebacks are often more wary, feeding less frequently and holing up in tight spots for most of the day. To entice small-stream trophies, you need to appeal to their predatory instincts, dialing in a presentation and lure size these fish can't resist. This twitchbait and teaser fly combination packs a one-two punch.

RIG IT Cut a length of mono from your main line (which should be around 8-pound-test) and splice it back onto the main line with two Uni knots, creating tag ends that measure 5 or 6 inches. Trim off only the tag from the main line close to the knot. Next, tie a twitchbait, such as the Rapala X-Rap, to the end of the spliced line. Now, tie a small Muddler Minnow or a white Zonker fly onto the remaining tag on the splice.

DIG IT Cast the rig upstream of holes, deep-cut banks, or slow runs, and aggressively jerk the rod three or four times to make the twitchbait dive (A). This mimics a baitfish (the twitchbait) chasing a smaller baitfish (the fly) and should get the attention of any bass holding within striking distance.

HOLD IT After those initial twitches, pause the rig, thus allowing the lure and fly to hover, then slowly rise up as they get swept along by the current (B). Smallmouths often attack at this point. Streams tend to feature smaller

baitfish than large lakes and rivers, so don't be surprised if the fly gets hammered. Even big bass will key in on tiny forage in this environment.

RIP IT If you don't have a strike during the pause, start quickly jerking the rod tip as you retrieve the lure back for your next cast (C). Sometimes any of the noncommittal smallmouths will be triggered to attack when it seems forage is trying to make a fast escape out of the area. Work the rig all the way back to the rod tip, as big bass may track the lure and fly for a distance before taking a swing.

154 HAMMER A BREAM BED

There's no finer way to usher in spring than with a floating foam spider tethered to a sinking ant. Start with formal attire: Tie on a black foam spider with white legs. Using an improved clinch knot, tie a 4-pound tippet to the hook bend on the spider; it should be just long enough to reach the bottom of the bedding area. Add the sinking ant and you're in business. It's a deadly tactic with spinning tackle, too. Just add a casting bubble a few feet up from the spider.

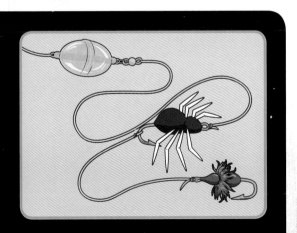

GRILL FISH WITH A TREE BRANCH

Leave the frying pan at home. In 60 minutes you can build a fire, clean your catch, weave a grill, and burn the dishes. Oh yeah, and eat the freshest fish you've ever tasted. These instructions are for a couple of eating-size fish for two people. But there's no limit to how big a grill you can weave from branches, so supersize this model for larger fish or cuts of game.

STEP 1 From a pliable willow sapling, cut the following: a Y-stick with a 12-inch stub and forks 3 feet long; two 20-inch branches; and six 14-inch branches. Snip off all twigs. Soak pieces in warm water.

STEP 2 Twist the fork branches into the shape of a racket. Start at the thick ends and move toward the tips, working them back and forth a bit at a time, being careful not to split the wood.

STEP 3 Lay a 20-inch branch across the center of the racket, then weave in the other 20-inch stick so they cross in the middle. Pre-bend the others so they can be woven in with enough tension to stay in place.

Top the fish with onions, lemon, and bacon. Or just scarf it down plain.

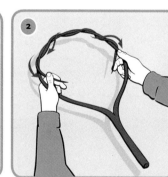

GET MINTY FRESH WITH MINNOWS

If you're looking to catch minnows for bait, you have a number of options, but here's an old favorite. Instead of baiting minnow traps with bread, cornmeal, or cat food, try using a fresh stick of chewing gum. Though minnows and shiners will swarm to the gum, they won't eat it. And since it doesn't dissolve, a single piece will effectively bait the trap for several days. It is by far the most effective and cleanest bait.

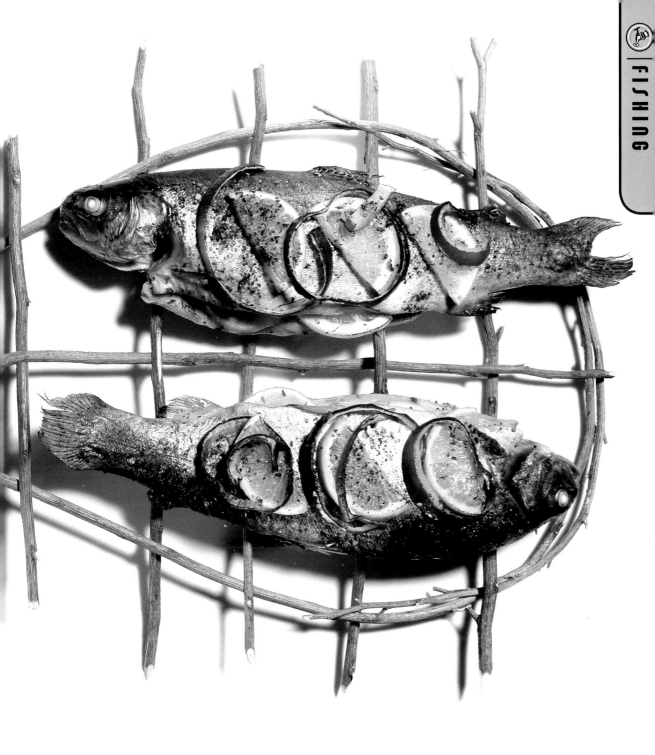

Dry ice is nothing more than frozen carbon dioxide, and nothing less than the solution to many cooler woes, including melting ice that creates a nasty fish-slime slush. Since dry ice sublimates, or goes directly from the solid to the gaseous state, it creates no meltwater. It's extremely cold—almost minus 110 degrees Fahrenheit. But dealing with dry ice takes some planning. Handle it with insulated or leather gloves or it will "burn" your skin. Keep children away from the stuff. Dry ice also expands approximately 800 times its original volume as it sublimates into the gas form, so cooler lids must be vented. And take care to crack a window if you drive with a cooler of frozen CO_2.

Here's how to turn your fishing cooler into a deep-freeze for the long run.

BLOCK IT OUT Two 10-inch-square blocks of 2-inch-thick dry ice (a standard 10-pound block) will keep 20 pounds of frozen foods frozen for approximately 3 days. To make dry ice last longer, fill dead air space with regular ice frozen in milk cartons or wadded newspaper.

THAW AS YOU GO Dry ice keeps frozen items frozen granite hard. Carry a small thawing cooler to thaw out foods as needed.

HAVE A COLD ONE Super cool beverages and nonfrozen items for extended periods with a 1-to-4 ratio of dry ice to regular ice. Wrap the dry ice in newspaper before placing in cooler.

PUT A TROPHY ON ICE To ship game and fish, use dry ice exclusively to prevent water spoilage of trophies. Be careful to wrap the specimen in a towel to prevent the dry ice from creating freezer-burn spots. Or mix dry ice and regular ice to save on shipping weight.

KNOW WHERE TO SHOP Dry ice is available in grocery stores in many southwestern states. Other vendors: ice companies and ice cream shops.

158 TRICK TROUT WITH THE RIGHT STICK

Stickbaits catch more and bigger trout than just about any other lure. The trick to being successful with these lures is making sure you match the style of stick to the size and speed of the water you're fishing. These three will come through in all kinds of rivers all over the country.

For clear, narrow pocket-water streams, you need a stickbait that won't splash down hard and can be worked effectively on a light rod. The 2-inch floating Yo-Zuri Pins Minnow only dives to 1 foot, so it doesn't hang up on the bottom often, and its thin-profile lip gives it a tight wiggle even when barely twitched. Work the Pins through seams and eddies with the rod tip high, twitching it gently.

On a stream with a little more width, depth variation, and structure, throw a 3⅛-inch Rapala X-Rap. What's great about this lure is its ability to suspend at any depth. The X-Rap is most effective when cast upstream, jerked to depth, and allowed to sweep downstream with an occasional twitch through likely holding water or around boulders and deadfalls.

Big-river trout hunters, especially in the South, might be married to their Smithwick Rattlin' Rogues, but the 4½-inch XCalibur EEratic Shad will put a hurt on heavy trout. The swifter the current, the more erratically it moves on the twitch, yet it's not tiring to work, which lets you cover more water without turning your arms to Jell-O. This lure shines in rivers with even flows and deeper runs where the trout hold in the main current instead of orienting to boulders, eddies, and fallen trees.

159 FILTER FISH-FRYING OIL

You can reuse fish-frying oil during a camping trip if you carefully strain it after cooking. Carry an empty container the same size as the original oil bottle. After you fry the day's catch, let the oil cool, then strain it through a coffee filter into the empty container. After the next night's fish fry, filter the oil again by pouring it through another clean coffee filter into the original bottle. You can repeat the process several times.

160 PRANK SOCIAL MEDIA PALS

Social media can turn you into a fishing hero or a former employee who's fish pics got you outed as a work-at-home poser. Here's how to post fish photos that supersize your catch while downplaying the fact that you boogied out early on a Friday afternoon.

GET RELATIVE Every fish looks bigger when photographed beside a toy-sized rod and reel. Pack one of those mini-micro-ultralight spinning or fly outfits to prop beside your catch. Turns a 6-inch bluegill into a true titty bream.

DELAY THE GAME When you post pics on the go, everyone—boss, spouse, buddies—is alerted that your nose is off the grindstone. Resist the temptation to post in real time. Lay down fake bread crumbs while on the water. "Deadline crunch today—hope I make that 3 P.M. cutoff!" and "Buried in this project for hours but light in the tunnel now!" will keep your pals from bugging you

since you are obviously sweating for The Man. Then hit 'em with that 8-pound hawg shot just past sundown. Use Instagram's "Hefe" filter to add sunset highlights, or throw them off the time trail completely with an artsy black-and-white filter.

HIDE THE SPOT Want to rub your big fish in your friends' virtual faces but without tipping them off to your favorite farm pond? Use the tilt-shift feature in the Instagram edit mode to blur out landscape details. Or haul in an inflatable palm tree for background foliage. The monkey gets them every time. "Man, that looks like Fred's pond, but I don't think there's a palm tree out there. And I would remember that monkey for sure."

161 MASTER THE ORVIS KNOT

Use this knot for tying small flies to light leader tippets, or spinning lures to light- or medium-size nylon monofilaments. It is usually 20 to 30 percent stronger than the popular improved clinch.

STEP 1 Extend 6 to 8 inches of line through the hook eye. Form a large loop with the tag end on the far side of the standing line.

STEP 2 Form a second loop by bringing the tag end around the standing line and back underneath and through the first loop.

STEP 3 Bend the tag end to the right and make two turns around the second loop. These turns must start from the far side of the second loop.

STEP 4 To tighten the knot, first pull in opposite directions on both the hook and the tag end. Then pull on the standing line to bring the knot firmly against the hook eye.

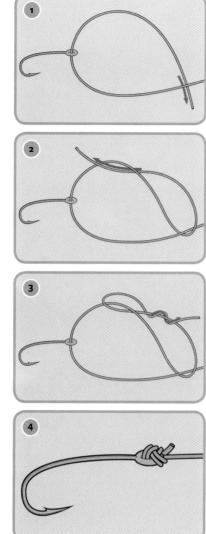

163 SCHOOL A KID ON FLY FISHING

Teaching your kids how to fly-cast doesn't have to be as trying as helping them with math homework. Approach the task like training a puppy: short, fun sessions with plenty of opportunities for success. Using kid-friendly gear is a huge bonus. Here's what to look for.

A soft action helps kids feel the flex and load. Resist the temptation to choose a super-short rod, which can be difficult to cast. Go for an 8-foot, 6-weight outfit.

Overline the rod by one line weight to make for easier casting and ability to feel the rod load.

Get a barbed fly stuck in your child's forehead and you can forget about a future fishing buddy. Only use flies with barbless hooks. For practice, tie orange egg yarn next to the fly to make it visible. On the water, cast big high-floating flies like Stimulators.

162 TRICK LUNKERS WITH A LANTERN

For several million years, there was only one way to fish at night: Hang a trusty double-mantle, white-gas-burning Coleman lantern over the water and get to it. The lantern hissed gently, its glow attracting baitfish and their bigger brethren, as well as hordes of mosquitoes held at bay with metal-melting concoctions of 100 percent DEET. That's how your granddaddy night fished, and his'n and his'n. And guess what? It still works today.

MAD RIVER EXPLORER DUCK HUNTER CANOE

Occasionally I make a good decision, a choice that betters the shape and course of life. For some folks, these transformative moments might come in the form of a marriage vow or a winning lottery ticket. For me, it was when I bought my first canoe.

It was a Mad River 16-foot Explorer, with a tough Royalex hull, and I splurged an extra few hundred dollars for the so-called Duck Hunter's edition. That canoe was clad in an olive green skin, and it featured cane seats, a portage yoke, and eye-catching slotted gunwales of dark-stained ash. What a beauty.

And that beauty goes beyond skin-deep. Despite its name, the canoe has shown its chops as an unsurpassed fishing canoe. I learned to stand up in a canoe and fly cast from that Explorer, on Van's Pond, where bass cruised lily pond edges and crappie skulked around Christmas trees sunk in the cold waters each January. In the early 1990s, as the striped bass runs came roaring back in North Carolina's Roanoke River, Scott Wood and I turned the Explorer into a poor-boy's striper boat. Our sole outfitting accessory: a disposable river anchor of a rope tied to a brick or cinder block. We turned plenty of heads in that canoe, the boat anchored in an eddy line, two guys standing up in one canoe, laying out 40-foot casts of lead-core lines.

One thing I love about the Explorer is its haul-it-anywhere, run-it-everywhere utility. The canoe features a shallow-V arched bottom that provides just a bit of tracking without sticking tight to logs and rocks, and while it's a bit squirrely underfoot, there's plenty of secondary stability to make the boat serviceable in whitewater and absolutely excel as a fishing craft. The Explorer is tough beyond description. On a rocky smallmouth bass river, I fear no jagged ledge. Outfitted with a side motor

mount, she's ferried me into salt marshes in search of redfish and speckled trout. She's not light at 70 pounds, but I can carry her on my shoulders no problem, and the boat will swallow 1,100 pounds of men and gear without a groan.

Over the years, that canoe has endured abuse that would have shredded lesser craft. Its inaugural float trip was down a small bony river in a summer drought. My buddy and I bashed the boat over rock ledges and through shallow boulder gardens, each scrape and smash a dagger to my heart as I imagined the shiny, smooth hull roughed up like a new truck in a demolition derby. That first day on the water wiped the newness from the hull, and from then on, the Explorer has been a true workhorse.

I've made only a few modifications. A few years back, I tired of replacing the cane seats and wove duct tape into a basket-weave pattern that is now a permanent fixture (see item 107). At some point I switched out the factory portage yoke with a fancy sculpted yoke I ordered from Canada and paid a bloody fortune to have shipped home. It comes in handy when I portage the canoe down closed country roads to the lake. In truth, however, the canoe is just so tough, I often simply load it with a morning's worth of fishing gear and lunch and drag it through the woods.

These days, fishing kayaks are all the rage, and I am charmed by their possibilities. There's a lot to be said for all the gizmos available to fine-tune a kayak for anything from pond crappie to bluewater sharks. But for 30 years that Explorer has helped me find fish, find hidden waters, and find my way. She's steady and quiet, tried and true. Occasionally, some other canoe nut will see that old Duck Hunter Explorer at the boat ramp or upside-down on my truck and offer an impressive pile of cash for the old gal. You should hear me laughing.

IT'S THE FIRST SHOT THAT MATTERS

The gun was a Remington Model 700 BDL Varmint Master, chambered in .22-250 and fired handloads that could flip a groundhog backwards out of its burrow at 300 yards.

If you could hit the target.

This was 40 years ago, and that was the gun that taught me how to shoot a rifle. I learned through equal parts humiliation and determination. My mentor, Keith Gleason, was a former U.S. Marine who didn't coddle the newbie. We cruised dirt roads in the rolling foothills along the New River where it stitched back and forth between North Carolina and Virginia, trading shots at whistlepigs in greening pastures. You got one shot. After that, hit or miss, you had to hand over the rifle. If I blew my chance, well, Gleason didn't care that I was a 13-year-old kid and he was a trained sharpshooter. Try harder, he'd say. And I would.

I learned a number of valuable lessons sweating over each shot, and one of them was about the proper role of hunting gear. Gleason tweaked handloads and fussed over ballistics tables, but when it came to putting lead where he wanted it to go, those tools only accentuated his skill. It was never the other way around.

It's too easy to forget that these days, when technological advances in gear make so many things seem all too easy. But good stuff works best when it works in tandem with finely honed ability. You can spring for the finest scope glass and bullet-drop compensating technology, but to shoot a rifle well, you still need good body mechanics, no flinch, and a trigger squeeze smooth as butter. All the recoil-dampening gas port tweaks in the world won't make a mallard any easier to hit when it's quartering away at 40 yards. Honeycombed risers and hybrid cams make it easier to hold a bow at full draw, no argument there. But it's pure skill that allows a bowhunter to thread an arrow through a tight slit in the dark timber.

More often than not, fine and fancy gear doesn't get the job done any better. What brings home the backstraps is knowing how to wring every drop of potential from the gear you have at hand. Like dragging a moose back to camp with a boat.

I was far up in northeastern Alberta when I heard about this, hanging on to a 20-foot aluminum skiff as Junior Adams, an XXXL-sized Athabascan Chipewyan native, gunned the 135-horsepower outboard. It was a 32-mile run to Adams' camp at a tiny Athabasca River village called Jackfish, set deep in the million-acre Peace-Athabasca Delta. As we made the run, Taylor Swift warbled from the boat's satellite radio, a duct-taped 1903 Enfield rattling against the windshield. When Junior said he kept the rifle handy in case a moose wandered out of the alders, I had to ask, "How do you get a moose home, when home is 30 miles down the river?"

"We drag them to the river with an ATV," Adams replied, "then we hook them up to the boat with a rope around the neck. It's a little hairy at first, but

once you get that moose on plane, it's like dragging a water skier back to camp!"

Of all the wonders of the sporting world, I'd like to see that at least once.

I've always been fascinated by hunters who fine-tune gear to very specific locations and hunting situations. It isn't always so dramatic as to involve a long rope and a 1,000-pound mammal. I remember a Quebec guide who made giant diving duck decoys for hunting out of traditional sinkboxes in the rough open waters of Lac Saint-Pierre. First, Roger Gladu had a local carver craft the perfect decoy—a tall, big-bodied bluebill that would show up on the white-capped lake. Gladu then made a mold of the decoy, and blew urethane foam into the mold. He had scores of the scaup, because divers like a big spread and his home waters ate decoys like peanuts. The decoys were practically the size of a garbage can. Each one was topped with hand-carved heads large enough to hide a softball inside. They weren't finely finished or artfully painted, but they matched the very conditions in which they were deployed: big, brawling, snotty waters.

I offered Gladu $50 for one. He couldn't do it. It'd be like a mechanic selling his favorite wrench. And to be truthful, I think a guy like Roger Gladu couldn't abide the thought that a working decoy he sweated over and designed to suck giant flocks of Arctic-breeding ducks from the sky would ride a bookshelf in some writer's office back in the States. I left empty-handed, but full of respect for a gear-hound like that.

That's one of the things I like the most about traveling North America for *Field & Stream*. I get to meet some of the most innovative people on the planet, and few of them are computer engineers. Most are wearing Carhartts overalls.

Like whoever figured out that you can sharpen a short, stout stick, thread it under the cartilage that runs on top of a doe's nose, and drag the deer to the truck with a DIY handle. Or thread a zip tie through the open spring in a clothespin, cinch down a handful of reeds in the zip tie, and clip the pin to a duck blind or treestand rail for a quick camouflage bundle. Pure genius. The same for the old Cajun squirrel hunter who mounted Vise-Grips to a pole barn and clamped squirrels in the pliers for quick cleaning. And the guy who invented the Butt Out tool—snicker if you wish, but any cheap plastic gizmo that makes it easier to remove the business end of a deer's digestive system deserves my undying gratitude. The value of a hunting tool has nothing to do with its price, but how well it solves a thorny problem or helps a hunter step up to the next level of skill.

Which is why that old Remington Varmint Master was the perfect gun for me, at the perfect time. While it was capable of more than I could do with it as a boy, it wasn't overly complicated. And most importantly, I saw it being used with skill that I could only dream of—and set my mind to replicate.

Even today, nearly 40 years after I last pulled its trigger, I can be at a gun shop, glancing down a line of 50 used rifles, and the first thing that catches my eye are those familiar white spacers between the stock and the butt plate, and Remington's distinctive fleur-de-lis flourishes in the grip checkering. All of a sudden, I'm back on the New River, crosshairs wobbling around a woodchuck burrow, counting heartbeats and squeezing the trigger between each throb. A lot has changed since then, but one thing hasn't: It's the first shot that matters.

164

STICK IT TO DOWNED GAME

Pick up a long stick and approach a downed big-game animal from behind. Watch for the rise and fall of the chest cavity. Closed eyes typically indicate a living animal. Never lay down your gun or bow until you use the stick to touch the animal's open eye. If it doesn't blink, you're good: Break out the skinning knife.

165 HOIST A DEER

I used to dread the backbreaking task of getting a buck up and over the truck tailgate solo. Until I discovered this trick.

STEP 1 Throw one rope over a branch. Tie one end to the rack and the other to the trailer hitch. Tie a second rope to the rack and toss the tag end over the branch.

STEP 2 Pull the truck forward to lift the animal off the ground. Secure the free end of the second rope to a tree or another object strong enough to hold the deer.

STEP 3 Untie the first rope from the vehicle. Back up, untie the second rope, and lower the deer into the truck.

166 TAKE A KILLER SELFIE

Taking a great selfie with your latest big buck is practically impossible unless you use a camera with a self-timer. Not all smartphone cameras come with a self-timer function, but many do, and those that don't can accept inexpensive self-timer apps. Add a small smartphone tripod and you'll be armed for taking boss self-portraits with your trophy.

This classic setup of the hunter approaching a downed deer is a snap. Focus on the deer's head and move back a few dozen feet for a more staged approach. That should put the deer in sharp focus and the hunter slightly out of focus for a dramatic view. This is one of the few times that having the hunter "skylined" against a light background is a good thing.

A shot as you drag the deer out of the woods can tell you an important part of the story. Use a small tripod to affix the phone to a sapling or tree branch. Frame up shots as you drag the deer towards the camera and away.

Another good shot that showcases headgear in a subtle way is attaching a permit to the deer's antler or punching a tag. Prop the smartphone on a pack or use a small tripod to frame up a shot of just your hands, a knife, the permit, and the deer's rack.

167 DECOY A PRONGHORN ANTELOPE

There might not be any more exciting archery hunts than decoying a lust-crazed prairie goat ready to stomp the life out of the life-sized decoy you are hiding behind. During the late-summer rut, dominant pronghorns gather harems of does during a brief 2- to 3-week period and chase away any other bucks that may horn in on their love nest. Even the less-dominant bucks are ready to fight at the drop of a decoy and run out across the plains—literally—for a no-holds-barred smackdown. Here's how you can dupe that goat with a decoy.

GO WITH A PAL Decoying works best when one person handles the decoy and a rangefinder while the other is dedicated to getting the shot. Trade off positions during the course of a day.

MAKE IT VISIBLE You have to be seen to be charged.

Set the decoy up on a ridge or swell where it will show up against the sky, or place it out in a flat open spot where there is minimal vegetation.

BE READY Your decoy might bring in a goat from the next county over or from just out of sight. As soon as the decoy is up, get on your knees and nock an arrow. Have your partner range a few clumps of brush or rocks so you'll have a rough idea of distance. It can happen that quickly.

DROP DOWN Speaking of knees, practice shooting from them, and practice shooting while leaning to one side to replicate working an arrow around a decoy.

GET AGGRESSIVE If a pronghorn buck is distracted by females, feeding, or another goat, go ahead and stalk close, hiding behind the decoy.

168 PACK STRING WAX EVERY HUNT

Place a big glob of bowstring wax on the E- or C-clip of your bow axle and you'll help to prevent a trio of noise problems. It stops the clip from rattling, it keeps debris and water out of the axle, and it will give you a handy supply of surplus wax in the field. Nick your string on a tree step or in some briars, or if dealing with a rest that suddenly develops a squeak, and you can reach up and grab a little wax to take care of the problem right in your stand.

169 CUSTOMIZE YOUR BOW SIGHT

Smaller .010 sight pins are all the rage, as they cover up less target surface than larger, more traditional .019 pins. But many shooters with less-than-perfect eyesight find the smaller pins tougher to shoot with, and some do find that they aren't bright enough in low-light situations.

Luckily, you don't have to take the one-size-fits-all approach. Many bow sight manufacturers offer models that take pins of multiple sizes. Set the sight up with larger pins on top and smaller pins below. That way you get the advantage of the smaller pin size at longer distances when the target picture is reduced, while retaining the brighter pin at the shorter distances you're more likely to shoot at in low-light scenarios. And while you're on the range, mix and match the pins. You might find that the smaller sized pin actually works better at super-short ranges of 20 yards or so. It's all about the individual shooter, and the right bow sight will give you all the flexibility you need.

170 READ A BLOODY ARROW

It's a very fortunate archer who recovers a bloody arrow, but now the tougher part begins: finding the deer and turning all that luck into steaks and roasts in a freezer. The first step is to examine that arrow for clues about where it passed through the deer. Find a strong source of light—sunlight or flashlight—and take a close look from nock to broadhead.

BLOOD Bright pink-red blood from tip to nock indicates a hit in the vitals. Frothy bubbles can suggest a lung hit. No bubbles indicates a heart shot. Dark red blood with no bubbles could indicate a liver hit.

HAIR Coarse brown hair can indicate a good shot if the arrow entered in the vitals. White hair suggests a low hit. Wait several hours before tracking.

BROWNISH OR GREENISH MATERIAL An arrow streaked with any brownish or greenish material is a bad sign. An arrow from a gut-shot deer might be flecked with stomach contents such as green leaves or little bits of any partially digested corns or soybeans. Lift it up to your nose and smell for a strong odor. This typically indicates a gut-shot deer. If gray or brown hair is on the arrow, that could mean a higher hit than white hair.

FAT Greasy streaks of fat or tallow can be a clue that the arrow passed through the deer's back or haunch.

171 PIMP YOUR .22

A dear uncle gave me my first gun, a J.C. Higgins Model 31 tube-fed .22. Manufactured by the long-gone High Standard Corp. and sold through Sears, that rifle was the kickoff to a lifelong rimfire romance in which fidelity has never played a role. Over the years I've wandered widely. My old high school flame was a Remington Speedmaster—another tubular semiauto. I had a serious college fling with a Browning 541T bull-barreled bolt action. Next came a steady relationship, sort of, with a succession of factory Ruger 10/22s. Right now, my current rimfire love is the equivalent of a trophy wife: a pimped-out 10/22 with aftermarket trigger, carbon-fiber barrel, rimfire-specific scope, and a few other whistles and bells that toll a death knell for squirrels. The highly customizable Ruger 10/22 has a screwed-in barrel and straightforward design that allows it to be inexpensively tinkered with from butt to muzzle. Here's what I did to my own Ruger. Now, how about yours?

→ **DROP-IN TRIGGER** Timney's one-piece drop-in trigger is set at a crisp 2 3/4 pounds, with no creep. Machined from 6061-T6 aircraft-grade aluminum, the action houses a trigger, sear, and hammer of heat-treated steel. Replacing the famously unimpressive factory 10/22 trigger is a snap. Punch out the two action pins, remove the trigger action, and replace the entire assembly.

→ **LAMINATED STOCK** With grain in their multiple layers of wood running in different directions, laminated stocks can offer you high strength, great stability, and good resistance to warping. I chose a straightforward lay-up, but there are lots of aftermarket stocks out there, from thumbhole stocks to Monte Carlo designs to lightweight configurations with skeletonized buttstocks and slotted fore-ends.

172 USE SNAP CAPS THREE WAYS

Snap caps are dummy rounds that cushion the fall of the firing pin so that firearms can be safely dry-fired. Some manufacturers recommend them, and others contend that are not necessary, but they are cheap insurance. Here are three ways to use snap caps.

PRACTICE MAKES PERFECT There is utterly no question that dry-fire practice will make you a better shooter. It's a great way to get used to the trigger pull of a new gun and a great way to keep muscle memory tuned up for pulling the trigger of an old favorite.

FLINCH TEST When practicing on the range, mix a snap cap in with your live rounds and you'll quickly uncover poor shooting technique when the pin falls on a dummy round.

ASSESS A USED GUN Thinking of buying a used gun? Run snap caps through the action to evaluate the trigger mechanism and ejectors.

→ **DEDICATED RIMFIRE SCOPE** The 50-yard parallax setting on the Nikon Pro-Staff 3-9X BDC 150 gives a squirrel hunter tack-sharp focus when he's searching for limb dancers squashed tight against a treetop limb, while the BDC reticle is calibrated for .22 Long Rifle ammo, taking much of the guesswork out of those long shots to the back of the woodlot.

→ **VOLQUARTSEN CARBON FIBER BARREL** At a short 16.5 inches long and just 23 ounces in weight, this match barrel changes the look and feel of a rifle like nothing else. The carbon fiber barrel shroud is put together with tension at both the muzzle and chamber ends to provide rigidity. For long walks in the squirrel woods, it's a delight. Such a light front end, however, is an acquired taste.

→ **PARACORD SLING** I like lightweight slings on my rifles. Choose your color, choose your swivels, choose between fixed length or adjustable. There are tons of options online. Mine is created with a standard weave for a supple feel, but the Double Cobra and King Cobra designs are pretty sweet, too.

173 RUIN A RIFLE BY BEING AN IDIOT

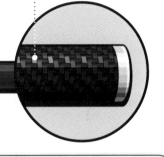

The last thing a bullet sees as it flees a rifle barrel is the crown—the very tip of the gun muzzle. The great majority of rifles' crowns are recessed at the bore to protect this precious aperture from any tiny deformations that can throw a bullet off. Any nick, or chip, or uneven wearing at the crown can spell disaster, and there are two very common culprits. Each is entirely avoidable.

TRUCK MUCK It is never a good idea to place an uncased rifle inside a vehicle, but it's an idiotic move to place a rifle muzzle down in the front seat so that the barrel crown grinds into all of that mud, grit, grime, and dried ketchup you store on the floor mat.

CLEANING DAMAGE An old adage holds that more guns are damaged by cleaning them than by using them, and this is what it means. When cleaning from the breech, be vigilant about pulling the cleaning brush or jag back into the barrel if it exits the bore. Use your fingers to carefully guide it into the barrel without coming into contact with the crown. The slightest ding can be a whitetail buck's best friend.

174 MAKE A EUROPEAN MOUNT DUCK SKULL

Here's how to turn a greenhead—or any other duck or goose—into your very own miniature European mount, complete with crossed upper leg bones and, if you're lucky, a snazzy bird band to bling it up.

I've used two methods of preparing the duck skulls: The first involves soaking the bones in hot water for days, painstakingly scraping away the flesh, then gluing the parts back together. Once I discovered the second, super-easy way, I'll never go back. It starts with a friendly phone call.

MEET THE BEETLES Flesh-eating dermestid beetles can clean off a duck skull in a matter of days. Plenty of museums and nature centers keep a colony or two of the dermestid beetles, and a modest contribution—say, $25—can often win you a spot in their beetle box. You will first need to skin the upper legs and then cut away most of the muscle, and skin the skull and cut out the tongue, but the bugs will do the rest. Another option: Inquire with a local taxidermist if you and your buddies can toss a few duck skulls and leg bones in with a load of deer skulls being prepped for European mounts. Tell the taxidermist there's no need to go through the degreasing process. You will do that yourself in the next step.

DEGREASE THE BONES Once the bones are back from the beetles, degrease them by soaking them in warm water and Dawn dishwashing detergent for a few hours. Rinse well. Dry in the sun. To further whiten the bones, soak overnight in hydrogen peroxide and set in the sun to dry. Use small dabs of wood glue to strengthen any loose joints. Brush bleach on stubborn brown spots, or go all natural. If you want, add a yellow bill with acrylic paint.

COME TOGETHER Cross the leg bones and use hot glue to hold in place. Once they're dry, build up a few layers of glue in the concave underside of the bill for a flat base, then attach the crossed bones to the back of the skull with more glue. Finish with a leather lanyard and duck band.

175 TUNE A DUCK CALL

Just about any duck call can be tuned to produce sounds that are higher or lower in pitch or have more or less rasp or squeal than what you get with the factory-tuned setup. It's neither terribly difficult nor terribly easy, which means that it's perfect for any duck hunter with shade-tree mechanic tendencies. Here's how.

SINGLE REED First, check to make sure that the call's wedge hasn't slipped or, if it's made of cork, dried out. If it won't seat firmly in the call, get a replacement from the call manufacturer. To give the call a higher pitch, use scissors to trim off a tiny sliver at a time, and reassemble the call and test it after each trimming. To add raspiness, rough up the toneboard with 220-grit sandpaper. Or dog-ear the front corners of the reed at a 60-degree angle with a tiny diagonal cut.

DOUBLE REED Pull the barrel off and take a quick photo of the insert so you'll have a record of the reeds' placement in relation to the wedge and toneboard. To tune, move the wedge back (to lower pitch) or forward (to raise pitch), without altering the reed arrangement. Test the call after each tweak. If the call still isn't to your liking, trim very lightly with scissors. Again, test after each adjustment. To add rasp, carefully offset the top reed slightly back from the lower reed. As little as $\frac{1}{32}$ inch may do it, so go easy.

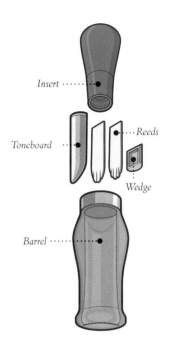

Insert

Toneboard

Reeds

Wedge

Barrel

176 BRUSH UP A DUCK CANOE

A correctly camouflaged canoe will put you so close to river ducks you'll have to give them a few seconds to open up the distance before pulling the trigger. An incorrectly brushed-up boat will get you just close enough to realize you should have done a better job with the canoe.

THE HULL TRUTH The long, smooth hull of a canoe will glint with sunlight and spook every duck on the creek long before you're close enough to shoot. Even a camo-painted canoe can use some help. Use one or two long pieces of camouflage netting to knock back the hull's shine. Drape the netting over the rails so that the bottom edge is barely above the water's surface. Start at the bow and extend the netting at least as far back as the stern seat.

FLOATING ISLAND Cut twice as much brush as you think you'll need. Use half of it to create a fan-shaped hide in the bow. Bend some limbs so they drape over the gunwales in order to break up your boat's outlines. Stand some brush up as far back as the center thwart, and drape a few branches out over the gunwales to shield the paddler's movements. Jam more cut brush behind the stern seat.

177 USE A DOG WHISTLE TO CALL A MALLARD DRAKE

That saucy loud mallard quack is made by the hen, not the drake. The quack of the greenhead is a soft, subtle, raspy whistle—*mweep-mweep-mweep*. At close range, it's a deadly finishing call, and you can make it with any pealess dog whistle. The specific tactic will vary depending on the whistle, but here's the general drill: Hum into the whistle, saying "mweep" with a deep, guttural tone. You might need to partially block the top air hole. Experiment with finger placement on the air hole and different versions of "mweep," "shweee," and "zsssoop" until you find the right tone for your whistle.

178 USE A POV CAMERA

Point-of-view cameras have transformed the outdoor experience, and hunters have latched onto these pocket-sized dynamos. Here's a grab-bag of tricks from GoPro engineers that go beyond the instruction manual. They range from common-sense tips to high-tech insights, and they'll make you a better videographer.

CARRY IT RIGHT Transport the camera with its battery separate. If you don't, then the camera or its WiFi can accidentally, and easily, turn on.

FIGHT THE FOG Waterproof housings are great, but be vigilant. Moisture captured inside the housing can cause the lens to fog, and it doesn't take a deluge. Damp fingers, humid air, and hot breath can all fog the inner surface of the lens. If available for your camera, carry anti-fog pads.

GET CLOSE Most of the time, closer is better, so put the camera right into the action. Let the dog lick and sniff it. Set it in a cooler and then toss in the ducks. A point of view 2 or 3 feet away from the subject is not too close for many shot opportunities.

CENTER IT If there is a large sweep of horizon in the shot, it is often best to try to have that horizon line in the center of the frame. That will keep the horizon line straight, instead of bowing with the wide angle.

CONTROL TIME Learn how to take and edit time-lapse sequences. Opinions vary about ideal intervals between shots, but do the math to figure out how long you'll need the photo capture to run in order to get the desired seconds of "video" out of the time-lapse clip. For example, at 30fps video playback, and taking a photo every 2 seconds, you'll get 1 second of video for each minute of photo capture.

ADJUST FRAME RATE In low light conditions, adjust the frame rate to allow the camera to capture more light per frame. In decent sunlight, 48fps is a standard setting, but don't be hesitant to crank it down to 24fps.

RELAX Don't let the camera get in the way of your fun, or your quarry. Practice at home so you can seamlessly integrate the camera once you're in the field.

179 USE GPS TO RECORD GAME TRAILS

The "track-back" or "path" mode in a GPS is one fantastic tool to mark both human and animal trails on your favorite hunting grounds. While scouting, turn the mode on as you walk any linear feature. Choose one color for human features, such as logging roads, ATV trails, and property boundaries. Choose another for game features, such as rub lines, primary trails, and faint buck trails. Now you will have a features map that makes it easy to plan entry and exit routes to your hunting locations.

180 CONTROL A SPINNING TURKEY

When it comes to turkey decoy movement, there can be too much of a good thing. Those super-lightweight foam decoys bob and dip in a slight breeze, but a decent puff of wind can send them weathervaning to all points of the compass—and spook any gobbler that's giving them a look. To rein in a spinning turkey decoy, tie twine to the tail and stake it loosely to a tent stake or nearby sapling. If you're caught in the turkey woods without twine, jab a pair of sticks into the ground a few inches to the left and right of the decoy's tail. That will give it plenty of room for lifelike motion without spinning like a top.

You can't keep up with all the advances in trail camera technology until you learn the language.

BLACK FLASH Typical infrared sensors emit a dull red or orange glow that can be detected by game; a black flash supposedly doesn't.

BURST MODE This setting shoots multiple images in quick succession when triggered.

DETECTION ZONE Cone-shaped area formed by the maximum distances at which the camera's sensors can detect an animal and shoot a photo.

MP Stands for megapixel. High-MP cams can produce higher-quality photos, but other factors also affect picture quality.

PIR Passive infrared sensors can detect the heat and/or movement of an animal and activate the camera.

RECOVERY RATE How long it takes a camera to rearm before taking the next photo.

TRIGGER SPEED Time elapsed from when a camera's sensor detects an animal to when a picture is taken. Speeds vary greatly, and fast is almost always better.

2012-10-16 3:53:26 AM   M 2/3   46°F

MC65HO COVERT

Bushnell   10-20-2012 18:28:29

Bushnell   10-20-2012 18:28:49

182 FINE-TUNE TRAIL CAMS

Here's how to snap a picture of a bruiser buck.

STEP UP Place each camera 6 to 8 feet high in a tree, with the lens angled slightly downward. Wedge a stick behind the camera to get the correct angle. You will get a much better field of view and also increase your chances of picking up bucks in the background. Plus, there's less chance of alerting deer with the camera flash.

QUARTER ANGLE One of the most common mistakes is to aim a camera perpendicular to the trail. A quartering angle is best for maximizing the time the deer stays in frame.

BUCK SHOT Place an additional camera on your stand tree, facing behind you, to capture savvy bucks skirting field edges and moving parallel to established deer trails.

TIME TRAVEL If your camera will run in both time-lapse and motion modes simultaneously, switch on both modes.

CHECKMATES Always carry spare memory cards and surgical gloves when you check cameras. It's quicker to swap cards than remove the entire camera, and surgical gloves will keep cameras and trees free of human scent.

184 TARGET SHOP AT WALMART

Looking for fun targets to shoot with a .22? Take a stroll through the aisles of your local superstore. There are plenty of cheap, reactive targets that will add pizzazz—not to mention a mini-explosion—to your next rimfire shooting session.

- Condiment packs
- Charcoal briquettes
- Animal crackers
- Eggs
- Kool-Aid ice cubes
- Figurines
- Sandwich baggies filled with white flour
- Cheap cookies
- Poker chips
- Baby carrots
- Cheap soda
- Golf balls

183 TURN A PISTOL INTO A SHOTGUN

Ranchers in serious snake country are known for toting revolvers loaded with rat shot for those too-close encounters with Mr. No Shoulders. There are plenty of myths and misinformation about shotshells for handguns, so here's what you need to know before plugging away with pint-sized shotshells.

MICRO-SHOT Pistol shotshells are loaded with tiny shot. In .22 and .22 Magnum, most shells are filled with tiny No. 11 or No. 12 shot. Step up to the larger calibers—9mms, .38s, .40s, .44s, .45s—and the shot size can creep up to No. 9. That's still pretty lightweight stuff.

BARREL BASHING It's a misconception that shooting rat shot in a rifled barrel will ruin the barrel. Lead shot won't damage a steel barrel. Shoot a lot of the stuff, however, and lead and plastic fouling could be an issue, so clean barrels with a bronze brush after firing rat shot.

SEMIAUTO PAINS It's true that the plastic-topped rat shot is a questionable load for your semiautomatic pistol. Even if the round cycles, there's a chance that the feed ramp or any other metal parts might tear the plastic cap and allow all the spilled lead shot to dump into the inner workings of a handgun. That's no good.

BOTTOM LINE Rat shot from these calibers is a decidedly short-range, very-small-game load. The shot cups spin from the rifling, so the pattern opens quickly. And the shot itself is too small to do much damage. They're great for bumblebees on the wing, blackbirds at 20 feet, and rats, mice, and snakes at super-close ranges. Not so much for something as tough as a squirrel.

185 USE AN OLD TIRE TO TEACH A NEW DOG TRICKS

The "place" command is a great tool to introduce to any dog, and it is especially good for retrievers. Waterfowl hunters often need their dogs to stay and work from a distance, be it 10 feet or 20 yards away. And retrievers should be comfortable sitting and staying on any less-than-comfortable structures, such as downed logs in beaver swamps or small platforms in marshes.

Use an old tire as a backyard "place" training tool. It provides a slightly elevated platform that helps a dog understand that this is its "place." Cut a scrap piece of plywood or even an old foam archery target to fit the top of the tire and secure in place with paracord. Ugly and effective.

ONE PLACE With the dog on leash and a treat in your non-leash hand, lead the dog to the "place" stand. Using the hand with the treat, point with your finger to the stand, say "place," and use the treat to guide the dog up to the stand. Give the treat the instant the dog sits. Repeat, repeat, repeat.

TWO PLACES Once the dog knows "place," set up a training route with multiple stations for the "place" command. Use another tire, a few cinder blocks, and other items that provide a well-defined place to sit. Once your pooch is solid on the command, add stations without any elevation, such as carpet squares.

TOUGH PLACES Add "place" stations that have a degree of difficulty or instability to your training route. Log rounds, overturned canoes, and upside-down coolers work well. While on walks, give the "place" command at park benches, retaining walls, and other similar structures.

186 TRAIN A DOG TO SCENT TRAIL

Early-season hunts often take place in the heavy cover of beaver ponds and thick timber. A good cripple dog is a major asset. To fine-tune your dog's nose, cut a piece of PVC pipe about 5 feet in length. (The diameter doesn't matter—use whatever you've got cluttering up your basement.) Run an 8-foot-long section of paracord or other cordage through the pipe, and tie a slip loop to one end. Attach the loop to a bird wing or training bumper treated with duck scent. Hold the pipe out from your body, and drag the wing or bumper along a scent trail through your yard. The pipe prevents your own foot scent from contaminating the trail.

187 MAKE A CANINE FIRST AID KIT

Think it's a dog's life? Try pushing aside briers with your own face. Packing a small, light first aid kit for your sporting dog can save a morning's hunt, or even your dog's life. All these items will fit inside a 1-gallon heavy-duty zip-seal bag.

BETADINE SOLUTION	4 ounces	Clean and irrigate cuts.
TRIPLE ANTIBIOTIC OINTMENT	1-ounce tube	Treat minor burns and cuts after cleansing.
HYDROGEN PEROXIDE	4 ounces	Clean wounds. Induce vomiting.
STERILE EYE WASH	1 ounce	Aids in removing foreign objects.
STYPTIC PENCIL	1 pencil	Stop bleeding in toepad and muzzle lacerations
SUPERGLUE	1 small tube	Close minor wounds in brier-torn ears and toepad.
GAUZE PADS	Ten 3- inch-square pads, two 2-inch-wide rolls	Stem bleeding, clean and dress wounds.
DUCT TAPE	5 feet	Emergency bandage. Use to hold gauze in place.
STERILE TAPE	1-inch-wide roll	Use to hold bandages in place.
TWEEZERS	1 pair	Remove splinters, pluck seeds from ears and nose.
BENADRYL	25-mg tablets	Treat insect stings, snakebite.
PLASTIC ZIP-SEAL BAGS	4 small bags	Emergency booties for injured feet; secure with duct tape.
NEWSPAPER	1 sports section, folded	Emergency splint for broken bones.

188

TEACH A DOG TO DIVE FOR DUCKS

Wounded ducks will frequently dive when a retriever approaches. Teach yours to match wits with these escape artists. Run an anchor line or paracord through the eye of a mushroom anchor, then tie one end to a training bumper. Use three times as much cord as the distance you can throw the anchor. Walk up to the edge of a pond, toss out your bumper with its anchor, and hold firmly onto the end of the line. Send the dog on a retrieve.

As he approaches the bumper, pull on the line so you pull the bumper under the water. You can bob the bumper up and down to encourage the dog. When he grabs it successfully, allow him plenty of slack for a drag-free retrieve.

189 STORE A DUCK IN PANTYHOSE

Don't be alarmed when your duck-hunting buddy breaks out a little lingerie while on your next trip to the marsh. Pantyhose can make a fine protective tote sack for ducks bound for the taxidermist, keeping their feathers slightly compressed and out of harm's way.

In the field, gently wipe off blood and soil. Don't worry so much about blood staining the feathers; the taxidermist can clean them up. Just mop off the excess. Gently tuck the head under the wing, and slide the entire bird into a section of pantyhose. You'll want a bit of excess hose on both ends, and don't tie off either end just yet. Store the bird where it will be protected on the way out of the marsh—in a cooler or rolled in a vest and tucked into a daypack.

At home, snip the foot end from the hose, roll it back slightly, and insert a wad of paper towel or a few cotton balls into the bird's beak to soak up any blood that might seep out during the freezing process. Gently tuck the head back into the hose and tie off with a knot. Wrap the feet in a damp paper towel and secure with a rubber band or twist ties. Tie off the feet end, and slip the duck into a zippered plastic bag. It should easily store in a freezer for six months. If you need to store it longer than that, take the bird out of the pantyhose and freeze the entire duck in a large plastic bag filled with water.

190 TUNE SHOTGUN SWING WITH A FLASHLIGHT

Proper shotgun mounting is critical to hitting targets consistently, and you can practice without ever firing a shot. Happily, a shotgun and the nearly ubiquitous Mini Maglite are all you'll need to kill hours working on shotgun technique that you might have otherwise wasted on yard work.

STEP 1 Check to make sure that the gun is unloaded. Check again. Put the gun down. Pick it up and check it again.

STEP 2 Wrap the shaft of a Mini Maglite with a single layer of duct tape and insert it into the gun barrel, lamp pointing out. The Maglite that uses AA batteries will fit a 12-gauge shotgun. The AAA-battery model works for a 20 gauge. Dial down the beam to its tightest point.

STEP 3 In a darkened room, start from the low ready position. Point the light up at the place where two walls meet the ceiling. Next, mount the gun slowly. The goal is to have a smooth mount so that the light will stay centered on the spot.

STEP 4 Now practice your crossing shots by tracing the line where the wall and ceiling meet. Now, move the muzzle along the seam, bring the gun up to your face, and track a smooth line across the entire room. Shotgun mounting is purely a matter of muscle memory, so repeat it often, past that point at which any family members become alarmed at your behavior.

192 TURN AWAY TICKS

Spring turkey hunting season is a prime time for ticks, and long after your gobbler is in the refrigerator, these nasty bloodsuckers will still remind you that you should've used duct tape. To keep any ticks from crawling into your pants and up your legs, seal pants from cuffs to boots with duct tape (matte black or camo), or stuff the ends of your pants into your socks and then seal up the seam with a strip of duct tape.

191 DISAPPEAR WITH ZIP TIES AND CLOTHESPINS

Make handy vegetation clips for camouflaging blinds and boats with zip ties and clothespins. Insert a zip tie through the opening of a clothespin spring, and cinch down handfuls of raffia, marsh grass, or holly twigs with the zip ties. Now you can clip instant vegetation to any surface grasped by the clothespin.

Slicing a turkey-camp tomato calls for a different solution than opening up an elk belly. Here's a guide to matching blade shapes and grinds to the task at hand.

BLADE SHAPES

The blade shape is the knife in profile. Does the tip sweep up or down? Is the point clipped? Is the edge straight or curved? It all matters, greatly.

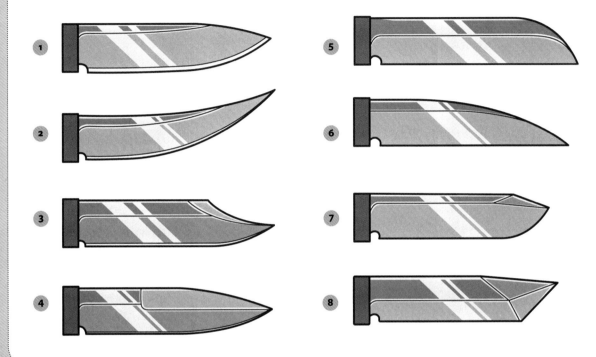

1 DROP POINT A downward convex curve along the blade spine forms a lowered point, creating a very strong tip. The drop-point blade is particularly suited for big-game hunting as the tip curves away from an animal's organs while field dressing.

2 TRAILING POINT An upward curve in the blade spine meets an upward curve in the blade edge to created a large belly for slashing. Good for some fillet knives and skinning knives.

3 CLIP POINT A general-use blade in which the spine of the blade drops to the tip for a strong piercing point with a slightly upswept belly. The clipped portion of the blade spine can be straight or curved and often holds a false edge. Bowie knives have a clip-point blade.

4 SPEAR POINT A stabbing blade, which is both spine and edge taper equally to a point.

5 SHEEPSFOOT Straight-edged blade with a spine that curves downward to meet at the blade tip. Originally designed to trim sheep hooves, this design does not have a sharp, piercing tip, making it a good choice for whittlers and boaters who must handle knives in unstable conditions.

6 WHARNCLIFFE Very similar to the sheepsfoot, but with a longer trailing point. Very efficient slicer.

7 SPEY Originally used to spey livestock, the blade spine terminates in a well-defined curve that meets another sudden upward curve at the blade tip. Allows for a fine degree of control with just a bit of a piercing tip.

8 TANTO These chisel-point blades are popular on tactical knives. Near the blade tip, the sharpened edge rises up at a sharp angle to meet the spine. This creates a blade that carries its thickness nearly to the tip for added strength.

BLADE GRINDS

The blade grind refers to the shape of a blade in cross section. Some grinds lean towards strength, and attempt to retain as much steel as possible. Thinner designs are designed for slicing.

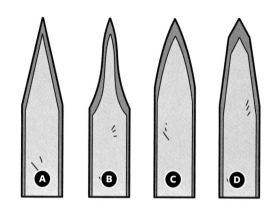

A **FLAT-GRIND BLADES** taper evenly from the start of the bevel to the cutting edge. There are several variations. Full flat-grind blades taper evenly all the way from the spine to the cutting edge, in the classic V-shape. In a high flat-grind blade, the bevel begins between the spine and the edge, but closer to the spine. In a Scandi grind, the bevel begins closer to the edge, below the midpoint between spine and edge. Flat-grind blades are easy to sharpen but dull more quickly than other grinds.

B **HOLLOW-GRIND BLADES** have a concave shape, as if a scoop of metal has been removed from the blade between the spine and edge. This thin, sharp grind produces an edge that slices easily, making it a common choice on a field-dressing knife. But the hollow grind will chip or roll over if it hits bone and can hang up in deep cuts.

C **THE CONVEX GRIND** arcs down from the spine as it tapers to the edge, thus creating a very sharp cutting edge that retains plenty of steel for strength. A convex grind is difficult to sharpen, but creates an edge with great durability and sharpness.

D **A COMPOUND BEVEL OR DOUBLE-BEVEL GRIND** is a secondary grind on the blade close to the edge bevel. This retains thickness for strength while allow for a thinner edge for sharpness.

9 **SKINNER** The full curving knife belly is perfect for long, sweeping motions, such as skinning big game.

10 **FILLET** A thin, flexible blade allows the knife to work over and around bones and fins.

11 **CAPER** A short, pointed blade with a slightly down-turned tip is easy to control in tight spots, such as removing the cape from an animal's head.

12 **RECURVE** The slight S-shaped belly forces the material being cut into the sharp edge. Recurves can be designed into most blade profiles.

194 MASTER THE GROUND-BLIND SHOT

The growing popularity of pop-up ground blinds has changed the game. Deer bowhunters are down from the trees, now joined by a growing number of gobbler hunters. But there's more to hunting from these blinds than simply sitting on a bucket with a bow in hand. Here's how it's done.

FIND YOUR BLIND SPOT Set up your blind between tree trunks and break up the horizontal outline of the blind's roof with cut brush.

GET BACK TO BLACK Wear a black facemask, gloves, and shirt or jacket to blend in with the blacked-out interior of the blind.

KNOW YOUR WINDOWS OF OPPORTUNITY Open the windows at 12, 3, and 6 o'clock. Sit in the back and raise your bow as the deer passes from an open side window toward the front.

BE A STRAIGHT SHOOTER Concentrate on keeping your back straight. Many shooters rely more on arm and shoulder strength than back muscles while sitting, so dialing down 5 or 10 pounds can help. And a shorter draw length can make it easier to reach full draw from a bucket.

195 USE SUPERGLUE

Servings that can hold peep sights, nock points, nock loops, and other aftermarket items will fray with hard use in the field. When they do, wandering sights or flapping serving threads will kill your accuracy. Toss a little tube of superglue into your hunting pack for instant field repairs of loose servings. Grasp the loose end of thread between thumb and forefinger. Pull taut and then place a drop of superglue on the serving. Once the glue sets, snip off the tag end and keep hunting.

196 USE CONFIDENCE DECOYS TO ARROW A DEER

How many times have you seen deer feeding calmly amidst a flock of turkeys? It might be time to take the hint. Turkey decoys are getting more and more realistic, with details from fully fanned tail feathers to wobbling heads. Using a fake turkey as a confidence decoy for deer hunting, especially while bowhunting, could give you the edge you need. Some hunters report that deer seem to be relaxed while in the presence of a confidence decoy, while others figure that it can hold a little bit of the deer's attention, thus making it easier to draw the bow undetected. In a field, crow decoys work, as well. But it is vital to keep those decoys scent-free—spray with scent killer and handle with gloves.

197 SHOOT TIGHTER GROUPS AT EVERY DISTANCE

It might sound counterintuitive, but archery field tests prove that a slim grip—or better yet, no grip at all—is a better grip. A thick, cushy bow grip feels great in your hand, but all that hand-to-bow contact creates opportunities for greater bow torque when you release the arrow. Shoot a few groups while your bow grip is on, then remove it and shoot a few more. You just might be surprised at the difference.

198 DRILL FOR THE SCAMPERING SQUIRREL

Given a solid rest and enough time to find a clear shot, most hunters can topple a squirrel from the treetops. The ones that get away are the ones that aren't in the treetops at all. They're the squirrels that show up close and scurry along a fallen log at 30 feet.

These squirrels never stop long enough to offer you a stationary shot. They can accelerate and decelerate like a pinball, and somehow they still have the ability to see you raise your rifle, which transforms them into a speeding, vanishing gray blur. The trick here is to shoot before that happens—meaning you have to hit that small, erratically moving target at relatively close range.

How to drill for this? Channel the spirit of a bocce ball champ, and bounce and roll a spherical squirrel-size target along the ground. You'll need a bucket of old tennis balls and a buddy to toss them, and make sure there's an appropriate background in order to absorb the bullets.

The thrower stands a yard or two behind and at varying distances perpendicular to the shooter.

STEP 1 Start out by tossing balls about 25 yards down the line. Each of the balls will cross in front of the shooter in near profile, just like that movement of an unalarmed but actively foraging squirrel.

STEP 2 Make each shot more difficult by having your thrower stand closer to the gun. With the balls coming from beside the shooter, the shot simulates those all-too-frequent times when you're busted by a feeding squirrel and he's hightailing it to the nearest tree. Your goal: three out of five hits on a bouncing tennis-ball squirrel.

CHALLENGE YOURSELF Once you're acing the tennis balls, switch to golf balls.

199 CALL SQUIRRELS WITH STUFF IN YOUR JUNK DRAWER

In his historic 1984 research paper on the language of gray squirrels, Dr. Robert Lishak identified four different alarm vocalizations. Avid squirrel hunters might be a bit surprised at such a low number. Personally, I know that squirrels have cussed me out using at least 83 separate potty-mouth squirrel-words. Point is, the limb dancer is a loquacious fellow, which can be his undoing. You can buy a squirrel call, but here are three ways to use common household objects to strike up a conversation with a tasty squirrel—just before you shut him up for good.

TOY SQUEAKER

Cut open squeaky dog and baby toys and you'll find a small plastic bulb. Its high-pitched squeak can imitate the distress call of a young squirrel in the clutches of a fox or hawk, and that racket draws other squirrels that are concerned or just plain curious. There are a few different sizes of squeakers, so experiment to find the pitch that works.

Works best early in the season, when young squirrels are still plentiful.

BOLT AND WASHER

Cutter calls involve a ridged rod and a striker and replicate the sound of a squirrel's teeth on tough nut hulls. For the rod, try threaded plastic or metal bolts or even the brass bolts that hold toilet seats in place. For a striker, use metal or plastic washers of varying thickness. In the woods, toss a few light rocks into the leaves, which sounds like nut fragments falling.

Try this technique after you've been busted. Sit quietly for 10 minutes, then lure the squirrel back into the open.

SPARE CHANGE

Something about the clink-clank of a couple of coins can turn a squirrel inside-out with curiosity. Rubbing the ridged edges of quarters together makes a sound not unlike a squirrel cutting nuts (poker chips are even louder). Or hold a quarter and penny between thumb and forefinger and rasp them together in short, quick movements.

This is a short-range game, which makes the one-handed quarter-and-penny call a deadly finisher.

200 BE THE TRIPOD

A wily old South Carolina squirrel hunter named Mac English perfected this rather unorthodox prone position. It is deadly, as your upper arm and entire upper body are in solid contact with the ground, bolstered by a bent leg that serves as an outrigger.

STEP 1 With your rifle in your left hand, lie on your right side. (Do the opposite if you're a lefty.) Keep your right thigh in a straight plane with your torso, and bend the right knee back at a 90-degree angle.

STEP 2 Cross left leg over right, placing your left foot across the right knee on or close to the ground. Move the rifle into position against your shoulder, keeping your upper right arm flat against the ground.

STEP 3 Hold the fore-end with your left hand, and position this hand against your left knee. You can make adjustments by shifting the left knee, keeping contact between the left leg and the right knee joint.

201 | BUILD A RABBIT GUM

Early settlers used fire to hollow out black gum logs and used the hollowed logs for bee hives, poultry roosts, and cottontail traps they called "rabbit gums." For the last hundred years, any country boy worth his snuff ran a line of rabbit gums to keep his family in fried bunny. Here's how to channel your inner Opie Taylor.

STEP 1 Saw a 10-foot 1x8 plank (A) as illustrated below. The 3-part trigger (B) mechanism can be made from a $1/2$-inch wooden dowel cut to 11 inches, and a 58-inch-long strip of $3/4$-inch x $3/4$-inch wood, cut as shown. Alternatively, the mechanism of lever (C), fulcrum post (D), and trigger can be whittled from a set of sticks.

STEP 2 Assemble the rabbit gum as shown, fastening the pieces with nails or wood screws. Be careful placing the trap door guides (E). It's important that the trap door slides freely in order to beat a bunny to the draw.

STEP 3 Place the rabbit gum along runs in thick cover, unbaited, for a week or two to get bunnies used to it. Lean a few saplings or handfuls of grass around the trap to break up the outline, but be sure not to impede the trigger mechanism.

STEP 4 Place bait between the trigger stick and the back panel. Try out aromatic goodies such as apples. Old-timers would use cabbage, turnips, salt—and carrots, of course. It's not a bad idea to create a trail of small bait pieces that leads up to the trap opening, and then crush a piece of bait and smear the scent along the inside of the gum to lead the rabbit to the point of no return.

TRY THIS NEW-SCHOOL TRICK

The back panels of rabbit gums are often built with plywood or planking. Instead, try making the back from chicken wire, hardware cloth, or some other sturdy see-through material. Ol' wabbit will feel much better when he can see all the way through the trap . . . And you'll be able to see what you caught before opening the door on a pissed-off possum.

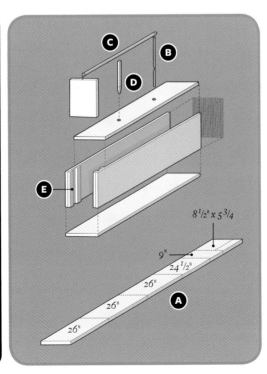

202 MOUNT A RACK ON A ROCK

For more than a year this 6-point rack, connected by its antler plate, had been relegated to a grimy corner of my basement. There it kept company with a few other racks that never quite made the mounting cut. But every set of antlers tells a story and deserves better treatment. One day, I kept telling myself, I'll do something with those horns. One day I did.

Turning that overlooked rack into a distinctive piece of sporting art took maybe three hours of work and less than $10 in supplies. I used a paving stone from a landscape supply shop. You won't believe how easy it is.

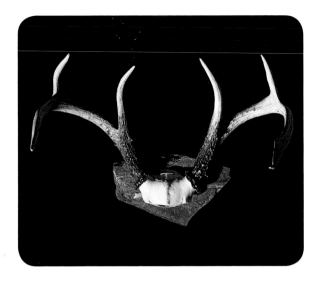

STEP 1 Cut away as much of the hide and flesh as you can, being careful not to score the bone with your knife. Soak the antler plate in a basin of water for two to three days. Scrape away as much tissue as possible.

STEP 2 Mix bleach and water in a one-to-one ratio, then carefully swab down or spray the entire antler plate with the liquid. Be very careful to keep it off the antlers or they will discolor. Repeat every 30 minutes or so until the bone is completely white. This might take one or more afternoons.

STEP 3 If the antlers have lost their color, use a woodstain to restore. Test it with a small spot on the back of the antler first, and use sparingly. Let it dry, then spray the finished antlers with a clear semigloss polyurethane.

STEP 4 Round off the edges and corners of the antler plate with a hand-held rotary tool, being careful not to breathe in the bone dust.

STEP 5 Drill two 1/4-inch holes through the top of the antler plate, approximately 1 inch apart. Drill another pair of 1/4-inch holes, about 1 inch apart, through the mounting board or stone.

STEP 6 Fasten the antler plate to the backing using a leather lace (wet it so that it dries tightly), tied on the back side with a very tight square knot. The lace also serves as a handy hanging loop.

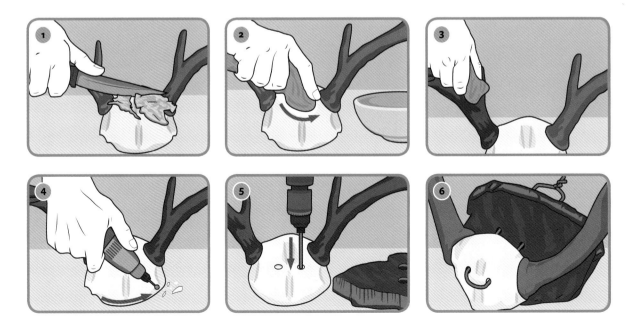

205
RIG A DEER DRAG

Have a few odd pieces of webbing and rope heaped up in the basement? Add in a carabiner to make a handy deer drag. First, lash the deer's front legs tight to the upper neck. Next, wrap a 6-foot loop of some webbing or rope around the antlers (if it's a buck) or its neck (if it's a doe), and tie an overhand loop in the end. Clip the carabiner onto the loop. Now run a 6-foot loop of wide webbing through the carabiner to form a pair of loops like butterfly wings. Slip a shoulder through each loop and stand up; the deer's head will lift up and off the ground. Head for home.

203 TRACK A BLOOD TRAIL

The same hydrogen peroxide your mother sprayed on skinned knees can help you track your next deer. The liquid will foam up on contact with blood as the peroxide reacts with the enzyme catalase, which is released when tissues are damaged. Take along a small spray bottle and you can use it to tell whether those tiny dark specks are blood from the deer you are trailing or just little leaf spots and pieces of dirt. Spray with a fine mist, and mark each positive result with surveyor's tape, because the hydrogen peroxide will remove small blood specks. It's a great trick for color-blind hunters.

204 LIGHT UP A HUNT

Stash a few glow sticks in your daypack. Down an elk or deer at dusk and it will soon get dark. Tie the glow sticks to branches to mark the blood trail. When the trail gets sparse, you can look back through the woods and the glow sticks will line up, giving you a general direction of travel. Once you find the animal, the glow sticks mark the route back to where you were when you shot.

206 FOOL WOOD DUCKS WITH A SPINNING DOVE DECOY

Spinning wing dove decoys can pull double duty in a duck swamp frequented by woodies. To raise the spinner above the water, cut a length of gray PVC pipe and sharpen one end with an angled cut. Push the pipe into the mud, then insert the spinner pole into the pipe. Dove spinners are small and light, so you can easily fit one into a daypack for those dawn hikes into wood duck swamps.

207 MAKE THE AWESOMEST DUCK WHISTLE ON THE PLANET

This loud, breathy whistle is a charmer for teal and wigeon. It's a snap to make with a few common tools and pairs of spent 12-gauge shells. Each requires either one low brass head shell (approximately 5/16 inch tall) and one high brass head (approximately 5/8 inch tall), or two low brass head shells. Whistles made from low or high brass heads will make different sounds, so keep a variety on your lanyard.

STEP 1 Heat up the brass head in the flame of a propane torch. Put on a work glove to hold on to the brass and gently remove the plastic case with pliers. Take out the plastic cup inside the brass head by reheating the brass, then scraping away the remaining plastic with a flat-tip screwdriver.

STEP 2 Place the brass head (with the primer down) on a 1-inch-thick stack of cardboard. Punch out the primer. Use your screwdriver to partially flatten the metal flanges that held the primer for each brass head. Hold the pair together and blow through the holes. The final sound will be louder and sharper.

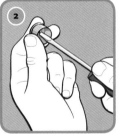

STEP 3 Widen out the rim of the high brass head to take the other head. Use a rotary tool to grind the rim of a 9/16-inch socket just slightly so that the ground rim will barely fit into the brass head. Lightly tap it with a hammer to widen the circumference of the brass, then remove. Lastly, tap one brass head into the other.

208 TRANSLATE A QUACK

Know a great duck caller? Have him turn a call around and blow his best hail calls and highballs with the insert against his lips. Now you know what to "say" into your own call.

209 SNAG DECOYS IN DEEP WATER

Pulling in dozens of floating decoys after a hunt is a task burdensome enough to make you forget all about the easy incomers you dispatched at dawn. But you can make quick work of the chore with these two tricks.

A GRAPPLE LINE Tie 30 feet of decoy line on to a 6- or 8-ounce lead sinker. Twist a half-dozen screws into the sinker at odd angles until each one protrudes by about 1/2 inch. To use it, toss the sinker at the decoys. All those screws will grab the onto the anchor line on the way to the bottom, and you can gently pull the decoy close.

B PADDLE PICKER-UPPER With a handsaw, a band saw, or a small handheld rotary cutting tool, cut a 1/2-inch angled slot 1 inch deep into each edge of your duck-boat paddle's blade. Slant the slots about 45 degrees away from the handle. File down the rough edges. The slots won't affect your paddle, and you'll be able to reach out from the boat and snag decoy lines from much farther away.

210 GLASS THE GRID

The hardest hunting lesson I ever learned was a result of missing the biggest deer of my life. My guide and I found a monstrous mule deer bedded down just within bow range of a cliff top. After a 90-minute barefoot stalk, I had the bowstring nearly anchored for a 15-foot shot—and then the really big deer snorted 40 yards away. Now, had I spent more time behind the binoculars and less time mentally clearing wall space in my office, I'd have seen both deer. Using this grid system would have done the trick.

STEP 1 Divide the field of view into an imaginary grid pattern. Begin reading it like a line of type: Move your eyes slowly from left to right along the uppermost grid cube until the horizontal line intersects with a vertical line. Move down slightly, then glass from right to left. Repeat this pattern till you complete a grid. Mounting binoculars on a tripod can be a huge help.

STEP 2 Between grids, give a quick look to open areas where any movement may be obvious. As the sun comes up, pay attention to west-facing slopes that stay in shade. Muleys will feed later in the morning if they can stay out of the sun.

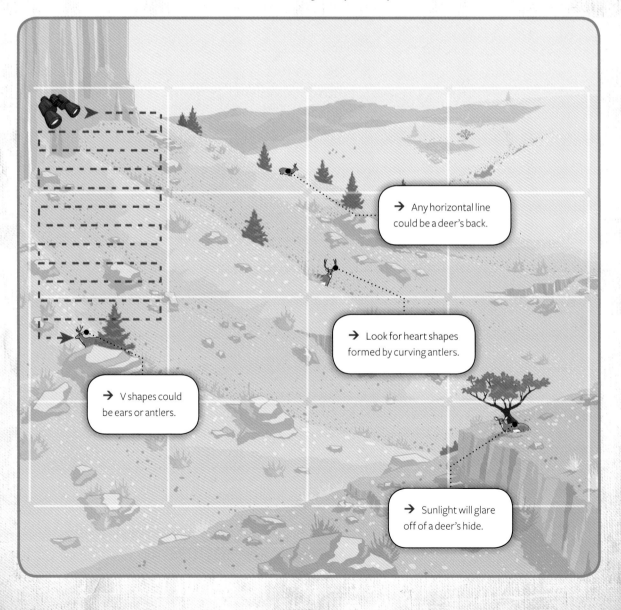

→ Any horizontal line could be a deer's back.

→ Look for heart shapes formed by curving antlers.

→ V shapes could be ears or antlers.

→ Sunlight will glare off of a deer's hide.

211 HOMEBREW DEER SCENTS

You can buy fancy commercial scents to lure out those big bucks, or you can make your own. Here are a few options.

EASIEST Stuff a pillowcase one-third full with aromatic vegetation from your hunt area, such as green leaves, pine needles, pieces of bark, moss, acorns—even dirt. Tie a knot in the top. Prior to a hunt, dampen the pillowcase with water and toss it in the clothes dryer with your clean hunting duds.

EASY Gather ½ gallon of acorns; add in a double handful of green pine needles if pines occur in your hunting area. Boil them gently in 1 gallon of water for 30 minutes. Let the mixture cool. Remove the nuts and needles, mash them, and boil again in the same water. Let the mixture cool, then strain it through cheesecloth. Store the liquid in a refrigerator. To use the cover scent, pour into a spray bottle.

NOT-SO-BAD Snip off one leg from a pair of hose. Remove the tarsal glands from a buck's hind legs by cutting around each gland, lifting it with rubber-gloved fingers, and then separating the connective tissue under the skin. Use a 10cc hypodermic syringe and needle to remove urine from the buck's bladder. Place the glands in the hose and knot closed. Squirt them with the urine and store in a sealed plastic bag in a freezer. Hang it by your stand during the hunt.

HARD Remove the tarsals from a buck, following the directions above. With a leather needle, thread the end of a 5-foot length of heavy monofilament through a gland; tie it off. Tie a loop in the other end of the line. Vacuum-pack the glands separately and freeze them. Before a hunt, thaw one out, then spritz it with urine scent and use it as a scent drag.

HARDEST Collect enough pine needles to fill a 5-gallon bucket. Boil in a large kettle with 6 to 7 gallons of water. Strain the needles out, then pour the liquid into a washing machine set at the lowest load setting possible. Toss in clean hunting clothes, and wash using the presoak cycle for a very intense pine scent. Clean the machine by washing a few old towels in hot, soapy water.

212 STICK A CALL TO YOUR COAT

Put a small, lightweight grunt call to your hunting jacket and you'll be able to call deer with a minimum of movement. Sew or glue a small strip of Velcro to the top of your jacket sleeve or upper chest, and then glue a corresponding patch to a grunt or bleat call. Now just a slight turn of your head will put that call into your mouth and keep both of your hands on the gun or bow.

213 MAKE A DRAG RAG

That first deer of the season will provide much-needed burger and backstrap, but if you're smart, it will also provide a pair of tarsal glands that will up your chances at tagging more deer. Remove these dark tufts of hair and skin with a sharp knife, wearing rubber gloves to keep them free of human scent. Toss in a zippered plastic baggie along with 6 feet of paracord, and store in a refrigerator or freezer. To use, simply tie a cord to the tarsal gland and knot it off on one of your belt loops. Drag it behind you on the way to your stand. Once near your hunt location, hang the tarsal gland from an upwind branch. You can get a couple of weeks of usage out of fresh tarsal glands by recharging them with a few drops of commercial doe urine.

214 MAINTAIN A MOUNT

Ol' Bucky not as impressive as he used to be? Lifeless eyes, dull hair, nostrils stuffed with cobwebs? Time to take 10 minutes and buff that deer mount into museum quality again.

STEP 1 Don't grind in dust and grime with a cloth. First, vacuum the entire mount with a shop-vac using a stiff bristly dusting head attachment. Go lightly, and move in the direction of the hair. Clean out the ears and nostrils.

STEP 2 Clean ear cavities, nose cavities, and open mouths with a blast of canned compressed air.

STEP 3 Wipe down antlers with a wet rag, let dry, then go over with linseed oil or a touch of non-yellow liquid floor wax.

STEP 4 Starting with the head, give the hide a light wipe down with spray furniture wax.

STEP 5 Clean glass eyes with glass cleaner and a pointed-tip cosmetic swab. Available at most drugstores, these swabs holds less liquid and reduce the chances of wetting the eyelids. That is a no-no, for ammonia in the glass cleaner can dry out those tissues.

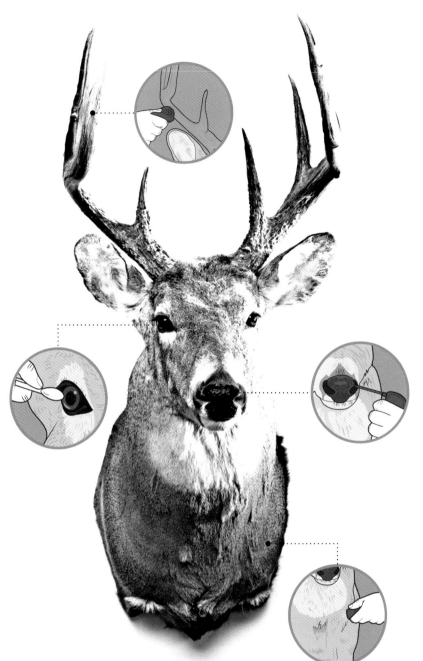

215 MAKE JERKY WITH A PENCIL

Here's an easy way to make jerky without using a dehydrator or smoker: Line the bottom of an oven with foil, spray the racks with cooking spray, and drape jerky strips over the racks. Dry at about 180 degrees, and prop the door open with a 3-inch pencil stub so the moisture can escape.

216 PACK A FIELD-DRESSING KIT

Store-bought field dressing kits often include a bunch of unnecessary items for a hunter who's faced with gutting a deer and getting it home. This DIY kit fits into a gallon-size plastic zippered bag, which also serves as a handy place to put down a knife while you're wrestling with a transcending colon. At the truck, stash 3 gallons of clean water for rinsing out the body cavity, and a hatchet if you want to open the pelvis.

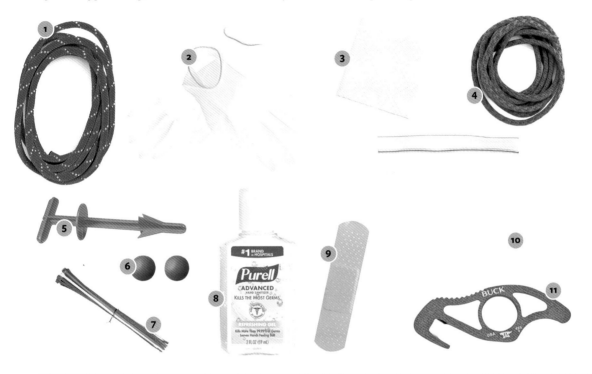

1 DEER DRAG Store-bought deer drags have a handle that makes them too bulky for this kit. Tie a loop in each end of an 8-foot length of 9mm climbing rope. Now you can slip a choker loop around the doe's neck or buck's antlers and cinch the other end of the rope around a sturdy stick for a handle.

2 LATEX GLOVES Lots of field dressing gloves go up to your armpit, to turn blood away from clothing and any open cuts. But wrist-high gloves have a better feel and grip and still prevent blood and nicked guts from infecting small cuts.

3 PAPER TOWELS I like to keep 15 paper towels, folded up, to use as cavity and hand wipes.

4 PARACORD Keep a 5-foot length of cord in the kit and use it to tie one leg to a sapling and hold it out of the way for easier gutting.

5 BUTT OUT 2 It works. Enough said.

6 IBUPROFEN If I'm farther than a few hundred yards from the truck, I make my back happy with a dose of Vitamin I within minutes of pulling the trigger.

7 ZIP TIES Tie off the intestinal canal with one hand. Snazzy.

8 HAND SANITIZER Bring a small bottle for field treatment of knife nicks and overall cleanup.

9 BANDAGES Pack these for knife nicks.

10 ZIP-SEAL BAGS Have two gallon-size bags for the heart and the liver.

11 GUT HOOK Tons of small gut hooks have hit the market.

217 CAMO PAINT A GUN STOCK

Think your old synthetic rifle or shotgun stock could use a modern face-lift? It's a snap for you to camouflage a stock with easily available hardware store spray paint and stencils you pluck from your hunting land. Instructors at the North Carolina Montgomery Community College Gunsmithing School dolled up these beauties and gave us their step-by-step plan. All you need is spray paints in three or four flat finishes (many hardware stores stock camouflage spray paint), a little bit of paint thinner, some paracord, and a few handfuls of leaves, pine needles, and grasses.

GATHER AND GLEAN Collect three species of local vegetation to use as custom stencils: a few medium-sized leaves; some pencil-thick vegetation, such as fern fronds; and finer materials, such as thin reeds and pine needles. Especially with pine needles and grasses, make sure there's plenty of open structure for the paint to get through.

PREPARE THE STOCKS Remove the barrels, actions, and sling swivels from the stocks. Degrease with a wipe of paint thinner. Use some masking tape to mask off areas that shouldn't be painted, such as the barrels' bedding channels and any action ports. Use a sharp X-Acto blade for precise cuts. Make a clothesline of paracord out in the workshop or backyard, and hang the stocks for painting. You can also paint them lying flat on some newspaper, but you'll have to wait till the paint dries to flip them over, and it's more difficult to match patterns on the two sides.

LET THE PAINT FLY Paint your entire stock black. Let dry. Now use the natural stencils. Start with the medium-sized leaves and a medium-dark paint, such as brown or olive green. Hold that vegetation very still up against the surface of the stock, and spray with a light back-and-forth action with the can about 6 inches away. Rotate the camo vegetation in all directions to prevent striping—everything in nature is random. Next, use your thin grasses and pine needles with a bit of light brown or khaki paint for added depth. Use just enough paint to get the desired effect; too much, and thick paint globs will crack upon drying. Finish with a coat of clear flat acrylic sealant.

218 CLEAN A TRIGGER WITH A TOOTHBRUSH

We fuss over our barrels and actions, but we give too little thought to the first line in a firearm's offense: the trigger. A gunked-up trigger might be, at best, cranky to pull and the root cause of a missed shot and, at the worst, the culprit of a shot that fails to go off at all.

Cleaning a trigger is as easy as degreasing it with lighter fluid, which doesn't harm the plastics, bluing, stock finishes, or epoxy. Lighter fluid flushes out the crap and leaves behind a slight residue that provides just enough lubrication for a trigger.

There are two ways to apply. The quick and easy way is to remove the bolt from a rifle, squirt the lighter fluid into the trigger assembly, and work the trigger as all that evaporating liquid works its magic. For a truly gunked trigger, such as a duck gun that's been hard at work all season long, remove the trigger assembly from the receiver. Flush it with lighter fluid, using an old, clean, toothbrush to flick out the grime. After it dries, use a can of compressed air to blow junk out of all the little nooks and crannies. Repeat as necessary.

219 HOLD BINOCULARS ROCK STEADY THREE WAYS

It's not easy holding binoculars steady over the course of a long glassing session for mule deer, pronghorn, and other open-country game. Here are three tricks to keep your glasses from shaking—and your arms fresh for holding a rifle.

A **RIFLE SLING** Use a long, wide binoculars strap like a rifle sling for some stability. Hold the binoculars horizontally, so that the single strap loops down towards the ground. Then, one at a time, insert your hands through the loop far enough that your elbows are inside the loop. Hold up the binoculars in a typical grip. The strap should wrap around the outside of your arms at your triceps muscle. Now spread your arms apart, tightening the strap across upper arms and chest.

B **HAT TRICK** Adjust a baseball-type cap so it fits a bit tighter than normal. Hold binoculars in a regular grip, then extend each middle finger over the cap brim and grasp firmly.

C **RECYCLE A HOCKEY STICK** Developed in Finland, a "finnstick" is a device that allows you to keep binoculars at eye-level without needing your hands. Make one out of a forked branch about 2 to 3 feet long (depending on your height). The fork holds on to the center barrel of the binoculars, while you hold the other end of the stick at waist height. In another nod to their Finnish roots, many birders use broken hockey sticks as DIY finnsticks.

220 FIX STOCK DINGS WITH AN IRON

If you view the minor dents and dings in a wooden rifle or shotgun stock as badges of field honor, then skip ahead to the next skill. If not, then grab a wet cloth, a clothes iron or soldering iron, and prepare to raise a little grain. By carefully steaming the dent you will cause the wood cells to expand, minimizing the blemish. This process works best on porous oil-based finishes. Lacquer finishes may need to be removed first, however.

STEP 1 Clean the dent to keep from steaming dirt permanently into the wood grain.

STEP 2 Wet a corner of a towel or cleaning patch with hot water. Place the wet cloth directly over the dent, and press with the tip of a clothes iron or soldering iron. Don't overdo it. A few seconds of steaming is enough.

STEP 3 Repeat as necessary. Depending on the dent and the wood, you might need to repeat twice, thrice, or a dozen times. Let the wood dry completely between treatments.

STEP 4 The steaming process tends to raise the wood's grain, so hit the raised grain with steel wool to buff it down.

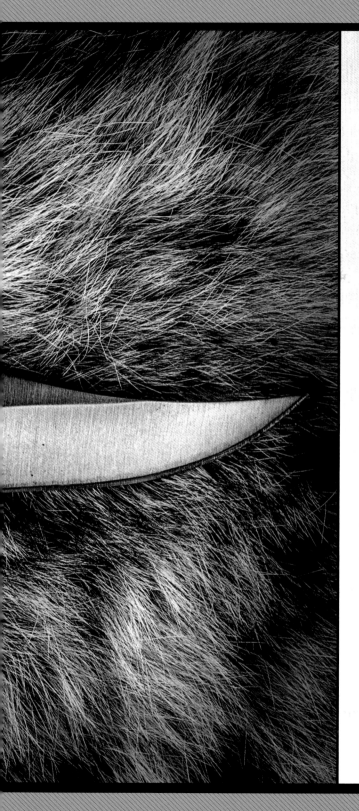

It was the first knife to catch my eye, and I wasn't alone. I was 12 years old in 1973, the year that Schrade Cutlery introduced its model 150OT, the Sharpfinger. This was one of the very first purpose-specific knives that I can remember—a knife made solely for gutting an animal lying on brown leaves, or stripping the hide from a beast swinging on a rope. It stood apart from a few centuries' worth of general-purpose American blades, the Bowies, faux-Bowies, and German-style hunters that were the coin of the bladesmithing realm in my youth.

To my young eye, the Sharpfinger was a bit of a global mash-up: an exotic blade shape, all swoopy and pointed like an Arabian knight's scimitar. The subtly textured thermoplastic handle scales looked like old bone but offered the sexy unbreakability of space-age engineering. Back in the day, the old Sharpfinger magazine ads would brag: "For small elephants and large squirrels." My dad bought one. I can still smell the leather sheath.

The Schrade Sharpfinger was crazy popular. (The knife was originally called the "Sharp Finger," but the name was changed to the one-word "Sharpfinger" in 1980.) Over the years a number of limited editions were pumped out to feed the public's nearly unlimited appetite for the knife. There was a "Grandad's" edition that looked even more old-timey—a knife with a faux-scrimshaw handle of fake whale tooth. The knives even caught on far outside the hunting world. Hells Angel founder Sonny Barber carried a Sharpfinger, and extolled the little blade in his memoir *Dead in 5 Heartbeats*. That did nothing to diminish public fervor.

Schrade churned the Sharpfinger out for almost 30 years, until 2004 when the company went bankrupt. The trademark has since expired, and these days Sharpfinger-type knives are pumped out of Chinese factories like cheap shirts. It seems the old Sharpfinger magic still cuts deep.

Today, I own a fleet of dedicated-purpose blades: skinners, capers, boners, gut hooks, bird knives, trout knives, camp knives, and survival knives galore. I like them all, and love a rare few. But it was that original Sharpfinger that sent the first chills up my spine. It was the first knife I ever paid for, bought with money saved from my newspaper route. It was a knife I simply had to have, no matter what. It was the first time I felt that way, but hardly the last.

221 DOUBLE YOUR RANGE WITH A BIPOD

Reaching out for long-range coyotes, varmints, and even open-country big game will require a rock-solid rest, and nothing does the trick like using a rifle-mounted bipod from the prone shooting position. There's a little more to mastering this two-footed rest than simply flopping on the ground with the bipod deployed, so here's the drill for the long-range game.

GO LOW The longer the legs, the more they will flex, and the shorter the legs, the more stable the platform. Adjust the bipod so the rifle is as close to the ground as possible without forcing you into an uncomfortable position.

NOT ROCK SOLID You'd never shoot a rifle rested on a rock, because recoil will jump the stock, sending your bullet high. It is the same idea with a bipod. Place the bipod feet on a surface with some give. Dig down to reach softer subsoil under a hard crust. At the very least, spread a jacket over an unforgiving surface and place the bipod on the material.

THE GOOD FLEX Once in position behind the bipod, seat the stock against your shoulder and push it slightly forward. This will "load" the bipod, seating the feet more firmly into the ground and reducing how much the legs will flex with the rifle's recoil.

REAR SUPPORT With the gun's forestock resting on the bipod, your left hand (for a right-handed shooter) needs something to do. Double down on bracing by using your fist to steady the toe of the stock. Reach under your right armpit, grab the rifle's rear swivel sling and make a fist. Make slight elevation changes in point of impact by squeezing or relaxing your fist.

222 USE BINOCULARS AS A SPOTTING SCOPE

Backcountry elk hunters and high-country sheep and goat hunters look to shave ounces from their loads, so converting binoculars for use as a spotting scope holds down weight and limited pack space. A couple of aftermarket accessories make the conversion work. The results aren't as clear and bright as a dedicated spotting scope, but not having to carry both binoculars and a spotting scope is a definite bonus for wilderness hunters.

MOUNT STEADY Tripod adapters allow binoculars to be mounted to the $1/4$-inch screw bolt of a tripod. Many manufacturers offer adapters specific to their models.

TWICE AS NICE Optical doublers double the magnification of binoculars, turning an 8X binocular into a 16X spotting scope, or a 10X binocular into a 20X elk-finder. The doubler typically fits over one eyepiece. Doublers are light enough you can toss one in your pack and, in a pinch, use it without a tripod. Just brace the device against a tree.

223 MAKE A PVC RIFLE REST

Carry a folding saw and this modified PVC T-joint, and you'll never be without your own shooting stick for long-range squirrel shots. Glue a 4-inch piece of 1 ½-inch PVC pipe into the branch of the T-joint (1), and pad it with black foam or camouflage tape (2). In the field, cut a 1-inch-thick sapling about 4 feet long. Slip the T-joint over the stick (3) so the padded branch juts off to the side—voilà, a mini shooting rail. To aim, grasp the stick and pipe at the proper level, cradle the rifle in the rest, and bring home the good stuff.

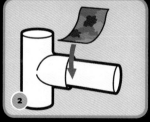

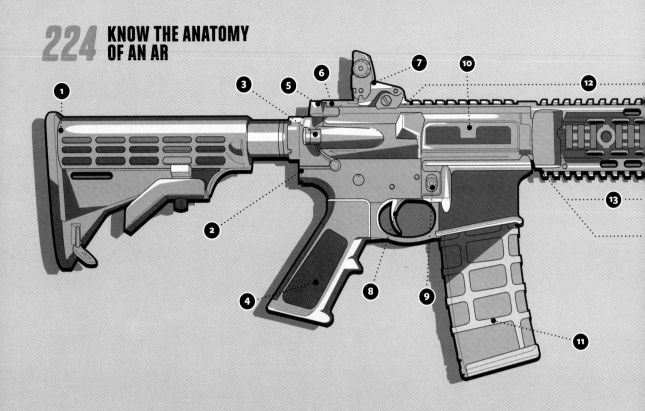

1 **BUTTSTOCK** Most AR rifles are sold with a collapsible, telescoping stock or a fixed stock; aftermarket options abound.

2 **LOWER RECEIVER** Includes the trigger assembly, magazine well, magazine, magazine release and latch, fire selector, bolt stop, and pistol grip.

3 **FORWARD ASSIST** Added to later models of the AR, and absent from some modern models; helps move the bolt forward when normal charging fails to fully chamber a round.

4 **PISTOL GRIP**

5 **CHARGING HANDLE** Used to open the bolt or chamber a round from a closed-bolt position.

6 **UPPER RECEIVER** Houses the bolt carrier assembly and attaches to the barrel.

7 **REAR SIGHT** Flip-down or fixed with multiple variations that serve as half the weapon's default iron sights.

8 **TRIGGER**

9 **MAGAZINE RELEASE** Button that releases the mechanism that locks the magazine into the magazine well.

10 **EJECTION PORT** Point where spent shells are ejected.

11 **MAGAZINE** External box magazine that stores the ammunition and feeds it into the firearm during cycling.

12 **ACCESSORY RAIL** Mounting system developed by the Picatinny Arsenal, the Picatinny Rail is a very simple, strong base for mounting sights. Many ARs have multiple rails for employing specialized sighting devices.

13 **FORE-END** Can include integral or attached rails for attaching lasers, tactical flashlights, and other accessories.

14 **BARREL**

15 **FRONT SIGHT POST** Typically a simple iron post sight, but may also include a luminescent element for low-light shooting.

16 **FLASH HIDER** Disperses burning powder gas, and thus muzzle flash, making it harder to spot shooter's position.

15

16

14

226 MAKE A TATER TREE

Nothing says "fun" quite like an exploding spud. This little homemade potato tree is the perfect target for all kinds of rounds ranging from rimfire to rhinoceros-worthy, and the raw materials might just be in your basement. All you'll need is a 4-foot or 5-foot section of 2x6. Make a sturdy base out of scrap lumber. Drive large finishing nails 1-inch deep into the upright. Jab potatoes to the nails and have at it.

225 GET OUT OF A JAM

Every once in awhile, especially when shooting large volumes of ammo or during rapid-fire shooting, you'll get a jam with your AR, and you need to clear it correctly and safely. Here's how.

When you first experience a malfunction, use the simple steps of the SPORTS method.

SLAP the bottom of the magazine. This ensures it is seated fully and correctly in the receiver.

PULL the charging handle completely to the rear and hold it there. The bolt should move back and expose the chamber.

OBSERVE the ejection port. See if pulling the charging handle ejected a live round or a spent cartridge that was holding up the works.

RELEASE the charging handle. If the jam has been cleared, this will fully lock the bolt forward and load a new round.

TAP the forward assist. This will help ensure the bolt is fully locked. Once the bolt is locked, pull the charging handle back slightly and do a brass check, ensuring a new round has been seated. Release it and allow it to snap closed fully. Remember to always keep the muzzle of the rifle pointed downrange.

SQUEEZE the trigger. Take aim and attempt to fire a shot.

If that doesn't clear it out, or if your charging handle can't be manipulated, you have a more serious jam, and it's time to take it to a professional gunsmith to have it serviced.

227 MAKE A HANDY BANDOLIER

Puppy eat one of your gloves? Use the other one as a handy cartridge carrier. Fill each finger with your favorite load, roll the glove up, and seal it in a zippered plastic baggie. Silent, weatherproof, and ready when you need it.

228 CLEAN A BLACKPOWDER GUN WITH A GUITAR

OK, so maybe not the entire guitar. But a guitar string makes a great cleaning rod for a fouled flash hole in the breech plug of a modern blackpowder rifle. Soak a short length of guitar string in solvent and run it into the flash hole to clear out the gunk.

229 USE SPIT TO SHOOT A BLACKPOWDER RIFLE

Anyone who's ever cleaned a blackpowder rifle barrel knows how much gunk a single shot leaves inside the bore. To maintain accuracy shot-to-shot, always "spit swab" after each pull of the trigger. It's easy and takes very little time. If you put an animal down, spit swab before approaching, in case you need an accurate second shot. And do this exactly the same way each time you shoot. A consistent spit swab will lead to consistent points of impact.

Keep a cleaning jag attached to your ramrod. After a shot, pop a .22 cleaning patch in your mouth, wet it with saliva, and wring it out by pressing between your tongue and the roof of your mouth. Run it down the barrel and out, and you're ready to reload. It's also a good idea to finger space your ramrod to stop the spit swab an inch or two above the vent hole. This will keep you from blocking that crucial port with powder crud.

230 STOP RAMROD BLISTERS

An old golf ball can make a great blackpowder ramrod grip. Simply drill a 1-inch-deep hole into the ball the diameter of your ramrod. Slip it over the end of your rod when it's time to reload and seat the next round.

231 MAKE A BUCK BED WITH A CHAIN SAW

Savvy big bucks are all about shelter. They like a thickly brushed spot with a view, just the kind of microhabitat you can create in 15 minutes with a chain saw. This is especially effective where an open oak flat offers little bedding cover. Provide a dense spot of brushy cover on the edge, and it's likely a buck will take up residence to scope out does feeding on the acorns.

It's easy. Locate two or three trees about 6 to 8 inches in diameter and growing 10 to 15 feet apart. Decide which direction you want each tree to fall.

To hinge-cut, use a chain saw to create a downward cut at a 45-degree angle on the side of the tree that is opposite of the direction you want it to fall. Make the cut at waist height or slightly higher. For larger trees, loop a rope around the trunk as high as you can reach, and have a buddy pull on the rope to prevent the saw blade from pinching. Such a helper can be useful even with smaller trees—the less that you cut through the trunk, the more future growth the tree will be able to maintain, which will keep the bed not only thickly vegetated, but provide browse.

232 STEER DEER WITH BUCKETS

When television host and Outdoor 3-D Archery World Champion Travis "T-Bone" Turner wants to steer a buck to his bowstand, he hits the woods with a stack of 5-gallon buckets. Bowhunters are often advised to learn exactly where a buck enters a field and sit just downwind. But not all bucks are so accommodating as to approach from the same spot every night. "He might show up within 100 yards of a certain tree, trail, or field corner," Turner says, "but that doesn't help very much when you're shooting a bow."

So Turner steers these deer to his stand with buckets. Yes, buckets. "They stack like traffic cones for easy toting, and to a whitetail they say, Detour—go that way." If a certain deer tends to show up anywhere along a 100-yard stretch of a field edge, Turner places a line of four or five of his 5-gallon buckets parallel to that stretch, 100 yards or more into the opening. He then hangs his stand along the edge of the woods, lined up evenly with the farthest-downwind pail. "When the buck comes out, he'll spot those buckets, be leery, and instead of marching into the field, he'll hug the edge and, with luck, walk right to you."

233 PRUNE AN APPLE TREE FOR DEER

Many overgrown farmsteads hold apple trees. When neglected, they produce few fruits. With a little pruning, however, they can churn out deer chow. Do it in late winter, just before the new spring growth. And then make it an annual event because the sucker shoots (skinny, whiplike branches) grow back.

CLEAR THE GROUND Remove all of the brush and saplings that are around the tree, at least to the canopy's drip line.

CUT THE DEAD WOOD Remove all dead wood, using a chain saw if necessary.

TRIM IT BACK Remove any and all sucker shoots. They sap growth, siphon off any needed nutrients, and will stymie the tree's ability to produce its fruit.

GET VERTICAL Remove any branches that grow horizontally, as the burden of apples can shear these off.

WEED OUT WEAKLINGS Pick the healthiest-looking branches to save, and remove some or all of the rest.

FEED THE TREE Fertilize with tree spikes made specifically for fruit trees.

234 MAKE YOUR OWN SCENT DRIPPER

Scent drippers work on a physical principle we all learned back in grade school: heated air expands. Sunlight hits the dark cloth, warms air trapped in the bottle, and pushes the scent out of the tube. Here's how to make your own. It's quick and cheap, so it's perfect for public land locations where some scofflaw could take a liking to your scent dripper and take it home.

YOU'LL NEED

a small glass bottle with cap • bubble wrap • tape • a power drill • 12 inches of ¼-inch outside diameter rubber tubing • zip ties • epoxy • string • dark cloth—maybe an old T-shirt you can cut up • flat spray paint in a dark color

AT HOME Wrap a small glass bottle with bubble wrap and secure it with tape. Drill a hole in the bottle top the same size or slightly smaller than the diameter of the tubing. Fasten a loop into the rubber tubing with a zip tie, leaving approximately 1 inch of the tubing extending below the loop. Thread the other end of the tubing through the bottle cap till just past flush. Epoxy in place. Once dry, wrap the bottle in black cloth and secure with string. Spray paint the bottle cap and tubing.

Experiment at home with how much scent to place in the bottle. Start at a quarter-full and place in sunlight conditions—ratio of sun to shade—that mimic those where you plan to hang the dripper.

IN THE FIELD Fill the bottle with the correct amount of scent. Hang from a limb. Return with rifle and gutting knife.

235 SHOOT FROM A LAYOUT BLIND

Layout blinds are popping up everywhere—in field hunts, sure, but also along pond edges, river islands, and marsh sloughs. Shooting from a layout blind is tricky because a shooter's range of motion is seriously limited. The basic rule is to set up with the foot end of the blind pointing to the right of where you expect the birds to land. Figure out exactly where your blind will be, then make a "hip hole" by digging out 4 or 5 inches of

dirt at the position of your butt. Once inside the blind, pull the knee of your shooting side up a bit, which will give you a bit of leverage to drive your backside into the hip hole as you sit up for the shot. When it's time to shoot, rise into position, then lean forward an extra inch or two to help absorb recoil, and concentrate on swiveling your entire torso with the birds instead of pushing the gun with your arms.

236 KNOW YOUR AR BIG-GAME CARTRIDGES

Hunters keep flocking to the AR platform, whether the game is long-distance varmints, hogs in the dark woods, or deer just about anywhere. New cartridges seem to crop up every year. Here are some of the best for modern sporting rifles.

.223 REM
Close to the 5.56mm, the .223 Rem. is safe to fire in a rifle chambered for 5.56mm, but it is not recommended to run 5.56 ammo through a .223 action. The .223 works for varmints but is too light—and often illegal—for deer-sized game.

.243 WIN
This necked-down .308 pushes a .243-caliber bullet fast and flat, making it a fine round for white-tailed deer (with the heavier 100-grain bullet) on down.

.308 WIN
Also known as the 7.62x51mm NATO, this cartridge is the little brother to the .30-06. Its accuracy is legendary among snipers and beanfield shooters, and it has plenty of oomph for 300-yard deer.

6.8 SPC
Designed as a longer-range cartridge, this .270-caliber round is super versatile, with muzzle energy between the .223 and .308.

7MM-08 REM
Flat-shooting and accurate, this necked-down .308 carries plenty of energy far down-range, making it a fine choice for beanfield deer, elk, antelope, and other big game smaller than brown bear and moose.

.260 REM
For shooters looking for relatively low recoil, the .260 offers that, plus much higher energy than the .243 Win.

.300 BLK
Many shooters like the load for its subsonic possibilities, but at fairly short ranges—200 yards or less—the supersonic 110-grain bullet is a great hog and deer load.

.338 FED
Another round from the .308 family tree, this one is necked-up to handle bigger game like moose and elk. Pushing bullets up to 200 grains, at muzzle velocities topping 3,000 feet per second, the .338 Fed. packs a wallop.

.450 BUSHMASTER
Dubbed the "Thumper," the large-bore cartridge provides knock-down-and-dead ballistics on large game out to 250 and 300 yards. Long-range hogs tremble at its name.

237 EARN THE RIFLEMAN'S MERIT BADGE

The official Boy Scouts of America Rifle Shooting merit badge is a prestigious one, conveying the hallmarks of practice, marksmanship, and respect.

Acing this badge's test means that you possess those fundamental skills required for shooting game—both big and small—in every corner of the continent: breathing control, trigger control, body positioning, and follow-through. There's a written essay test that leaves no doubt as to whether you know the difference between a squib and a hangfire. You had better bone up on rifle cleaning, gun safety, and local laws, too.

That's before you even pull a trigger. And pull it you will. The Boy Scout test involves 40 shots. Not a one can be a clunker. No wonder the test put many a young man in a cold sweat. It's not easy, whether your scouting days have just ended or are only a misty memory. Mop your brow, and get started.

This is a three-part challenge—shooting a tight group, adjusting the sights to zero, then punching high-scoring holes in an NRA bull's-eye.

STEP 1 Decide on a preferred shooting position, either from a benchrest or supported prone, and set up an NRA smallbore or light rifle target 50 feet away. You have to fire five groups, with three shots per group, each of which can be covered by a quarter.

STEP 2 Adjust the sights to zero in the rifle. Get ready to sweat.

STEP 3 Fire five more groups, with five shots per group. No fliers and no excuses—every single shot has to meet or exceed these scores:

- NRA A-32 target: 9
- NRA A-17 or TQ-1 target: 7
- NRA A-36 target: 5

CHALLENGE YOURSELF Stand up and man up. Get off the bench and shoot your group from a standing position.

238 BRIGHTEN YOUR RIFLE SIGHT

When the front blade of a rifle's open sights goes dull, brighten it up with a bit of sandpaper or emery cloth. Polish away the bluing from the top of the front blade and paint it with fluorescent paint or even nail polish. Now you have a bright spot to settle into the rear notch.

239 SHOOT WITH TWO EYES

Closing the weak eye robs you of depth perception and slashes field of view dramatically, which means you can miss important variables, such as wind gusts at the target's location . . . or the fact that an even larger buck stepped out of the woods 10 feet away. If you shoot with one eye closed and then open both eyes, it will take a few seconds for your brain to sort out the differentiated views and those few seconds can be critical. And perhaps most important, shooting with one eye closed leads to what Gunsite Ranch founder Jeff Cooper calls "getting lost in the scope." You see the animal with both eyes, pull the gun to your shoulder, and then waste valuable seconds waving it around trying to find the target. For those who have shot one-eyed for years, opening both eyes is easier said than done. The off-season is the time to kick the habit.

METHOD

1 AT THE RANGE Start off with two strips of masking tape on the outside of the nondominant-eye lens of your glasses. This helps to prevent the double image that is so bothersome to shooters. As you get used to keeping both eyes open, switch to frosted tape, then try a smear of petroleum jelly. Gradually reduce the amount until you need none.

2 AT HOME Back up range practice by dry-firing your rifle. Mount the rifle, acquire the target, then shift your attention between the view in the scope and the other eye, to pick out all the details of the environment surrounding your target. The trick is to do this while maintaining a strong "cheek weld"— never lifting your face from the stock.

240 SAVE YOUR EARDRUMS FOR A QUARTER

I keep foam earplugs stashed in my hunting jacket pockets, blind bags, and gun cases. The low-pressure polyurethane memory foam is made to compress easily and re-form in the ear canal for a tight fit that blunts any sound. Covered with a skin of slick material, they are easier to insert and much more comfortable to wear than the bargain-basement PVC stopples. They offer a noise reduction rating (NRR) of up to 32 decibels, and they make high-repetition shooting safe and comfortable. I make sure to plug up any time I share a blind with a ported gun.

The trick is getting the plugs deep enough into your ear canal. You can't just stuff them in like shoving letters into a mail slot. Here's the drill: Roll the plug in between your thumb and your first two fingers. Be careful not to roll a wrinkle into the plug. Roll it gently with increasing pressure until it's a third the original size.

Start with your right ear—hold up the plug in your right hand while still gently rolling it tightly between your fingers. Reach over the top of your head with your left hand and pull the tip of your ear lobe upward to open up your ear canal. Now, insert the small end of the ear plug deeply, retaining enough of the larger end to easily grasp and remove.

Repeat with the other ear. And don't wait. Proper insertion takes two hands and more time than you have when the ducks are coming.

241 SHOOT A DOUBLE GUN FOR PLANTATION QUAIL

Many quail plantations ban the use of any semiautomatic shotguns in favor of double-barreled side-by-sides or over-unders. Part of the reasoning has to do with conservation: Limiting a shooter to two shells for each covey rise reduces the number of birds taken. Double-barreled guns are also shorter, which means they are easier to maneuver in thick cover; and well balanced, which makes them a pleasure to carry hour after hour. But there are other reasons a "twice-barrel," as one of my old Southern hunting pals calls them, are the go-to gun for Southern quail shoots.

SAFETY Quail hunting often involves a number of living creatures other than quail, from additional hunters in the party to pointing dogs, flushing dogs, horses, and mules. There's no safer way to carry a shotgun than to carry a double gun broken open.

SELECTION Most double guns allow the shooter to select which barrel to fire first. In modern shotguns with screw-in chokes, this allows shooters to customize varying chokes for the hunting situation—for example, a cylinder bore in the first tube for close-flushing birds, followed by a tighter modified choke inside the second barrel for the next shot at farther distances. The double trigger guns can provide an instant choice simply by moving your trigger finger. The shotguns with barrel-selecting buttons aren't quite as quick.

SHOT SIZE The double-barreled configuration also gives shooters the ability to load barrels with different shot sizes. That's a bonus for waterfowlers.

242 REMOVE A RECOIL PAD

There are plenty of reasons to remove a recoil pad, from replacing the existing pad to accessing the spring on a recoil-operated shotgun. First, however, you have to solve the riddle of the invisible screw slots. Many recoil pads are affixed to the stock with two Phillips-head screws, which are recessed deep into the pad and fit flush against a stiff spacer that lies next to the stock butt itself. You might never find them—or even know they are there—until you find the tiny slits or channels that allow a screwdriver access to the screw heads.

To sleuth out these hidden slits, try this: With the butt end of the stock between the fatty bases of your thumbs, use your thumbs to apply outward pressure to the face of the recoil pad. Start at one end and work your way down. The screw slits or holes should peek open just enough to be visible. If that fails, pull the tip of a large flat-bladed screwdriver over the pad to reveal the holes.

To insert a screwdriver, use a drop of dishwashing liquid or oil on the tip of a Phillips-head screwdriver, and push the point into the screw. It is critical to avoid stripping the screw head, so be sure to carefully rotate the screwdriver back and forth to feel for a tight fit. If you feel much wiggle in the screw tip, use a slightly larger screwdriver.

While you have the screws out, perform a little bit of maintenance: Paint the threads with a silicone-based waterproofing agent before replacing them.

243 BUILD A GUNSMITH BOX

I keep a basement table cleared off and dedicated for gun cleaning. (It's an old family heirloom—a gorgeous walnut drop-leaf—please don't tell my mother.) At least one gun cradle is deployed at all times, which makes after-the-hunt cleaning sessions much more convenient. Here's a list of items I store in the gun cradle or in a nearby tote.

TOOLS AND BASICS
- Gun cradle or two. Maybe three.
- Wheeler Deluxe Gunsmithing Screwdriver Set. The absolute foundation.
- #1 Phillips-head screwdriver for removing recoil pads. The Wheeler set with the interchangeable tips has a flange that prevents its use for this.
- Large flat-blade screwdriver
- Socket wrench with extension for removing stock bolts
- Roll pin punches
- Allen, Torx, and hex wrenches
- Needle-nose pliers
- Rotary tool with attachments
- Old toothbrushes
- Pointed cosmetic swabs. Not ear swabs, but the pointed ones made of denser cotton.
- Cleaning rods, brushes and wool mops
- Cleaning patches
- White hand towel. Useful as a mat on which to place small parts.
- Small flashlight
- Nut pick
- Small mountain of rags
- 0000 steel wool

GADGETS AND GIZMOS
- Trigger-pull scale
- Boresighter
- Scope bubble level

SPRAYS, GOOPS, AND LUBES
- Gun oil in various forms—spray and bottle
- Solvents in various forms—spray and bottle
- Choke-tube grease
- Bore-cleaning compound
- Break-Free CLP
- Loctite Threadlocker Blue
- AquaSeal for sealing recoil pads and screws on a duck gun's synthetic stock and adding grip to gun slings
- Cans of compressed air
- Lens cleaner and tissues
- Lighter fluid

244 MAKE A DIY TARGET STAND

This target stand holds a pair of furring strips upright for easy target attachment. Assemble as shown. For a more permanent stand, glue the PVC pipes into place with PVC glue. For an easily transportable stand, toss all the components into a bag and push the pieces into place once you're out on the range. Staple the cardboard to the furring strips and attach targets. It is, literally, a snap.

YOU'LL NEED

2-inch PVC pipe cut to these lengths: four 16-inch pieces, two 20-inch pieces, two 26-inch pieces • 4 PVC elbow joints • 2 PVC T-joints • two 1-by-2-inch furring strips • one 24-by-36-inch piece of flat cardboard

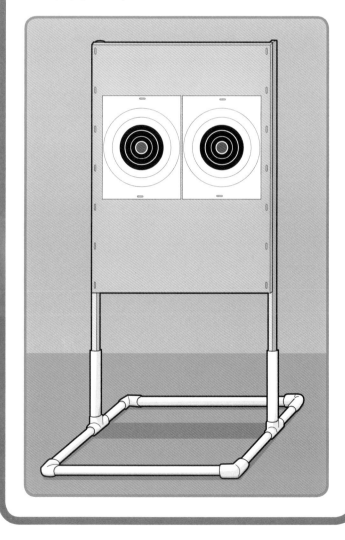

245 MAKE A TRAIL TAPE DISPENSER

By the midpoint of the hunting season, most hunting packs will contain messy wads of surveyor's tape. The stuff is indispensable for marking trails and tracking wounded animals, but the rolls unroll, twist, and get caught in pack zippers, and they become a nuisance when you're trying to fish out a small strip. Create a quick fix with an empty 35mm film canister: Stuff the canister with surveyor's tape, cut an X into the top, pull a tag end of the tape through the slit, and cap off the canister. It will work just like a box of tissues: You can pull out what you need, and no more. And they're small enough to stash in a shirt pocket or hip belt pocket, where it's ready to go.

246 STOP GUN-SLING SLIP

Nylon and paracord gun slings are light, but slippery. Add in traction with bands of a silicone sealant such as Seam Grip or Aqua Seal.

247 FLAG A DUCK

Your buddies might snicker when you bust out a duck flag in a timber hole, but soon enough they will be asking you, "Where can I get one?" Goose hunters have long used flags to pull honkers into gun range, but I've flagged ducks in open country and tight timber with very positive results. Don't forget the camo—head to toe, nose to fingertips. After all, you're asking those birds to practically look you in the eye.

GIVE A FLAP Grab the flag firmly, raise it over your head, and shake it vigorously as you flap it down toward the water. Picture your mallard back-flapping hard as it descends the final 10 feet to land. You can see the flash of those white underwings in even the shadiest corners of a swamp, and that's what you want to replicate. Repeat three times quickly.

PLAN YOUR SALUTE As the ducks begin to close the distance, they'll be looking right down at you. Similar to calling, you should work the flag only when the ducks are "on the corners" as they loop around the decoy spread. When the hunting slows down, however, you shouldn't be afraid to give the flag a hearty flapping every few minutes to grab the attention of cruising mallards you might not see.

DO THE WAVE If you and a buddy are hunting out in thick timber and beaver swamps, a pair of flaggers can mean an especially deadly strategy. Stand about 5 to 10 feet from each other, and shake the flags in a row-row-row-your-boat round style: As one flag nears the water, that's when the other flagger starts his turn. This sequence helps simulate one duck following another to the honey hole.

248 COOK A DUCK WITH A STICK

My hunting partners and I watched in amazement as our Athabascan Chipewyan guide cooked a whole duck on a stick. The bird self-basted in its own dripping fat, which scorched in the fire and sent seasoning plumes of smoke up around the meat. It is not required that you put on a moosehide hat that has been sewn by your mother while cooking a duck this way, but it doesn't hurt. Total cooking time will be about 20 minutes.

STEP 1 Cut a 1-inch-thick green stick 18 to 24 inches in length. Sharpen one end. Gut and pluck the duck.

STEP 2 Remove the feet and the wings. Our host left the bird's head on, an impressive but not necessary flourish. Butterfly the duck through the breast, not the back. To do this, insert a stout knife along one side of the breastbone keel, cutting all the way to the backbone (A).

STEP 3 Loosen up the bones and flesh by working the duck back and forth between your hands, like trying to break a stick. Place the duck on a flat surface and press with the palm of your hand (B).

STEP 4 Skewer the duck by running the stick in and out of the breast meat on one side of the keel, and then on the other. Anchor the stick in the ground at a 45-degree angle to the fire, 6 inches to a foot away from the heat source (C). Cook breast side to the fire first, and rotate once.

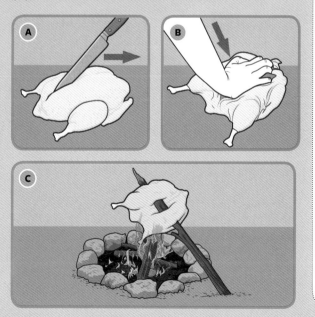

249 MAKE A DUCK HUNTER'S FLOATING TABLE

This floating table is a duck hunter's rip-off of the classic swimming pool beer pong table. All the pegboard holes drain any water that slops onto the table, so it will keep your shells, calls, gloves, and other items high and dry in a flooded swamp or timber hole. The pipe insulation serves as edge bumpers and keeps items from sliding off and provides a bit of outrigger flotation. Make the table long enough and it'll float a gun, as well. Pretty swanky.

YOU'LL NEED

a couple of pool noodles • a sheet of plastic pegboard in a dark color • black foam pipe insulation (the kind with the slit) • zip ties

STEP 1 Cut pool noodles into three pieces that are 4 inches shorter than the full length of your pegboard table top. Cut pipe insulation to the proper length to slip over all four table top edges.

STEP 2 Using zip ties, attach pipe insulation all the way around the pegboard.

STEP 3 Using zip ties, attach your pool noodle sections. Place one lengthwise down the center of the pegboard, and two other sections down the long edges. If more flotation is needed, simply attach more pool noodle sections.

250 COLD-PROOF YOUR SHOTGUN

Some of the best duck hunting takes place in some of the worst conditions for your shotgun: bitter, bone-numbing, oil-thickening cold. Semiautomatic shotguns in particular are at risk for freezing up in temperatures that drop into the teens or even lower. The first aid that some hunters turn to—additional lubrication of the action—is actually the worst possible solution you could use. Lubricants can thicken, especially when mixed with powder residue and grime, and gum up the action. Here's what to do to make sure your scattergun performs in the next "polar vortex."

STRIP THE OIL Disassemble the barrel, receiver, and action. Spray metal parts with Break-Free CLP. Wipe all excess oil away, and wait a few minutes. Now give the parts another good wipe. Use cotton swabs to soak up any excess pooling in nooks and crannies. You want to remove any and all oil. In the field, a squirt of lighter fluid can serve as an emergency de-gunker.

DUST BATH Use powdered graphite to dust primary action parts such as bolt rails and ejection latches.

OUTSIDE STORAGE Many problems occur when a warm gun is brought into cold, outside air. Moisture condenses on metal gun parts, then freezes in the field. The night before a hunt, store your gun safely outside.

251 PUT MORE SPRING IN YOUR SEMIAUTO SHOTGUN

Duck hunters who frequently go wading in beaver swamps, timber holes, and deep impoundments should take a harder look at those springs in recoil-operated semiautomatic shotguns. Gunstocks often take a swim, and a plastic stock is not impervious to the elements. Water can seep in at the recoil pad and at the sling swivels, and once it's in, it can rust recoil springs that compress inside the stock.

Here's how to make your shotgun beaver-pond worthy. Access the spring tube and get it cleaned up. Replace the factory spring with a new one or, even better still, one made of stainless steel. While reassembling the shotgun, waterproof the hollow synthetic stock by laying down a bead of AquaSeal silicone sealant around the recoil pad seam and the holes for the sling swivel.

252 MAKE EXPLODING FLASH TARGETS FOR AN OLYMPIC-STYLE SHOOT

Those big clouds of clay pigeon dust you see on shooting shows aren't there because the shooters center every shot. Those puff balls are "flash targets"—modified clay birds that carry an extra payload of colored dust. You can pay a gazillion dollars for commercially available flash targets, which are hard to find. Or you can make your own with common clay pigeons, carpenter's chalk dust, newspaper, and glue. Get a buddy or two together for an assembly line and crank them out fast and cheap.

STEP 1 Gather the essentials. Lots of common items will provide the cloud of colored dust, including flour and baking soda. Probably the best is carpenter's chalk—it's cheap and readily available, and comes in bright colors. You'll need spare cardboard like a shoebox, or perhaps construction paper. And some kind of glue—white glue, carpenter's glue, or barge cement will all work.

STEP 2 Cut cardboard or paper circles slightly larger in diameter than the raised rim that runs around the cupped dome on top of the clay bird.

STEP 3 Fill the dome with a few spoonfuls of colored powder. Run a bead of glue around the raised rim. Cap with the paper circle and press with fingertips. Set a half dozen on a flat surface and top with a heavy book to seal the bond.

253 SHOOT OLD-SCHOOL

The advent of in-line muzzleloaders fueled a blackpowder craze that's still going strong. New powders, bullets, and ignition systems make it easier than ever to shoot—and clean—a modern smokepole. Here's what you need to know to turn back time and go hit the woods with your own front-stuffer.

A FLINTLOCKS Traditional flintlocks fire when a cock, holding a fixed piece of flint, strikes a metal plate called a frizzen, sending sparks downward into an external flash pan filled with powder. The powder ignites, sending a tiny piece of the inferno through a small hole in the barrel called a touchhole. This flash ignites the main powder charge behind the bullet.

B PERCUSSION CAPS Introduced in the early nineteenth century, percussion cap firearms soon replaced flintlocks. A small cylinder of copper or brass holds a tiny load of impact-sensitive explosive. The cap is placed over a hollow metal nipple. When the hammer strikes the percussion cap, the flash ignites the main powder charge.

C IN-LINE MUZZLELOADERS The blackpowder arms modern era began in 1985 when a Missouri gunsmith, Tony Knight, debuted an in-line muzzleloader. Moving the percussion nipple from the side of the combustion chamber to directly behind the powder charge meant the flash would travel in a direct line—ergo "in-line"—to the powder charge. The innovation kicked off the current revolution in blackpowder firearms. More recent models include both bolt and break actions, with screw-in breech plugs that make loading and cleaning much simpler than ever before. Most in-line muzzleloading guns use 209 shotshell-styled primers.

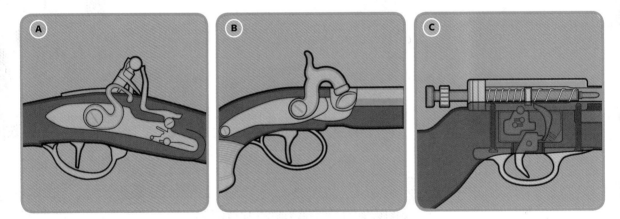

254 TRY A BLACKPOWDER PELLET

The new kids on the muzzleloading block, pelletized powders come in tablet form. Instead of measuring a charge of loose powder in a powder measure and then pouring it into the barrel, a shooter simply drops a number of pellets down the barrel before seating the bullet. Fans love the ease of reloading, while critics argue that pellets crack and chip, eroding accuracy from shot to shot. Pyrodex and Triple Seven come in pellets, with other popular choices including IMR White Hots and Shockey's Gold Sticks.

255 TAKE A BLACKPOWDER POWDER

While generically the guns discussed here are all called "blackpowder," in fact you have a number of options. True blackpowder is an ancient mix of charcoal, sulfur, and potassium nitrate. It is a "fast-burning" mix that ignites easily. Classified as an explosive, blackpowder comes in several grain sizes. FFFF is the smallest grade commonly used, favored by flintlock shooters as a flash pan powder. FFF is the go-to for muzzleloaders of .45 and smaller, while .50 caliber shooters tend to load up with FF powder.

Many modern shooters use Pyrodex, a substitute that is very close in burn characteristics to blackpowder. Slightly more difficult to ignite than blackpowder, Pyrodex can be more safely stored and shipped. It is not classified as an explosive, so it is more widely available than blackpowder.

While Pyrodex remains the top choice, other various powder-substitute brands, such as Triple Seven, Goex Clear Shot and Black Mag3, have plenty of fans. Most are formulated without charcoal or sulfur, which makes them easier to clean than other powders. Newer gun-powder products such as Blackhorn 209 and Black MZ are even cleaner-burning and produce high velocities, and have improved resistance to humidity and moisture. There is disagreement about how closely these various propellants simulate true blackpowder in volume and burn rates, so use product-specific guidelines when calculating loads.

256 KNOW YOUR BLACKPOWDER PROJECTILES

Blackpowder rifles require their own particular projectiles. Here are the ones you're likely to see.

ROUND BALL This traditional bullet is seated in a cloth patch, which serves as a type of gasket to seal the bore and engage the barrel rifling. It's most often used in traditional flintlock and percussion cap guns.

CONICAL BULLET Elongated conical bullets weigh much more than round balls of the same caliber and shoot harder and fly flatter.

SABOTED BULLETS The bullet fits into a plastic

cup, or sabot (from the French term for "shoe"), which engages the barrel rifling. The sabot allows lighter, faster bullets of slightly smaller diameters than the barrel. Many saboted bullets are made with copper jackets like conventional centerfire ammunition, making them extremely accurate and deadly at ranges Daniel Boone only dreamed of.

POWERBELT A mash-up between the elongated conical bullet and the sabot, PowerBelts feature a plastic base that expands to seal the bore, then pops off during flight. They can be more easily loaded than other bullet types.

Round Ball

Conical Bullet

Saboted Ball

Powerbelt

257 USE A LINEMAN'S BELT

A linesman's belt, or climbing belt, will not only make climbing trees and hanging tree steps, sticks, and stands much easier, it will make this inherently dicey activity much safer. Typically, the belts are a loop of rope, webbing, or sometimes leather, with a carabiner at each end. The belt encircles the tree at a height just above your waist, and then connects to loops on a safety harness. This not only provides a safety catch should you slip, but allows you to lean back and work with both hands. You'll need a safety harness built to accept a linesman's belt, but most

have the two required connections, as do many harnesses specifically made for tree stand hunting.

To use a lineman's belt, put on a safety harness. Attach one end of the belt to a harness loop above the point of one hipbone. Swing the other carabiner around the tree, grab it, and clip it into the harness loop on the other hipbone. Lean back and the loop supports your weight. Many belts come with a set of Prussik loops that allow you to adjust the angle of lean. The most comfortable will be between 25 and 30 degrees.

258 MAKE YOUR OWN SCENT-KILLER

Even if you shower in no-scent soap right before your hunt, the little bit you sweat going to your stand will turn into a powerful stench to deer. That's why many hunters compulsively use commercial scent killers. The problem is that their cost can make you apply them sparingly, which is like putting deodorant on only one armpit.

Here's a simple homemade scent killer. Hydrogen peroxide kills the bacteria and fungi that turn sweat into a deer-busting funk, and baking soda deodorizes whatever sneaks by.

YOU'LL NEED

2 cups (16 ounces) 3% hydrogen peroxide • 2 cups (16 ounces) distilled water • ½ cup baking soda • 1 ounce unscented shampoo or unscented hunter's body wash

MIX Gently combine all of the ingredients in a large bowl until the baking soda dissolves. Next, pour this mixture into a 1-gallon container with a lid, such as a milk jug. Let it sit for three days with the lid on loosely to allow gases to escape.

BOTTLE Fill a plastic bottle that has a trigger sprayer with the scent killer. It must be clean, so buy a new one from a hardware store or online.

WIPE To make your own scent-killing wipes, place plain brown multifold paper towels—the kind that come in stacks, not on a roll—in a small plastic tub with an airtight lid. Cover them with your scent killer and let it soak in. Pour out excess liquid and replace the lid. Now you can wipe down boots, bows, and stands, and even use a towel or three to neutralize the sweat that you'll produce while shinnying up that perfect white oak.

259 MOUNT A MEAT GRINDER FOR EASIER GRINDING

Hand-cranked meat grinders are efficient and last forever, but they do require a very sturdy attachment to a very sturdy table. If you don't want to permanently bolt a grinder to a table, you can easily mount the grinder to a separate board, then C-clamp the board to an existing table. Voila—an instant grinding station.

For a mounting board, avoid cutting boards made of multiple wood pieces; all those forces exerted by the grinder chewing through gristle will split them easily. Go for a solid cutting board, or better yet, a good solid 1-inch-thick polyethylene cutting board or kitchen laminate such as Formica or Arborite. Place the grinder on the board. Leaving room for four C-clamps that will attach the mounting board to your table, mark the foot holes, and drill them out. Use machine screws with lock washers and bolts to attach the grinder to the board. Now you can C-clamp the grinder to a kitchen table, deck railing, or work bench, and never buy sausage again.

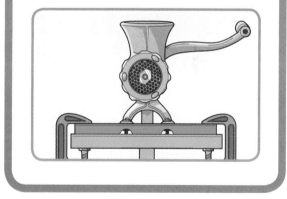

260 PROTECT YOUR TURKEY-CALL STRIKER

The plastic caps that come with cheap ink pens are perfect for capping the tip of a turkey-call striker, protecting it from dings and chips in you vest pocket, or oil from your hands.

261 HUNT ON SNOWSHOES

Floating over deep snow in pursuit of snowshoe hares, coyotes, and deer is a classic method of hunting, and easier than you think. A revolution in snowshoe design has spawned a wide variety of high-tech aluminum snowshoes, but the ancient wooden snowshoe still gets the nod for many hunters.

CHOOSE THE RIGHT SHOE A very big advantage to wooden snowshoes: They are sneaky-quiet in the brush. Smack into a rock or sapling with wooden snowshoes and you'll hear a dull thud. Do the same with some aluminum snowshoes and the loud metallic thwack will spook every animal within a quarter mile. The modified or elongated bearpaw style offers plenty of flotation, a slight lift to the tip for maneuvering through brush, and a stable enough platform that you can use to step on top of downed trees in tough cover.

TURN AROUND The toughest snowshoe maneuver is turning around, and it's particularly challenging for hunters who don't have the advantage of poles. It's similar to pulling a 180 on skis: keep one planted, lift the other foot high over the snow, and put it down at a right angle to the other. Bring the other foot around, and repeat for the full 180.

TAKE A SEAT A bearpaw snowshoe makes a handy seat with a built-in comfy backrest, perfect for watching forest openings and open glades. Stick one snowshoe vertically into the snow for a backrest, and use the other as the seat. Kick out a comfortable footrest and sit down.

262 KEEP HUNTING CLOTHES CLEAN IN CAMP

Most hunting camps will have most of what you'll need to jerry-rig a washing machine in the field. Just provide baking soda or your own scent-free washing detergent and you are ready to rid your duds of cigar smoke, sweat, and spilled bean dip.

Grab a 5-gallon bucket and the camp plunger.

Disinfect and deodorize that plunger by filling the bucket with boiling water. Add a bit of baking soda or detergent and work the plunger up and down to clean. Now replace the water with clean water and more baking soda or detergent, toss in your clothes, and churn your way to clean. Rinse with fresh water.

263 RE-PROOF WAXED COTTON

First-generation waxed cotton was just sailcloth smeared with fish oil, so don't go whining about the relatively low maintenance requirements of modern waxed-cotton duds. Heavily used clothing needs re-proofing once a year or so, and it's easy. It's best to do this during summer, when warm temperatures keep the wax soft and workable.

CLEAN IT Clean the jacket (A) with cold water and a soft cloth or sponge. No soap, ever. Let the jacket dry.

WAX IT Place a tin of wax dressing in hot water and allow the wax to warm into a semiliquid state. Warm the jacket, either by placing it in a sunny spot or by stuffing it into a couple of pillowcases and tossing it in the dryer (B).

FINISH IT Roll a soft cotton cloth into a tight roll (C); use rubber bands to hold it in shape (D). Use this to work the wax into the jacket exterior (E). Concentrate on a small area at a time, and pay close attention to seams, worn spots, and creases. Go for even coverage, and wipe excess with another clean cloth. Use a blow-dryer to finish the wax (F).

NEW-SCHOOL TWIST You can use re-proofing wax on other 100-percent cotton apparel, so give your favorite hunting cap an old-school spa treatment. While waxed cotton won't breathe quite as well as nontreated cotton, your broken-in lid will turn away showers and wear a retro patina.

264 SILENCE YOUR ZIPPER

Zipper pulls made of metal or heavy plastic can clink and clank just enough to spook game. Give them the silent treatment with a little electrical heat-shrink tubing. Just slip it over the zipper pull and hit with a lighter. The tubing shrinks when heated and provides a sound-dampening cover. Or cut the pulls off and replace with paracord or loops of old fly line.

265 KEEP CALLS CLEAN

Plug your duck, goose, owl, predator, and crow calls with a wine cork. Now you can stuff them into your filthy pockets without fear of dirt sticking in the reeds.

266 MAKE A FROG GIG

These are the nights to channel your inner Huck Finn. Frog gigging feeds the stomach and the soul, because there's something downright spiritual about a lily-fringed frog pond on a new-moon night. You can use a retro cane pole—or you can get fancy with this telescoping gig fashioned from a 16-foot collapsible bream pole. It's perfect for any small-boat frogman, plus the golf-course gigger who needs a pole that will fit in a car. Once armed, get to it. Gigging a gigged-out pond is like batting cleanup in a game of spin the bottle.

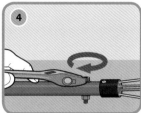

SBT Outdoors gig head

 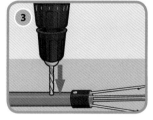

STEP 1 Remove the butt cap from the bream pole, then slide out the rod-tip end of the nested sections. Replace the cap.

STEP 2 Saw off the front end of the pole at the point where it snugly fits inside the gig head. The gig head sold by SBT Outdoors is the best I've seen and has replaceable tines sharp as a surgeon's scalpel.

STEP 3 Drill a ⅛-inch hole through the gig shaft and pole. Remove the gig head and coat the inside with epoxy.

STEP 4 Affix the gig head to the pole using a ¾-inch-long 6-32 stainless-steel bolt, a washer, and a locking nut. Let the glue set, and you're done.

267 PREPARE YOUR FROGS

To clean your frogs, remove the legs above the hips. A perfect cut helps keep the legs attached. Pull the skin down to the ankle and cut off the feet. Dredge legs through a milk-and-egg bath, then batter. Fry in hot peanut oil.

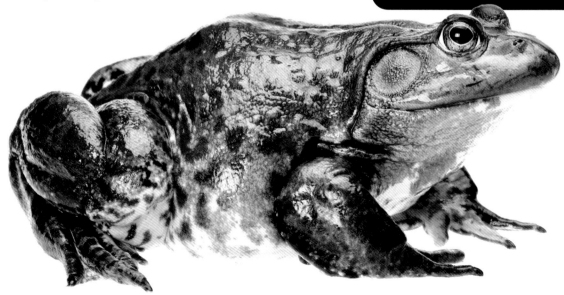

268 MARK YOUR POT CALL

There's always an area on the surface of any pot-style turkey call that will produce the best sound. To mark it, rotate the call so that the sweet spot lies between the thumb and index finger of the hand that holds the pot. Then use a knife to score the sides where those fingers lay. Now, you can easily orient the call to make the best tone without ever looking at it.

269 MAKE YOUR OWN LAYOUT BLIND

Will that brand-new $450 layout blind with spring-assisted doors and integrated camouflage work better than these ones? Probably. Will it work $450 worth better? Ask the geese.

A CHEAP Go comfy with a camp chair that folds all the way flat. Wrap the exposed metal on the frame with camouflage duct tape, walk into the field with a handful of long black cable ties, and brush it up. Do your best not to doze off.

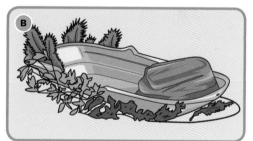

B CHEAPER Buy a plastic snow toboggan in a dull color, or spray-paint it. Use it to haul your gear and decoys across the field, then toss your hunting pack into the top for a pillow, and cover it all up with some camouflage material and vegetation cut from the field.

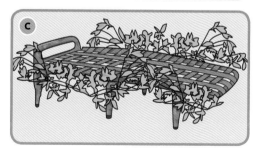

C CHEAPEST Find an old beach or lawn chair. Cover exposed metal with camouflage duct tape and weave green paracord line through the webbings for additional tie-ins for natural vegetation. Line it with an insulated camping pad or a camouflaged space blanket, brush it up, line down, and bring home pâté!

270 SHOOT A SUPER-MODERN ARROW

Hurtling along at 270 feet per second and faster, tipped with a cutting head capable of slicing a 2-inch cross through the entire body width of an elk or bear, the modern arrow is a technological wonder. Like supermodels, they keep getting lighter, stronger, faster, thinner—and more complicated.

→ **BROADHEADS** While open-on-impact broadheads often outsell fixed blades, not everyone is convinced they fly better. They may not penetrate as well, either. But they do offer one advantage: wicked wound channels. Open-on-impact broadheads are getting ever larger, with cutting diameters well over 2 inches. If your arrow drifts back and hits the liver, that could make a difference.

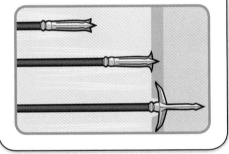

→ **SHAFT** Microdiameter arrows will have smaller shafts of stiffer materials that can lead to greater arrow penetration. Arrows with a varying spine rating seek to tame the flex that occurs when the enormous load of energy is applied at the release of the bowstring. Double and even triple spine arrows are on the market. Stiffer back sections take up the force, while lighter middle and forward sections contain most of the flex.

→ **FLETCHING** Short 2-inch vanes are stiff and tough and have nearly replaced 4-inch vanes. Most factory arrows have straight or offset fletching, but helical fletching gets an arrow spinning more quickly for greater stability. New high-speed photography has some arrow designers rethinking the role of fletching in windy conditions and longer distances.

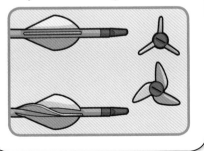

→ **NOCKS** Lighted nocks help you track the arrow's flight.

271 GET THE PERFECT NOCK FIT

Little things matter, especially when you're trying to send an arrow toward a target half a football field away. Change your arrow nocks every year, and change every nock at the same time. Nocks can loosen and lose their grip, and inconsistency between one nock and other will definitely show up down range.

272 CALL A TURKEY WITH A PEACOCK

Owl and crow calls are the go-to locators for shock-calling roosting toms, but pressured gobblers can clam up after being hammered with who-cooks-for-you hoots day after day. Switch to a pileated woodpecker, a coyote, or a peacock call to trick closemouthed gobblers into giving up their position.

273 TUNE UP A BOX CALL

The box call contains several of the elements of a fine musical instrument, and like Charlie Daniels warned Johnny to "rosin up your bow" for his fiddle duel with the Devil, a box call benefits from a little preseason TLC. Here's the 5-minute drill.

STEP 1 Clean it. First, put down the sandpaper. You want to clean the wood sidewall rails, not reshape them, and sandpaper will do both. Lightly rub the rails with a Scotch-Brite pad or other scouring pad designed for non-stick pots.

STEP 2 Rechalk the bottom of the paddle with a bit of carpenter's chalk or a chalk made specifically for turkey calls. Blackboard chalk contains wax, and that will deaden the call. Some callers shy away from chalk of any kind and go with Daniels' advice and use pine rosin instead.

STEP 3 Work the call a few times, then look closely at the underside of the paddle. Are there shiny spots? That means grime or grease still soil the sidewalls. Back to step one.

STEP 4 The tension screw on a box call lid has been set precisely by the call maker, but over time, the screw can turn and affect the call's sound. To adjust, first mark the exact position of the screw with a black marker. Tighten first, since it is more common for screws to loosen than to tighten. Give the screw the slightest turn, and test for call tone before making any other adjustments.

274 BLOW A WINGBONE YELPER

The beauty of a wingbone call is the organic feel to its sound, which can fool toms sick and tired of the calls hunters today carry around in their magnetic vest pockets.

PUCKER UP Insert the call's small end between your lips—either in the middle, or slightly off to one side—and form a very tight seal. The call should just barely extend into your mouth.

GRAB HOLD Grip the larger end of the call between the base of your thumb and forefinger. Create a flared bell with this hand, and cover with the cupped fingers and palm of your other hand. Open and close the hand positions for a variety of sounds.

PLANT A SMACKER To create short clucks, suck air in as if you were making kissing sounds. For yelps, extend the kissing inhalations and suck in air, then drop the lower jaw to create the two-note break of a hen yelp. Practice makes perfect. Tell your spouse you are getting ready for your anniversary night.

275 MAKE A CINDER BLOCK PIT COOKER

Here's a great way to go whole wild hog and construct a backyard pit using easy to find materials. And you won't need to store a full-blown pig cooker in the driveway for 12 months a year.

YOU'LL NEED

40 cinder blocks • A grill platform—either borrow the grate from a friend with a "real" pig cooker, or MacGyver your own out of nongalvanized expanded metal (galvanized metal will emit toxic fumes when heated) • Extra-heavy-duty aluminum foil or roof sheeting of nongalvanized metal • A shovel or two • One heckuva pile of wood—better get a half-cord, just to be safe; or augment with charcoal • BBQ sauce for basting

BUILD IT

Clear an area of level ground of any combustibles like leaves, sticks, or leaf litter. If not level, shovel out a flat spot. To construct the firepit, lay out a rectangle of cinder blocks in the pattern shown.

On each short end, leave a cinder block "A" out of the pattern. You'll add heat to the firepit by moving out that particular cinder block below "A" and shoveling coals into the fire through the opening.

On the ends of the long sides of the pit, turn the cinder blocks marked "B" sideways so the holes are exposed. You can regulate heat by regulating airflow through these cinder blocks. Cover the holes with other blocks or a board as needed.

Once you are ready to cook, a grill grate or expanded metal platform will rest on this platform. If an expanded metal platform isn't strong enough to hold the pig, add 3 pieces of rebar across the width.

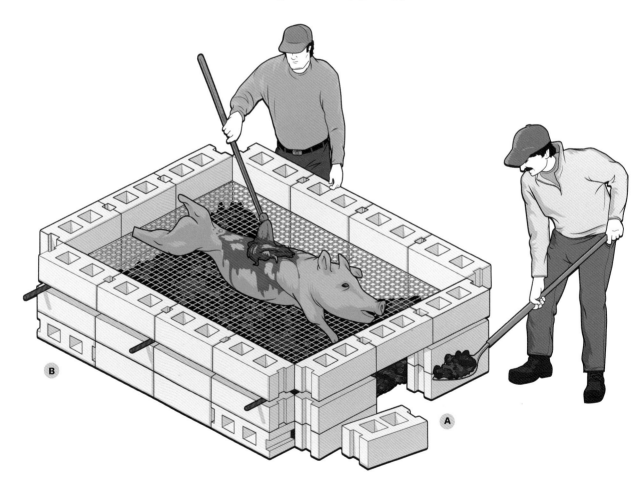

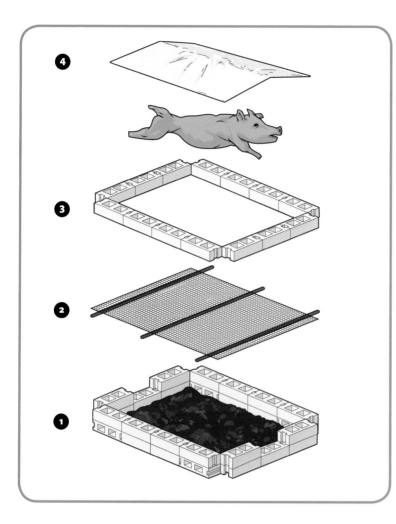

④

③

②

①

276 KEEP WILD GAME FRESH

Your trophy is now heaped on the counter top in small mountains of meat. Here's how to keep the meat fresh-as-the-day-it-was-butchered if you plan to eat it in . . .

1 WEEK

There's no need to freeze it for such a short time period. Keep the meat well wrapped, and in the coldest part of the refrigerator, far away from the door.

1 MONTH

Center the meat in laminated freezer paper. Fold the short ends over the meat and turn the package over on a countertop, keeping it in contact with the counter to push out air. Once it's flipped, use your fingers to press the air out of the sides as if you were sealing an envelope. Repeat twice more and tape the flap.

1 YEAR

A vacuum sealer sucks all the air out of packages, staving off freezer burn and saving freezer space. If you don't have a vacuum-sealer, freeze each cut in water. Place the meat in a zip-seal freezer bag, and fill the bag with ice water. Press down on the bag as you seal it so that water spills out of the top, driving air out of the bag. Also, I like to mark each package with the date, the cut, and a detail about the deer, such as "7-pointer by the swamp gate." That way I can relive the memory with each morsel.

TO COOK

Build a ginormous fire inside the pit and allow it to burn down to coals. You'll want about four inches of hardwood or charcoal briquette coals on each end of the pit. (Essentially, divide the pit into thirds longitudinally: the shoulder end, the ham end, and the rib middle. You'll use little direct heat under the middle third.) You'll also want a nearby auxiliary fire that will produce more coals that will be shoveled into the pit on an as-needed basis.

Place a whole wild pig or other animal skin-side-up on the grate. Now add the third and final layer of cinder blocks, on top of the others. This will hold a layer of aluminum foil or metal sheeting above the swine. Cover the entire grill. If using aluminum foil, you'll need to be very careful to knock down flare-ups with water so the foil won't ignite.

From here on out, it's a mix of art and experience. What you may lack in either you can make up with trial and delicious error. Figure on 6 to 8 hours of cooking, depending on the size of the animal. Keep most of the fire's heat under the hams and shoulders. When you think you're about halfway there, use a couple of shovels to help lift and flip the pig. Baste liberally. All helpers get to eat the ribs, which are ready first. The whole hog is done when the interior temperature of the hams hits 180 degrees Fahrenheit.

KIMBER MODEL 84M

I wanted a treestand rifle, a lightweight gun short and compact enough for thick woods hunting but with enough oomph to touch a buck snacking on cut corn 200 yards distant. I didn't need a shoulder cannon. I wasn't interested in the short mags and beanfield ballistics. I simply wanted a gun to have and to hold from this day forward, and something I could perhaps eventually give over to a young deer hunter coming up the trail. I didn't have all of the money in the world, but I'd squirreled away enough for something a little special. So, I wound up with a Kimber Model 84M in .308. I dare you to try and take it from me.

The 84M is built around the .308 Winchester, which is beefy enough to suit my needs perfectly. The action has just enough length to handle that cartridge, and no longer, and the barrel is just long enough to maximize ballistics for those bullets. A gorgeous satin-finished walnut stock carries a match chamber, barrel, and trigger. The barrel is glass-bedded and matte-finished. I like its three-position safety. The gun weighs just 5 pounds, 10 ounces, and is made in America. It is one sweet rifle.

This rifle is unlike all of my other deer guns, and that's just how I wanted it to be. My very first deer rifle was a beloved behemoth. I was young and had big dreams, and I'd fallen under the Jack O'Connor spell of the hot caliber that could do it all—the 7mm Remington Magnum. For my college graduation gift, my entire extended family put into the kitty and out came a Weatherby Vanguard. Built in '83, that gun must have weighed 83 pounds. It was too much gun for Southern woods hunting, a bit too fancy for a journalism graduate getting by on 12 grand a year. But that Weatherby wasn't just

my deer gun, but my dream rifle. One day, I'd haul it out West for elk. One day, I'd settle it across a heavy pack for a long shot at a tundra caribou.

One day it was all too apparent that it was too much medicine for my style of woods hunting. I went the opposite extreme on the next deer rifle. After my shoulder grooved from the Weatherby's bulk and weight, I settled on a lever gun—the Marlin 336 in .30-30, which was seeing new life thanks to the recent introduction of Hornaday's LeverEvolution cartridges. I ordered up the rifle in snazzy stainless steel. O'Connor would have kicked my butt, and I would have deserved the trouncing. The Marlin made a fine treestand deer rifle, as long as the sun wasn't shining. I loved that gun and still do, and tried to love it without a roving eye. But two deer busted me in a single week, thanks to that stainless steel. We had a quick divorce, and I went looking for a trophy wife.

Hello, sweet Kimber. That .308 has filled my freezer three winters running, and my most recent whitetail with the gun is the most memorable one yet. By the time I caught a glimpse of the 9-point swamp buck he was quartering away, 80 yards out and about to disappear into a canebrake. I had to lean farther out from the treestand than I wanted, and twist farther to the right than the textbooks say I should, just to thread the barrel through a screen of muscadine vine. Thanks to that short, light rifle, I caught the deer in the last half-second of opportunity, and pulled the trigger the instant the scope reticle crossed into the vitals. The buck fell in his tracks.

So far, my match with the Kimber seems to be made in heaven. I'm thinking the marriage will last.

THE WORST IT CAN GET

I'll tell you how bad it got. The last time I saw my son, Jack, he lay gasping by the trailside, face ashen and fearful, his head cradled in the arms of my wife. Two other hikers kneeled beside them. One had a different brand of rescue inhaler than the one we typically carry, and thank God for that. Our albuterol wasn't working. Maybe the terbutaline would. That was four, maybe four-and-a-half minutes ago, and when I left them, I could not tell you if Jack would be alive when I saw him again.

Now my daughter, Markie, has vanished around a bend in the trail. I tried to keep up, but she is a cross-country runner and my knees are wrenched. When I told her to run, run like she'd never run before, she vaulted through the forests below Wyoming's Teton crest with the winged feet of Mercury.

Now I sank to one knee and prayed. That was the best I could do. My son clinging to life in my wife's arms, my daughter running for her brother's life. That's how bad it got.

Few of us appreciate how quickly life afield can turn south. When we're headed out for elk camps and high-country lakes, swamp rivers, and salt marshes, we plan and pack for rough weather, rough roads, high water, poor fishing, flat tires, blown zippers, ripped tents, broken rods, and all the other evil contingencies that threaten to derail a blissful fishing or hunting trip. But when it comes to planning for situations where life or limb lie literally in the balance—and not just the fate of a wet sleeping bag—too many of us give it short shrift. A bottle of ibuprofen, a wad of old Band-Aids, maybe a tube of antiseptic cream, and we are out the door.

It can get bad in the blink of an eye. I've been carted off a dove field unconscious, dragged to the truck by my pal Scott Wood, who thankfully didn't wait for the ambulance to show up. I hazily recall a mid-highway ambulance transfer, injections, the world fading in and out of pure black and fuzzy light. The culprit: the sting of a single ground wasp.

I've been on the other side of the examination table, too, field-treating all manner of ills. I've closed up gashes with superglue, carved away portions of infected toenail and flesh and disinfected the remains with whiskey, closed wounds with butterfly closures snipped from duct tape, removed treble hooks buried to the bend, forced food into companions stooped over in a hypoglycemic bonk. None of this stuff is rocket science. Read, think, prepare. Once, in the midst of a horrific climbing accident, I rolled my brother over on his back so he wouldn't drown in a pool of his own blood. I compressed the gashes in his forehead and rib cage to stem the bleeding as he coughed bits of lung in my face. We immobilized his back as best we could and raced for help. Our simple, straightforward, right-out-of-the-books first aid probably saved his life.

As Markie dashed down the trail, I turned to pick my way back toward Jack and Julie. Already my mind was sifting the details, trying to figure out where this went wrong. Thanks to a late, wet spring in the Grand Tetons that year, the pollen load was epic. Bump a pine tree on the trail and yellow sheets fell. Every breeze sent paisleys of whirling pollen wafting through the woods. Jack suffers from the occasional allergy attack, so we always carry an inhaler. But he's a strong hiker, and we didn't think twice before setting out to retrace a favorite 14-mile loop. My mistake. A big mistake. On the far side of Jenny Lake, miles from help, the asthma attack was instant, and instantly life-threatening.

Within minutes, fleet-footed Markie made it to a floating dock that served a park boat for tourists who didn't want to hike all the way around the lake. Fortunately, a seasonal ranger was there, and radioed to park headquarters. In no time flat, a rescue boat was in the water.

Meanwhile, Markie and I made our way back up the trail to Jack. I hobbled up the final rise, heart in my throat, with no clue as to what I would find. As I rounded the trail, I saw Jack sitting upright—the other hiker's rescue inhaler worked. Jack still struggled for every breath, but there was color in his face, and he gave me a weak wave. Julie shook her head in relief. The evacuation team arrived, hooked Jack up to oxygen, lashed him to a backboard, and headed down the trail. Five hours later we were out of the clinic and back at camp, knees still weak from having dodged the bullet.

I may not know how to set a compound femur fracture—although I do think I could perform an emergency field tracheotomy if pressed—but this much I do know: There's space in every tackle pack for a wilderness first aid kit. They don't make a duffel bag that can't swallow one more fist-sized lump— Benadryl, an EpiPen, an emergency survival blanket, another bundle of firestarter. This is the time to take the time to read up, bone up, and be prepared. Fishing and hiking and camping and hunting aren't any more dangerous than a high school football game. But guess what's on every sideline of those Friday night lights? An ambulance with the engine running.

It's up to us. You and me. And I can tell you just how bad it can get out there.

Thankfully, the digital age hasn't rendered the USGS topographic map obsolete. In fact, it's now more important than ever to know how to decipher cartographic symbols, because topo maps are now accessible by desktop, laptop, tablet, and smartphone. Here's how to read the lay of the land . . . literally.

GENERAL MAP DESCRIPTORS Along the top and bottom of most maps are helpful blocks of information.

The map series relates to how much land area is covered by the map. The most detailed paper maps are 7.5 series maps, which cover 7.5 minutes of latitude and 7.5 minutes of longitude. Converted to miles, that covers a land area of about 9 by 16 miles. The 7.5 series was completed in 1992 and was recently replaced by the digital National Map.

Declination is the difference between true north and magnetic north, in degrees. The farther north your location, the greater the declination—and the greater the need to

adjust when navigating by map and magnetic compass. Scale is marked at the bottom of the map.

COLORS Background colors typically relate to vegetative cover.
- Green: Woods, forests, and scrublands.
- White: Open or semi-open lands, such as grasslands, agricultural lands, and deserts. Could include rock outcroppings.
- Gray: On maps with large blocks of public lands such as national forests and national parks, gray will indicate private inholdings within public boundaries.

CONTOUR LINES These are imaginary lines that trace elevation above sea level. Contour lines that are close together indicate steep land, and the closer the contours, the steeper the terrain. Cliffs can look like nearly solid blocks of merged contour lines. Contour lines that are farther apart indicate flatter lands.

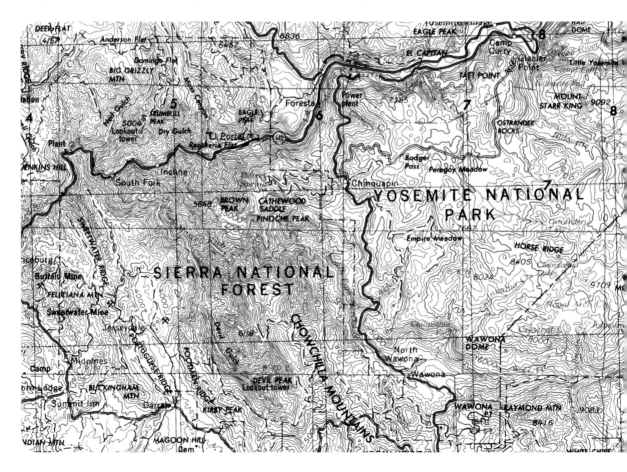

There are three types of contour lines. Indexed contours will typically be marked with numerals that indicate elevation. Often, each fifth contour line is an indexed contour. Between the heavier indexed contour lines are lighter intermediate contours. These are not marked with elevation, but help express the general steepness of the terrain. In very flat areas, maps might be marked with supplementary contours, which appear as broken dashes. They indicate an elevation change of half of the total between the contour lines on either side.

Ridges will appear as a series of Us and Vs that point towards lower elevations.

The highest elevation contour on a ridge, hill, or mountain will be marked by a closed circle of contour lines. Sometimes the very peak will be marked with the elevation and an X.

A gap, pass, or saddle appears as an hourglass, where the contour lines from opposing ridges nearly touch.

WATER FEATURES All water is marked in blue. Small streams are marked with a single blue line.

Intermittent streams are marked with a blue line broken by three dots.

Swamps and marsh are indicated by a blue pattern that looks like tiny cattails.

MAN-MADE FEATURES Most man-made features are marked in black. Buildings and smaller structures are marked with squares of varying sizes.

ROADS AND TRAILS Large interstate and divided highways are marked in red. Other roads are marked in black. Secondary gravel and dirt roads are indicated with parallel lines. Broken parallel lines mark unimproved or 4WD roads.

Foot and horse trails are marked by dotted lines.

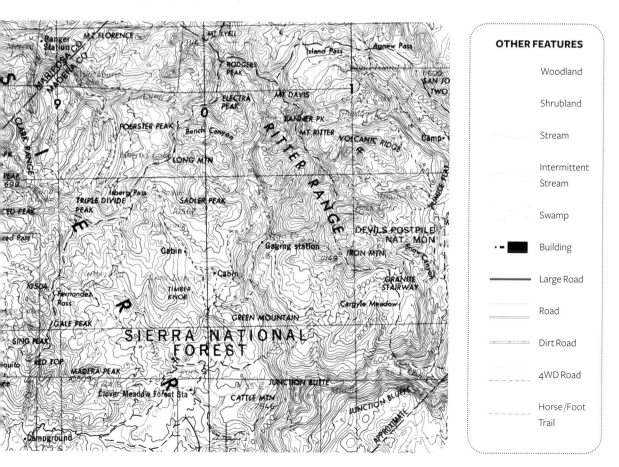

OTHER FEATURES

Woodland

Shrubland

Stream

Intermittent Stream

Swamp

Building

Large Road

Road

Dirt Road

4WD Road

Horse/Foot Trail

270 EVALUATE A BUBBLY COMPASS

The liquid that's found inside most compass housings is a specialized mineral oil. Its two main purposes are to dampen excessive needle movement and prevent static electricity from throwing off the bearing. Bubbles can form in two ways: At high altitude or in extremely cold temperatures, the liquid can contract, leaving a bubble. Or liquid can leak out of the seal or a tiny crack in the housing. Compass air bubbles are very common and won't affect the compass unless they are so large—say, a quarter-inch in diameter—that the movement of the direction arrow is impeded. If your compass develops a small bubble, place it in direct sun. The heated liquid in the housing will then expand to its original volume. If the bubble continues to grow, it's likely that there's a tiny leak in the housing. If this is the case, you should simply replace the compass.

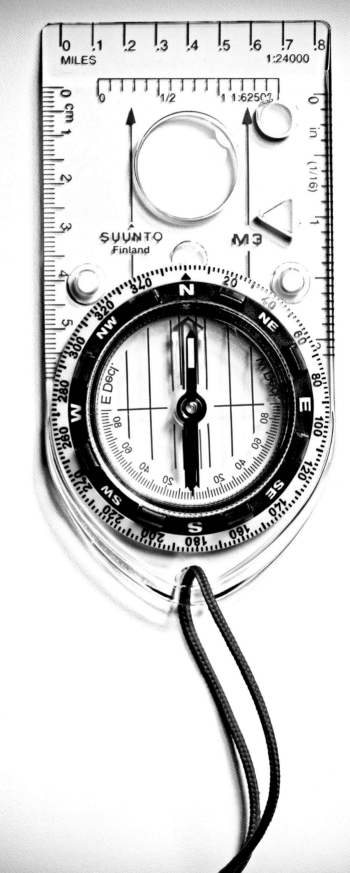

279 TREAT A SNAKE BITE

Snake bites require prompt attention, so don't hesitate to begin moving towards medical facilities ASAP.

STEP 1 Remove jewelry and clothing such as boots and socks immediately. Once the bitten area swells, they can constrict tissues and hold venom in place.

STEP 2 Clean the wound lightly. Do not flush with water and do not apply ice.

STEP 3 Affix a wide, flat constriction band a few inches above the bite. Two fingers should slide easily under the band.

STEP 4 If a pump suction device is available, use it with the first 5 minutes after the bite.

STEP 5 Immobilize the bitten area with a loose splint and keep it lower than heart level.

STEP 6 Get to help. If the victim can be carried, do so. If the victim must walk out, first sit calmy for 20 to 30 minutes as the venom localizes at the bite site. Stay calm and walk out. Try to avoid unnecessary exertion.

281 SAVE YOUR BACKTRAIL ON A GPS

One of the most useful features on a modern GPS is the ability to save the track or trail you have traveled. This will allow you to easily return to your starting point, or to duplicate the route of travel at a future date. Track logs are, basically, electronic bread crumbs that the GPS drops at various intervals of time and location. They are fabulous tools, provided you know how to operate the function on your GPS unit.

Look for a menu heading that reads "track log," "track recording," or something similar. Turn the function on. Now the GPS will record a track point at predetermined intervals. The default settings are likely something along the lines of one point for every 25 meters traveled or whenever there's a significant change in your speed or direction. For most of the applications this works well, but there may be times when you want to drop more or fewer bread crumbs. If your route needs a finer scale—say you are trying to stay in a narrow creek channel on a flooded lake—then you should set your GPS unit to record more frequent track points.

Another setting to consider is "record" mode. Choose "wrap" to keep the display on and the track log will keep continually operating, even if it fills up and needs to overwrite your starting data. Choose "fill" if you do not want the starting data to be overwritten. The unit should sound an alarm to let you know when it's reaching its storage capacity.

Once set, let the track log function keep you on track. When you arrive at your destination, don't forget to save the track if you want to keep it for future use.

280 CREATE A WHIRLING PROPELLER OF SIGNAL LIGHT

A small flashlight or chemical light stick is a pretty good signaling device, but you can supersize the effect with a small length of paracord. Simply tie an 18-inch length of cord to the light, and whirl it in a circle. Now you will have created a pulsing light source some 40 inches in diameter. Do the same during the daylight with aluminum foil or other shiny objects.

282 SHARPEN A SERRATED KNIFE

I'm a fan of the half-serrated blade. They cut like a small saw, and I use mine to saw off small branches when clearing shooting lanes, shear handfuls of cattails for duck blinds, cut a length of cordage, and more. You can't sharpen serrations with a flat stone, however. The serrated blade will still do a decent job even when dull, so many folks don't bother to sharpen them at all. But you should, and here's how.

Get a progressively tapered diamond hone made specifically for serrated blades. They're cheap and very effective.

Think of the hone as being cone-shaped. Match the diameter of the cone to the scalloped portion of the serration—this is called the "gullet" (A).

A tapered sharpener will easily match a wide variety of blade gullet sizes.

Essentially, you are sharpening teeth, one at a time. Holding the hone at the original angle of the serration's edge bevel, place the small end of your tapered hone into the gullet, and then push the hone down until the entire width of the serration is nearly filled with the hone (B). That's the stroke you'll want; Repeat until you can feel a fine burr on the flat back side of the blade.

Move down the blade, sharpening both sides of each serration. When you are finished, flip the knife over and grind off the burr with a ceramic rod or fine sharpening steel (C).

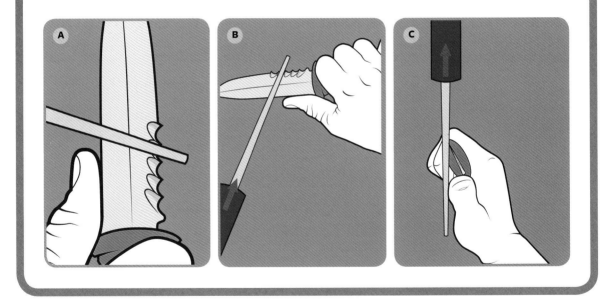

283 SUPERGLUE A CUT

So-called superglues were first used in Vietnam to close wounds and stem bleeding. The medical formulation, called Dermabond, is a slightly different composition that minimizes skin irritation, but as many an outdoorsman will attest, plain old superglue holds a cut together better than a strip bandage, and instances of irritation are rare. Always use an unopened tube of glue. Clean the cut and pinch it shut. Dab a drop or two of superglue directly on the incision, then spread it along the length of the cut with something clean. The watertight result seals out infecting agents.

284
CHECK A KNIFE FOR NICKS

To check sharpness, turn the knife edge so the very edge of the blade is facing you. Hold it under a strong light and look carefully at only the thin edge if the blade. A sharp edge will look like a thin black line. Any reflection spells trouble. Dull spots will shine. Minute nicks or burrs will be visible as tiny glistening points of light. If you see them, head back to the stone.

I can't recall a time when I didn't pack a space blanket as part of a survival kit. There are two reasons for this: First, ounce for ounce—all 3 of them—space blankets provide more protection from the elements than any other item. And second, I came of age during that glorious era when all things associated with "space travel" carried the panache of a dozen LeBron James, with a hundred-fold the gravitas.

Space blankets were developed in the 1960s after a heat shield on the Skylab—America's first space station—began overheating. NASA turned to a company that made Christmas tree tinsel to recreate a type of heat-deflecting parasol for the space module. The material used also evolved into personal emergency blankets for astronauts—the space blanket.

The manufacturing process is pretty straightforward, though not simple. Pure aluminum vapor is vacuum-deposited onto an ultrathin sheet of plastic. The result—a sort of souped-up aluminum foil—packs down to a tiny size, turns away wind and rain, and will reflect more than 95 percent of body heat. They have been a fundamental part of survival kits for a half century.

These days, the original space blanket is still out there, in a sea of knock-offs. It packs down to the size of a deck of playing cards, and unfolds large enough to wrap up a couple of lost and shivering hunters. Like many survival items, it is a tool, not a miracle. If you are wet and lying on the snow, you will not be warm in a space blanket. It's part of the puzzle of staying alive. You'd better have fire and water, as well.

The space blanket has also evolved into a related item, a heavier, far more durable version that goes by various names—sportsman's blanket and all-weather blanket among them. This is what many people think of when they think of a space blanket. They are puncture resistant, with reinforced edges and grommets. When folded, they are maybe 4 times the size of the original space blanket. I've used all-weather blankets as a tarp, emergency blanket, roof during a hailstorm, and makeshift bivvy sack. I've used them as a canoe sail and an erstwhile cooler—stuff a dressed deer with ice, wrap with an all-weather blanket or two, and I can age a deer for up to 4 days in the back yard. My very favorite way to spend the night outdoors is to spread out an all-weather blanket, toss my sleeping bag on top, and sleep under the open sky. I can look up at the heavens and watch the stars and thank the lucky ones for the space blanket under my back.

What's worse: the bite of a bullet ant or the hemolytic horrors of a bald-faced hornet sting? Ten fire ants on your big toe or one giant tarantula hawk with its rear-end sunk deep into your thigh? While assigning a pain factor to a "holy-$#&@!-that-hurts-like-#%*&!" insect sting won't mean that the agony goes away, it's still fun to try to figure out just where your torment fits on the Schmidt Pain Index of insect stings.

Yes, there actually is such a thing. Developed by Justin O. Schmidt, an entomologist at the Southwest Biological Institute in Tucson, Arizona, this index is used to rate the various degrees of perceived pain visited upon a person by the large number of stinging hordes that have stung Schmidt and his colleagues over the years.

Schmidt's index rates those stings on a scale of 0 to 4; I've provided the real-world context.

PAIN FACTOR INDEX

0 — Imperceptible. You don't even know you got stung.

1 — One sweat bee or a single fire ant. Aggravating. Swat-worthy. Continue your normal activity.

2 — The honeybee's signature sting. Involuntary jerking of limb. Howl of pain. Application of wet tobacco.

3 — We're talking harvester ant. Pain that endures for 4 to 8 hours. Associated with snarling obscenities, much hopping up and down. There could be tears. Your fishing trip is over.

4 — Only 3 critters are known to be capable of delivering such a life-changing wallop: the tarantula hawk, warrior wasp, and bullet ant. Of the three, only the tarantula hawk (pictured right) is found in North America. Schmidt described Level 4 pain as "a running hair dryer has just been dropped in your bubble bath."

286 PREPARE FOR ANAPHYLAXIS

While you really shouldn't ignore the possibilities of a fatal encounter with a wolf pack, enraged polar bear, or—if you are in the Florida Everglades—feral Burmese pythons, the far more serious threat to outdoorspeople comes in the form of winged venomous arthropods. Severe allergic reactions to insect stings and other complications from allergens can lead to anaphylaxis, which includes a sudden drop in blood pressure and difficulty breathing. In extreme instances, the reaction can kill within half an hour. This is not to be taken lightly. Anyone can have a life-threatening allergic reaction to an insect sting, even if they've never had a problem with stings before. Avid backcountry travelers should know how to treat the condition.

BE PREPARED When traveling with new companions, ask if anyone has issues with insect stings or other allergic reactions. If so, find out if they carry an epinephrine auto-injector, such as an EpiPen. If you like to travel widely in the backcountry, it's a good idea to carry one with you.

ACT QUICKLY Be alert to the first signs of a bad allergic reaction: skin reactions such as itching (especially around wrists, the insides of elbows, and on the face), hives, pale skin, or swelling of the lips, throat, or anywhere on the face. Be aware of any constriction of the airways or any trouble breathing, a weak pulse, or vomiting or nausea. At the very first sign of any of these indicators, take action. Do not wait to see if symptoms worsen.

GET HELP Head to emergency medical facilities, whether a hospital or doctor's office. If in the backcountry, begin an evacuation plan: Contact emergency personnel about the potential need for rescue, and plan on where the rescue will take place. My son's life was once saved because we split the family into two teams: My wife remained with my son while my daughter and I immediately raced towards the nearest backcountry ranger station.

PERFORM FIRST AID Administer an over-the-counter diphenhydramine such as Benadryl. While this won't be sufficient on its own to ultimately stave off a severe case of anaphylaxis, it is a first step. The liquid form is the fastest. Prepare to perform CPR and rescue breathing. Prepare to administer epinephrine via auto-injector.

GIVE EMERGENCY TREATMENT If the victim begins to experience trouble breathing, use the epinephrine auto-injector. Do whatever you can to get the person to medical personnel. Time is absolutely critical here. If the situation warrants, perform CPR and rescue breathing. Administer additional epinephrine if available.

BOTTOM LINE There are only limited actions you can take when faced with this situation. You must act early and decisively. If there are no emergency medications available, you should factor this in when you're deciding to reach out to emergency officials.

287 CALL FOR RESCUE WITH A NUT

If you're lost or hurt with no signaling device, head for the nearest oak tree. Find a fresh acorn and remove the cap. (The larger the acorn and cap, the lower the pitch of the corresponding whistle.) Form fists with your hands and pinch the cap between your thumbs and index fingers with its open side facing you. Create a Y with your thumbs by rotating wrists outwards. Now, rest the first joints of your thumbs against your lower lip and blow hard. Adjust the angle of the cap until you sound like a referee's whistle.

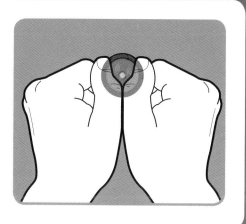

288 SEND A MARITIME DISTRESS CALL

If it's time to call in the Coast Guard, don't just jump on the radio and cry for help. Following the formal Distress Message Format will help ensure that search and rescue teams have the vital information they need to haul you out of the soup. Take a moment to calm yourself, then transmit the following broadcast.

SPEAK SLOWLY AND CLEARLY "MAYDAY," repeated three times, followed by the VESSEL TYPE AND NAME, repeated three times. For example: "MAYDAY, MAYDAY, MAYDAY. THIS IS THE POWER VESSEL FISH FEVER, THE POWER VESSEL FISH FEVER, THE POWER VESSEL FISH FEVER."

FOLLOW WITH PERTINENT INFORMATION IN THIS ORDER

1 LOCATION Give position in latitude/longitude, GPS, or LORAN lines if known. Or give a distance and bearing from a geographic point, as in, "We are 3.5 miles southeast of Big Inlet."

2 WHAT IS WRONG "We are sinking." "We are on fire." "We have a heart attack victim on board."

3 WHAT TYPE OF ASSISTANCE YOU NEED "We need an emergency rescue ASAP." "We need medical personnel." "We need firefighting equipment."
The number of persons aboard and the condition of any needing assistance.
The present condition of your vessel.

4 DESCRIPTION OF YOUR VESSEL Length, type, does it have a cabin, how many masts, color of hull, identifying trim.

5 YOUR LISTENING RADIO FREQUENCY

6 WHAT SURVIVAL EQUIPMENT YOU HAVE ON BOARD Survival suits, PFDs, emergency rafts, personal locater beacons or EPIRBs.

7 A PLAN FOR SUBSEQUENT RADIO CONTACT

289 HURL A ROPE

There are plenty of times when you might need to throw a rope—to a buddy on a boat dock, over a tree limb so you can raise a deer off the ground, or as I experienced once in northern Alberta, to a hunting partner stuck so deep in the muck it took three of us to pull him out. But we could do that only after we weighted the rope end with a knot that provided enough mass to be tossed to our stranded pal. He was quite appreciative.

A standard heaving-line knot doesn't add quite enough bulk and weight for such a heavy-duty, get-me-out-of-here-before-I-drown-in-the-mud rope hurling. But this supercharged version does. Before you try it, here's one must-know knot factoid: A bight is a loop in which the line ends do not cross, like a U.

READY Make two bights in the end of the rope. This results in three "rungs" of rope. Leaving plenty of line in the working end for the wraps, weave the working end under the middle rung and over the bottom rung. Then loop it around the back of the knot and bring it between the top and middle rungs.

SET Wrap all three rungs six to nine times. On the last wrap, thread the working end through the loop.

THROW Tighten by pulling alternately on the standing end of the line and the bights on each end of the knot. To throw the rope, stack it at your feet, starting with the end of the line you'll be holding so that it uncoils tangle-free.

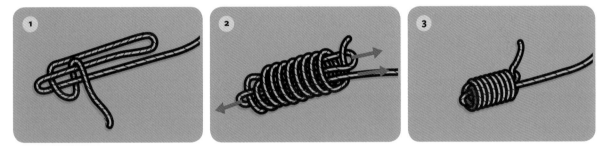

290 FREE A GROUNDED BOAT

If you run your boat aground on a mud flat or sandbar, being able to free the craft can mean the difference between a close call and a long day in broiling sun. If you've run too far up the shallows, you can't push the boat backwards because the transom digs in. I got to learn this myself at 4 A.M. at the mouth of the Atchafalaya River on Louisiana's Gulf coast. To free up our duck boat, we dug a trench beside the boat (A), as close to the craft as possible and parallel to the keel. Then we rocked the boat side to side (B) and slipped it into that deeper channel next to the boat. If that hadn't worked out, we could have backed out (C) or extended that shallow trench a bit further to deeper water. We were lucky; we got free in about a half hour . . . which was bad news for the ducks.

291 CARVE A FUZZ STICK FOR A FAST FIRESTARTER

A fire-starting fuzz stick, or feather stick, is a super tool for starting a blaze and hard to beat for teasing flame from wet wood. It's not as simple as scoring a few flakes into a twig, however. With just a little practice, you can carve a fuzz stick in 90 seconds or less, and putting a mass of thin, spark-catching curls on a stick of wood is nearly as impressive as the flames it will produce. Here's the drill.

STEP 1 Split soft wood such as pine, spruce, or aspen into a foot-long length, 1 to 1¹/₂ inches on each side. Choose a knot-free stick that has a long, straight grain. Flat-ground blades work better than hollow-ground, but experiment to find a knife that you can control with steady pressure.

STEP 2 Wedge the stick between your chest and a tree trunk, or hold it firmly against a chopping block at a 45-degree angle. Lock your wrist and use slow, steady pressure to push the knife edge—starting at the middle of the stick—down the corner to shave a thin, curly strip. Bring the knife back up to the starting point, rotate the stick very slightly, and begin another. Avoid sawing back and forth, but experiment with the orientation of the knife tip to create curls that trend toward one side or the other. Point the tip down and curls will come off to the right. Point the tip up and the curls will shave off to the left.

STEP 3 Longer, thicker curls are needed to ignite larger kindling, but to boost the fuzz stick's spark-catching ability, finish off with short, super-fine curls. Done with one corner? You're not done yet. Rotate the stick, and work up another.

292 MAKE FIRE WICK AT HOME

Fire wick—a wax-impregnated cotton string used to start fires—will burn for several minutes, and it's a snap to make at home. Use a thick laundry string, commercially available candle wicking, or other 100-percent cotton cordage. Melt paraffin wax in a double boiler, slowly, never allowing it to smoke. Dip cotton string into the wax slowly, using pliers to hold one end (A). Remove by dragging the string over the edge of the pot (B) in order to wring excess wax from the wicking. Hang the wicking by a nail (C), let it cool, then snip into 2- to 3-inch pieces. Store in small zip-sealed plastic bags or water-proof match cases.

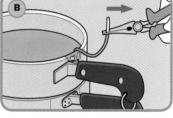

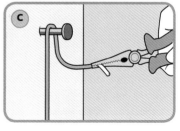

293 IMPROVISE SNOWSHOES

Got paracord? Got a knife? Then you have all you need to lash together a set of emergency snowshoes. Here's how.

STEP 1 Cut a couple of flexible branches, each at least 3 feet in length. Then, cut a couple of small pieces about 6 inches each, and a couple of about 10 inches.

STEP 2 Bend each long branch into a teardrop shape, and lash it together at the narrow end.

STEP 3 Lace paracord in a zigzag pattern the entire length of each shoe.

STEP 4 Test the snowshoe's size.

STEP 5 Add some bracing crosspieces where your toe and heel will fall.

STEP 6 Lash your boots to the snowshoes.

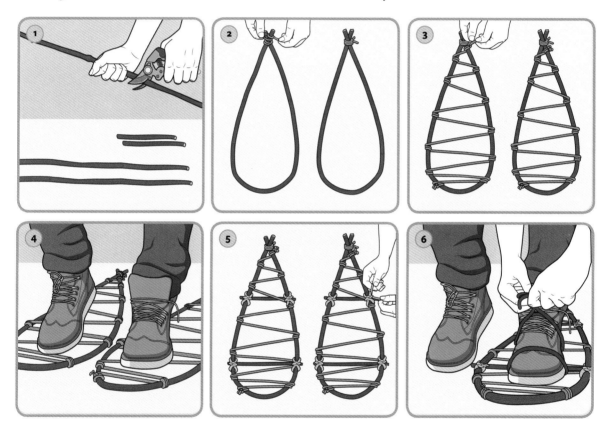

294 STAY FOUND FOR LESS THAN 10 BUCKS

Pin a simple bubble compass to the front of your coat and you'll circumvent half of the problems that lead to getting lost. Look for one that has luminous readouts and liquid dampening. The rotating sphere remains upright, so you can glance at the compass for a quick bearing read whether you're on the trail or hanging one-handed from a cliff.

295 SURVIVE A STRANDING

If you get stuck in your car during white-out conditions, here's some advice to help get you home warm and dry.

Keep the gas tank at least half-full during winter. You'll need the fuel so you can remain warm in a survival situation, and more fuel in the tank will help in preventing condensation of water, which can lead to your engine failing at cold temperatures.

Always inform someone where you are driving and when you are expected to return, or leave them a detailed note. If stranded, stay with the vehicle, which is much easier for rescuers to spot than a person stumbling through snow. Hike to find help only if odds of your rescue are remote or if help is in close range and you know exactly where it is.

Clear snow, dirt, or ice from the tailpipe of a stranded vehicle to avoid getting carbon monoxide poisoning. Crack open a window on the lee side of the car when running the motor or before you light a stove, candle, or space heater.

If high winds are sneaking in through the car doors and seals, use snow to seal the cracks. Avoid sweating, however, and use a sun visor as a snow shovel to keep hands dry.

Wipe off head and tail lights so searchers can spot your vehicle from a distance.

Run the motor no more than 10 minutes an hour to conserve fuel.

Tie a brightly colored shirt or reflective cloth to the antennae or roof rack and raise the hood to signal that you are stranded.

296 TEST A KNIFE WITH A NEWSPAPER

Your daily newspaper is packed full of plenty of critical information—including three tests that will tell you just how sharp you've gotten your knife.

Ⓐ LET IT BITE Hold a single page of newsprint up at a 45-degree angle at shoulder height. Rest your knife blade on the edge of the paper at a shallow angle, and slice. A sharp blade will immediately bite into the newspaper and begin a clean cut. A dull blade will skip along the edge, or tear into the paper.

Ⓑ WATCH IT GLIDE As the knife blade bites into the paper, it should easily glide with no significant sticking points. Run the entire length of your blade through the paper. If the blade cuts cleanly then hangs up, that may indicate a tiny nick or burr at that spot on the edge of the blade. Listen to the glide as it cuts: The higher the pitch, the sharper the blade.

Ⓒ MAKE A FILET The sharpest knives will literally filet newsprint. Tear off a notebook-sized piece from the newspaper. Hold the knife horizontally, one hand around the handle, the other thumb on the blade spine as a guide. The palms of your hands will hold the paper firmly on a table or desk top. Try to slice a tiny half-pea-sized piece of newsprint without cutting all the way through the paper, like removing the skin from a fish. Success? That is one sharp knife, alright.

297 ESCAPE FROM WILDFIRE

If it seems like wildfires are becoming more common, it's because they are. A warming climate and drought across much of the American West makes wildfire a growing threat to wilderness travelers.

When fire conditions are high, remain vigilant. Situational awareness is your first line of defense. At the first sign of smoke, start making a plan. Even if the fire is distant, know that the powerful updrafts of a blaze can send embers for long distances and ignite a secondary blaze nearby.

PLOT AN ESCAPE ROUTE Look for a route that heads downhill, but avoid canyons, deep gullies, and draws. Heated air can rush up these natural chutes.

Stay away from resinous trees such as fir. When heated, expanding tree sap can cause trees to explode.

Try to make it to a wet area—a swamp, stream or marsh. Jump in if flames get close.

IF FLAMES CLOSE IN Shed your pack and as much synthetic clothing (nylon, Gore-Tex, etc.) as possible; it will melt quicker than most natural materials will catch fire. Find the lowest spot you can, ideally in a clearing or field as far from trees as possible. Kick away as much flammable material as you can to create a 20-foot-diameter circle. Dig a shallow trench and keep the soil nearby. If the flames come, lie face down and scoop dirt over your body. Bury your face in a bandana or piece of cloth. If the heat gets unbearable, that's precisely the point at which you must will yourself to stay down.

298
MAKE A
WICKED SLINGSHOT

Slingshot aficionados turn out sturdy handmade models capable of firing heavy slugs at 225 feet per second—fast enough to take down game from squirrels to wild turkeys to ducks on the wing. Here's the drill on crafting the world's most awesome slingshot.

FRAME IT Dogwood, hickory, and oak make the best frames. You don't have to find the perfect Y-shaped fork. The typical right-hander will hold the slingshot in the left hand, so look for a fork where the main branch crooks to the left at 30 degrees or so, but a fork goes off to the right at a 45-degree angle. Cut the frame and let it dry for three weeks.

POWER UP A number of companies sell ready-made replacement bands with pouches attached for slingshots. The trick lies in a strong connection: An inch and a half from the top of each slingshot "arm," drill a hole that's slightly smaller in diameter than the band. Bevel the end of the band with scissors and thread it through the hole—a pair of hemostat clamps will make this easier. Snip off the bevel. Next, take a dried stick slightly larger in diameter than the inside diameter of the tubing and carve two half-inch-long stoppers to a point. Plug each end of the tubing with a stopper.

299 MAINTAIN A KNIFE CLIP

To keep a pocket clip from loosening and falling off, treat the clip screws with a threadlocker such as Blue Loctite. To remove the pocket clip, place the knife in a small box so you won't lose the tiny clip screws as they are being removed. Choose the right screwdriver. Most quality knife clips are attached with Torx screws. Find the right size, then try one size larger. The Torx screw head indentations can get gunked up with soil, thus making a smaller size driver head appear to be the correct one. Take out the screws and clean them. Then, put a tiny drop of threadlocker on each screw and replace them. The compound will set the screws with a tight grip.

300
START A FIRE WITH A FLARE

An emergency road flare will burn in just about any conditions, and will stay lit long enough to dry out some small pieces of soaked wood. Pack a few in your vehicle, your boat, and cabin survival kits.

301 REMOVE A FISH HOOK

Getting hooked is a rite of passage for anglers. It's going to happen eventually. The worst case I ever saw involved my buddy who was asleep on his boat. In the middle of the night he rolled over onto a jointed Rapala plug, and stuck two of the hooks into the back of his thigh—to the bends—and he was wrapped up in a blanket to boot. By the time he stumbled into my tent the flesh around the hooks was swollen and leathery. That was ugly. Still, if you've got a Woolly Bugger in your thumb, a crankbait hook in the leg, or a spinnerbait in your arm, there's no need to quit fishing. Here's how to remove a hook sans screaming and get back in the action.

STEP 1 Snip the hook or lure free of the main fishing line to get rid of any tension. If possible, detach a treble hook from its lure and clip off any of the hook points not stuck in your person. Next, cut a 15-inch strand of line from your reel and tie the ends together to create a loop.

STEP 2 Double the loop of fishing line, then pass it under the bend in the hook close to your skin. The line should be resting against the hook bend. Push down on the eye of the hook. This raises the point—better aligning it with the hole it made when entering.

STEP 3 Now, take a deep breath, and in a single, quick, sharp tug, yank the line straight back. (This step is often best executed by a fishing partner.) As with a Band-Aid, the faster you pull, the less it hurts, often popping right out without causing pain. If the wound is still bleeding, apply pressure until it stops. Put on antiseptic ointment and a bandage before you get back to fishing.

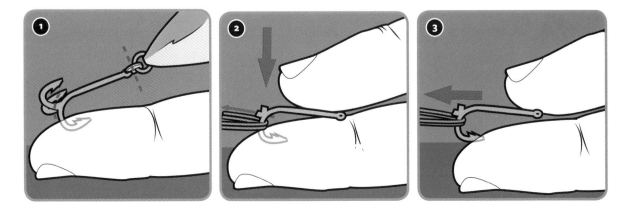

302 CATCH FISH WITH A TRIGGER SNARE

Trigger snares are among the most basic and effective tools for obtaining survival food, and just about everyone has seen photos or illustrations of these snares set along game trails and logs where small animals frequent. But the same primitive technology can be used to catch fish. Here's how.

STEP 1 Find a sapling located approximately 4 to 6 feet from the bank of a body of water. Look for places where fish congregate—deep holes on the outside of stream bends, near blowdowns where trees have fallen into the water, and other structures.

STEP 2 Carve the trigger. You'll need a simple one made of a base peg and a hook. Cut a notch into both. Tension from the bent sapling will keep the trigger "cocked" until a fish takes the bait, pulling the hook free of the peg and snapping the bent sapling upright.

STEP 3 Tie a cord from the top of the sapling to the top of the trigger hook. Tie a hook to one end of the fishing line and bait it. Tie the other end to the bottom of the

trigger hook, where it fits into the notch, making sure you have enough line to reach into the water. Now, bend the sapling over, pointing straight towards the water. Pull the trigger hook straight down to the ground—that's where you pound the trigger base into the ground. Set the snare trigger by fitting the notches together.

STEP 4 Carefully place the baited hook in the water. Be gentle so that you don't spring the trap.

303 CONSTRUCT A FISH WEIR

Every year, biologists with the Alaska Department of Fish and Game count rainbow trout, Dolly Varden, and salmon, by using fish weirs in migration streams. In a days-long survival situation you can build such a fish trap to help fill your belly.

In a shallow stream, build a weir with a low stone wall that extends out into the stream. The migratory fish will swim into the trap. Once enough fish are in the trap, close off the entrance. Water flowing through the weir will keep fish alive for several days.

304 STOP BLEEDING

Instead of using a tourniquet if you injure a limb, apply direct pressure to the wound with a cloth or even your hand. Wrap a some kind of bandage all the way around your limb. If the bleeding keeps up, put more dressings on top of the old ones, and elevate the limb if possible. Wait until the bleeding stops, then attempt to hike back to your car.

305 PACK A 1-DAY SURVIVAL KIT

Here are suggestions for an Altoids survival kit. Choose as many as you think you'll need and can fit. Wind the paracord outside the can to keep it securely closed.

SHELTER AND FIRE
- Butane lighter wrapped with duct tape (Duct tape is an excellent fire accelerant.)
- Spark-Lite wheel flint
- Tinder-Quik fire tabs
- Wire saw

WATER AND FOOD
- Potable Aqua iodine water purification tablets
- Nonlubricated condom for carrying water
- Fishhooks, sinkers, 2 dry flies, 2 wet flies
- 10 feet 24-gauge wire for snares

SIGNALING AND NAVIGATION
- Button compass
- Signal mirror (Use the top of the Altoids can for a signal mirror. Punch a hole in the middle as a sighting hole.)

MEDICAL
- Antibiotic ointment
- Butterfly closures

MULTIPURPOSE
- Single-edged razor blade
- 10 feet of monofilament fishing line
- Small pencil
- Waterproof paper, 2 small sheets

306 PACK A 3-DAY SURVIVAL KIT

Place all items inside a 1-gallon zippered plastic bag, then place in a small waterproof stuff sack or fanny pack.

SHELTER AND FIRE
- Space blanket
- Butane lighter wrapped with loops of rubber inner tube (Inner tube makes a great fire accelerant.)
- Spark-Lite wheel flint
- Tinder-Quik fire tabs
- Waterproof matches
- 1 garbage bag, rolled up tightly
- Wire saw

WATER AND FOOD
- Potable Aqua iodine water purification tablets
- Nonlubricated condom for carrying water
- GSI Outdoors foldable cup
- Fish hooks, sinkers, 2 dry flies, 2 wet flies
- 10 feet 24-gauge wire for snares
- Instant coffee
- Vacuum-packed beef jerky

SIGNALING AND NAVIGATION
- Compass
- Headlamp
- 2 glow sticks
- StarFlash signal mirror
- Signal whistle

MEDICAL
- Antibacterial wipes
- Antibacterial ointment
- Butterfly closures
- Gauze and tape
- Ibuprofen
- Benadryl
- Artificial tears for irrigating eyes

MULTIPURPOSE
- 50 feet of paracord (Mil-spec 550 cord has seven smaller lines inside the nylon sheath.)
- Aluminum foil for reflector oven
- Needle and thread
- Safety pins
- Spare knife
- Small pencil
- 5 sheets waterproof paper
- 10 feet of monofilament fishing line
- Superglue
- Surgical tubing (Use to suck water from shallow seeps, as a tourniquet, or to blow spark to flame.)
- Red crayon (Mark trees as you move, and use it as a firestarter.)
- Duct tape and wooden tongue depressor (1-inch strips of blaze orange duct tape serve as firestarter or route markers. Shave tinder from the tongue depressor.)

307 PACK A 1-WEEK, MULTIPERSON SURVIVAL KIT

Place all items in a waterproof stuff sack. Each group of items (Shelter and Fire, Water and Food, etc.) could also fit into a separate stuff sack.

SHELTER AND FIRE

- All-weather blanket
- Butane lighter wrapped with loops of rubber inner tube (Inner tube makes a great fire accelerant.)
- Spark-Lite wheel flint
- Tinder-Quik fire tabs
- Waterproof matches
- Wire saw

WATER AND FOOD

- Water treatment filter bottle (With these, you can drink straight from the stream.)
- Potable Aqua iodine water purification tablets
- Nonlubricated condom for carrying water
- GSI Outdoors foldable cup
- Fish hooks, sinkers, 2 dry flies, 2 wet flies
- 10 feet 24-gauge wire for snares
- Instant coffee
- Vacuum packed chicken and salmon.
- Pasta

SIGNALING AND NAVIGATION

- Full-sized compass
- Personal Locater Beacon
- 2 Flashlights: headlamp and small handheld
- Handheld flare
- StarFlash signal mirror
- Signal whistle

MEDICAL

- Antibacterial wipes
- Antibacterial ointment
- Butterfly closures
- Gauze & tape
- Ibuprofen
- Benadryl
- Imodium
- Artificial tears for irrigating eyes
- DenTec Dental First Aid Kit (Repacked into single zippered baggie. Includes a dental pain medication, cracked tooth and filling repair kit, and special tooth saver container for dislodged teeth.)
- SAM splint (Moldable aluminum alloy sheets between closed-cell foam provide support for a variety of bones and joints.)
- Azithromycin (A Z-Pak from your doctor will treat a number of backcountry ills: strep throat, sinus infections, bronchitis, ear infections, and some skin infections.)

MULTIPURPOSE

- Bush knife
- 100 feet of paracord
- Surgical tubing. Use it as a straw to suck water from shallow seeps, as a tourniquet, or to blow a spark to flame.
- One complete set: synthetic insulated top and bottoms, and socks, vacuum bagged
- Travel toilet paper
- Small pencil
- Waterproof notepad
- Small photo of loved ones (According to survival experts, thinking of family and friends keeps survival instincts strong.)

308 BEAT THE BUGS

A challenge in many survival situations is dealing with hordes of mosquitoes, black flies, and other biting, stinging pests. Here's what to use for a natural smokescreen.

CATTAIL While all parts of the plant are edible, burning the dried flower spikes will turn away mosquitoes.

SAGE The aromatic twigs and leaves burn quickly, so collect a large pile.

POOP Aboriginal peoples the world over burn buffalo, cow, and horse poop as an insect repellent—if the bugs get bad, so can you.

309 MAKE A SWISS SEAT

You can make an emergency climbing harness in the field with a carabiner and just 12 to 14 feet of rope. Use it to rappel down a cliff or as a backup for when you get to your treestand but realize you left your harness at home.

STEP 1 Find the middle point of the rope, make a loop there, and place this loop at the hipbone of your off-hand side with the closed section of loop pointing up (A). Bring one end of the rope around your back, above the hipbone, and all the way around to your front. You'll have one longer and one shorter length of rope.

STEP 2 Cross one length of the rope over the other twice. Let the ends of the rope drape between your legs (B).

STEP 3 Pull the ropes through your legs and around each buttock, angling towards the side (C). Pull the end of each rope under the waist rope, then back under the buttock section, and tie a half hitch around the rope angling across each buttock at the waist rope (D).

STEP 4 Bring the free ends of rope together at the hipbone on your weak hand side. Tie them together with a square knot, and lock each running end with a half hitch (E). Clip a carabiner into both the twisted rope section and the upper waist rope (F).

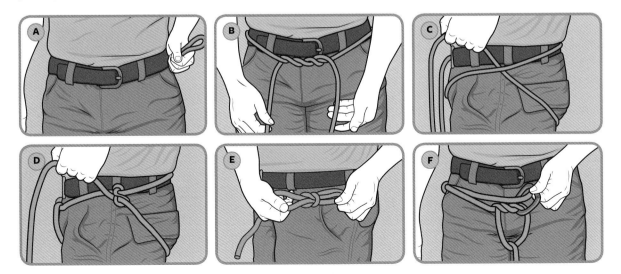

310 RIG THE Z-DRAG

Hardcore white-water paddlers use the Z-Drag to free kayaks and canoes that are pinned to boulders in heavy current, but this simple mechanical advantage system is also useful for dragging or hoisting anything heavy (stuck ATVs, dead game off a cliff, a tree atop your buddy's legs) short distances. With a minimum of gear, the Z-Drag gives you a 3-to-1 hauling advantage, so you can be thrice the man when the chips are down.

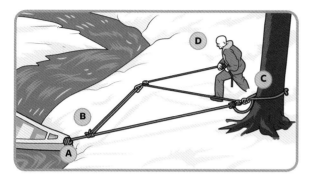

about 75 feet of hauling rope • two 12-feet-long sections of 5-mm rope tied into loops • about 10 feet of strong webbing or rope for an anchor loop • 2 carabiners • 2 petzl ultra legere pulleys, clipped to each 'biner

STEP 1 Tie the hauling rope to the stranded item (A). Using one of the loops of 5mm rope, tie a Prusik knot to the hauling rope close to the stranded item and clip a carabiner to the loop (B).

STEP 2 Tie an anchor loop around a strong anchor point, such as a tree trunk or a vehicle and clip a carabiner to the loop (C). Run the hauling line on the pulleys as shown. Use the other 5mm-rope loop to tie in a second Prusik knot to the hauling rope between the stranded item and through the anchor loop, close to this second carabiner. This will serve as an emergency braking device.

STEP 3 Stand next to the anchor point and pull on the working end of the hauling rope (D). There is no primary braking device on a Z-Drag, so hold the haul rope tight once you've pulled. As you take in line, have a partner slide the first Prusik loop down the hauling rope and toward the stranded item. If you're on your own, tie the pull rope off to a tree once you've retrieved the stranded object.

311 MAKE WATERPROOF MATCHES

These easy-to-make firestarters provide an all-in-one solution to starting a blaze: ignition, accelerant, and fuel in a single handy, cheap package. To use, scrape the wax off the tip and strike against a rock. Each match will burn for five minutes or better.

strike-anywhere matches • paraffin wax • cotton yarn or wicking • straight pins • aluminum foil

STEP 1 Tie an overhand knot in the yarn at the base of the match head, and wrap the match shaft. Tuck the tag end of the yarn under the last wrap and pull snug. Cut excess yarn.

STEP 2 Melt paraffin wax in a DIY double boiler. Select an old pot that will nest in a larger pot. (A clean coffee can works in a pinch.) Fill the larger pot about half full with water and place on medium heat on the stove. Place the wax in the smaller pot and place this double boiler in the larger pot. Pay close attention. Paraffin wax has a low flash point and can burst into flame when overheated. When fully melted, move the setup off the heat.

STEP 3 Insert a straight pin into the nonstriking end of a match, and dip the entire match in the wax for a few seconds. Set on the foil to harden. Dip every match several times to build up a waterproof coating that also serves as fuel. After the last dip, remove the pin and tamp down the moist wax to seal the pinhole.

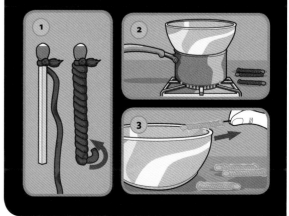

312 STAY ALIVE WITH TOILET PAPER

Get stuck in your car in a blizzard? You can create an emergency heater out of toilet paper, a coffee can, and rubbing alcohol.

First, crack the windows on each side of the car to let in some fresh air.

Loosen the cardboard tube from a toilet paper roll by kneading the roll in your hands, then remove the cardboard tube. Place the toilet paper in an empty coffee can, a one-quart paint can, or a similarly sized clean metal can.

Pour rubbing alcohol into the can, soaking the toilet paper. Carefully light the top of the paper. It should produce a hot, clean flame.

When the edges of the toilet paper turn brown, blow out the flame. Let the can cool, add some more rubbing alcohol, and relight.

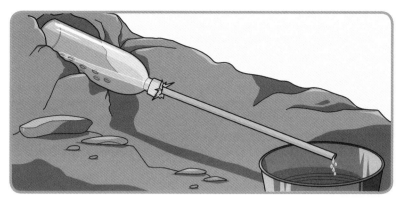

313 MAKE A SURVIVAL FAUCET

In a survival situation, every drop of found water is critical. The problem is that many springs and seeps put out a tiny trickle of water that is difficult to collect. Here's how to turn a weak spring into a survival faucet.

STEP 1 Dig a small basin where the water is seeping from the ground or dribbling over a rock.

STEP 2 Punch holes into the bottom of a spare water bottle or other lidded container. Wrap the container with a clean cloth and secure with cord. Cut a hole in the cap just large enough to insert some kind of tubing. A hollow reed will work, as will an aluminum tent pole. Stuff some clean vegetation around the tubing to seal up the hole. Place the water bottle firmly into the depression with the cap and tubing facing downhill. Anchor it with a log or stone to press the bottle into the bottom of the basin.

STEP 3 Run the tubing downhill into a collecting bucket. Treat or filter before drinking.

315 SHAVE THE DAY

Pencil shavings make great tinder. Just toss a pocket-size pencil sharpener and a stub of a good ol' No. 2 into your pack and you'll never be without a handy source for fire-building. Or simply shave thin curls with a knife.

316 REUSE A SHOTSHELL

To keep matches dry and handy, fill a spent 16-gauge shell with matches and top it with a spent 12-gauge shell. Wrap the seam between the shells with a few layers of duct tape to waterproof the case and provide a handy source of fire accelerant.

314 SCROUNGE UP SURVIVAL WIRE

You might know that 550 paracord is made with a sheath, inside which are 7 to 9 strong inner cords that are perfectly sized for things like snare loops, fishing lines, and small-diameter lashings. Here are other sources of wire and cordage to seek out in a survival situation.

- Got a power cord? Remove the twisted copper strands.
- Got headphones? Separate each wire.
- Got a spiral-bound notepad? Pull out the wire and straighten for nooses.
- Got a ballpoint pen? Remove the spring and straighten.
- Are you wearing a bra? If it's an underwire bra, remove the wire.
- Got a busted radio? There's wire inside.
- Are you wearing shoes? You have snare loops on each foot.
- Did you pack dental floss? It can be used as light lashing or fishing line.

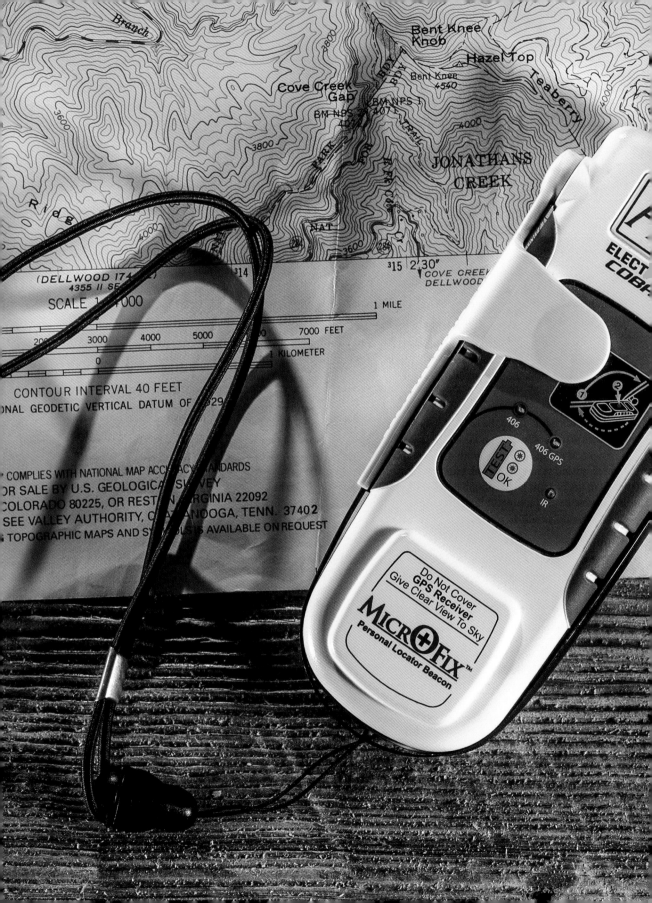

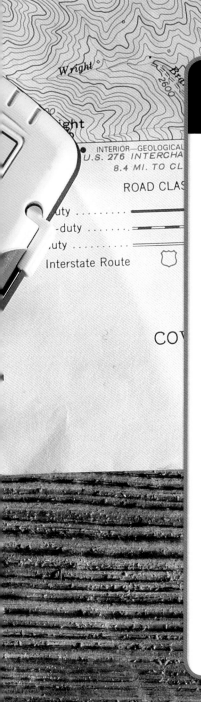

MY TOOL:
PERSONAL LOCATOR BEACON

When my wife gave me a personal locater beacon (PLB) for Christmas, my first reaction was one of mild annoyance. Didn't she trust me to be able to get myself out of an emergency? That ignorant response was soon replaced with thanksgiving. The more I thought about it, the more it made sense. What if I broke a leg and couldn't move? What if the canoe flipped with one of the kids and I was knocked unconscious on the way overboard? What if I had a heart attack on the back side of my hunting lease and no one was around?

Ask yourself any of those questions, or any like them, and you'll soon understand that carrying a PLB is pretty smart. It's overkill— until you're in a situation that could kill you. I now toss that PLB into my hunting pack or fishing bag every time I head out the door.

There are two broad types of these beacons. In addition to the PLB there is its marine kin, the EPIRB, which stands for Emergency Position Indicating Radio Beacon. PLBs are more mobile and are designed for folks who are hiking or otherwise away from marine environments, while EPIRBS typically have features associated with boating, such as automated strobe beacons, flotation, and a longer battery life that transmits for 48 hours as opposed to 24. When activated, all of the devices interface with the international Search and Rescue Satellite Aided Tracking System, called COSPAS-SARSAT. A combination of NOAA polar-orbiting and geostationary satellites detects the distress signal and relays that information to first responders on the ground in the area of the emergency. The better ones are GPS enabled, which can cut rescue time dramatically. These are not toys. By law, owners are required to register the devices with NOAA. At the end of 2013, the database contained more than 400,000 registrations.

PLBs are not available so you can call in water because you are thirsty. They are to be used in grave circumstances only, where there is a clear peril to life or limb. Once you hit that button, there's no cancel function, and the next thing you see might be a rescue chopper overhead with an SAR team rappelling down on ropes. In certain circumstances, that might be the only ticket to tomorrow. My wife knew what she was doing: giving me the gift of one more chance.

317 SPRAY A BEAR INTO RETREAT

When in bear country, I am never farther than 12 inches from the largest can of bear spray I can buy. I have it on my belt when fishing, on my pack strap when hiking, by my head when sleeping, and by my feet when my pants are around my ankles as I answer nature's call. When I see fresh signs of bear—rolled-over rocks, scat, torn berry bushes, gleaming white fangs surrounded by patches of snarling brown fur—I unholster the spray and hold it in my hand. In test studies, bear spray stopped charging grizzlies 92 percent of the time. It's estimated they can prevent injury 98 percent of the time. Pretty good odds.

To use effectively, practice with two cans of inert bear spray. It's not difficult, but shaking knees and a pounding heart won't make it any easier. Here's the drill.

DRAW Practice readying the can by taking off the safety strap, pushing the nozzle safety clip free, and grasping the can with two hands. If pack straps hinder you, move the straps or tuck them away. Speed is of the essence. A charging bear can move at 44 feet per second.

AIM LOW Pace off 50 feet away from a shrub, tree, or some other inanimate object. Practice by drawing the can

and spraying a short 2-second burst, moving the can from side to side. Aim slightly below the target. Bear spray will billow up from the ground into the bear's face. Aim too high and the bear could run under the spray.

STRIKE TWICE Practice discharging a second plume of spray to back up the first. Yell loudly while aiming. If this were a true attack, you would drop your pack and begin backing away.

GO ALL OUT Practice emptying the can to get a sense of the total load available. Most cans will spray for about 9 seconds. In a true attack, your last step will be to empty the can in the bear's face.

QUICK DRAW Now repeat the drill, but imagine close quarters: You're surprised by a bear so close there's no time to draw. Practice discharging the can from the hip or shoulder strap.

318 SPARK FIRE WITH A KNIFE

Use a high-carbon steel blade, or scrounge up an axe head or steel file. Find a hunk of hard stone. Flint is a classic; quartz, quartzite, and chert also work well. Stay away from round rocks; you will need one with a ridge sharp enough to peel slivers of metal from the steel. Add highly flammable tinder. Start sparking.

STEP 1 Hold the stone up with the sharp ridge extending out from your hand horizontally.

STEP 2 If you're using a fixed-blade knife, wrap up the sharp edge with a piece of leather or cloth. Using the back of your blade, strike the stone with a glancing, vertical blow.

STEP 3 Depending on where your sparks land, hold down a piece of char cloth, tinder fungus, or Vaseline-soaked cotton ball under your thumb and on top of the rock, or set the fire-starting material on the ground and aim the sparks down toward it.

STEP 4 Strike the stone, spark the tinder, and gently blow into a flame.

319 TIE THE KNOT THAT FIXES ALL

A shear lashing mends a broken tent pole or hiking staff. It rigs a long pole from two shorter ones. Lash three poles together with one-half of this handy knot, and you have a tripod.

Place the butt ends of two poles parallel to each other. Tie a clove hitch around one pole, then wind the rope around both pieces for a distance equal to the diameter of the two together. Finish it off with another clove hitch. Repeat on the other end.

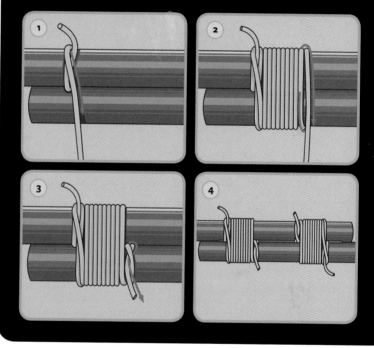

320 PREVENT A GUTPILE MAULING

When you're dressing big game out in remote bear country, it may often become necessary for you to leave a part of the meat in the woods. Here's one way to avoid an unhappy encounter with a bear that's found your animal: Before leaving the meat, tie a brightly colored rag or piece of T-shirt around a sharp stick. Drag the rag through the carcass to infuse it with blood, then drive the stick into the ground near the carcass. When you return, approach from downwind and use binoculars to see if the flag has been disturbed. If so, stay away.

321 OPEN A CAN WITHOUT A CAN OPENER

When the zombie apocalypse reigns in the streets—or you stumble into a remote cabin after having been lost in the woods for a week—being able to open a can of food without any utensils will put you at the front of the survival line. All you need on hand is your food can, a flat rock or piece of concrete, and enough remaining muscle strength to rub the can just the right way.

Most canned foods are made with a rimmed top that is crimped closed with an extra layer of metal. It might be hard to see, but it's there, and once you remove that thin layer of metal from the rim, the top will pop off.

You'll need to find a hard, flat surface such as slate or other flat rock, or a piece of concrete or a smooth brick. Be sure that surface remains steady, turn the can upside down, and grind the top rim vigorously back and forth (A). You might see liquid dribbling out; that indicates progress.

At this point you can turn the can right side up and pry the lid off by sticking a knife blade into the open seam (B), or keep on grinding it until you see that you've removed metal from all the way around the rim. Turn the can over and squeeze the sides of the can to pop the top free (C). Be very careful—all that grinding has created sharp metal edges.

322

MAKE A DUCT TAPE BUTTERFLY BANDAGE

A butterfly bandage is used to pull together the edges of a wound for quicker, cleaner healing. Here's how to make one on the fly.

Clean the wound thoroughly and dry the skin.

Cut a strip of duct tape 1 to 1½ inches long by one-quarter to ½ inch wide. Using sharp scissors or a knife, make small cuts to create two tabs in the middle of the bandage (A).

Fold one tab in so the two sticky sides are together (B). Fold the other tab over the first (C) to create a nonadhesive strip in the that will not stick to the cut.

Stick one end of the butterfly bandage to one side of the cut, pinch the cut together, pull the bandage across the cut, and stick the other end in place. For larger wounds, additional butterfly bandages can be used like sutures.

323

COOK FISH ON A LOG

The modern variant of planked fish involves a store-bought cedar board and a stainless steel backyard grill. It wasn't always so. In a survival situation you can cook planked fish without any utensils at all. Trout and panfish are small and thin enough to cook quickly, and fat enough to stay moist in the heat of an open flame. And you don't even need a carefully squared plank.

First, split an 8- to 12-inch log round in half. (Stay away from the wood of pine and other conifers.) No way to split wood? No sweat. Just use a round log. Whittle a half-dozen 2-inch wooden pegs with one sharp end. Clean the surface of the log and lay out the fish, either whole or skin side down. With the point of a knife, poke through the fish to mark the log where the pegs should be, remove the fish, then use the tip of a knife to drill a starter hole for the pegs. Replace the fish and then tap the pegs into place.

Build a teepee fire so the flames rise at least to the level of the fish, and scoot the fish in place. If needed, chock the log with a rock or stick.

324

MAKE A DUCT TAPE BOWL

Tear off two pieces of duct tape in equal lengths, about 18 inches long. Sit down on the ground with a bent knee. Form a cross with the tape, with the intersection of the cross on top of your knee, sticky side down, and press the tape against your leg. Make a bowl shape by wrapping your pants leg with more tape until you have it sized just right. Carefully remove the tape bowl, and add more duct tape to the interior to waterproof the bowl.

INDEX

A

acorn cap, whistle from 287
allergic reactions 286
antlers, mounting 202
apple trees, pruning 233
arbor knot 120
archery hunts. *See* bowhunting
AR rifles
  anatomy of 224
  cartridges for 236
  jammed 225
arrows
  broadheads 270
  fletching 270
  modern 270
  nocks 270, 271
  reading bloody 170
  shaft 270
ATVs, mud-proofing 47
automotive foam tape 67
axes and hatchets
  bits of 58
  handles of 58
  head patterns for 56
  parts of 57
  sharpening 61, 63

B

backpacks
  buying 22
  rigging, with paracord 72
backtrolling 126
bait
  catching 115, 117, 118, 156
  crickets as 122
  minnows as 156
  raising your own 114, 116
  salmon-egg 123
  tips for 124
bandage, butterfly, from duct tape 322
bandoliers 227
batteries, reviving 37
bears
  avoiding encounters with 320
  spray 317
Bimini twist 86
binoculars
  grid system for 210
  holding 219
  as spotting scope 222
bipods 221

biscuits, baking 44
blackpowder rifles
  cleaning 228
  history of 253
  pellets for 254
  powder options for 255
  projectiles for 256
  ramrod grip for 230
  spit swabbing 229
bladders, sanitizing 38
bleeding, stopping 304
blinds
  camouflaging 191
  layout 235, 269
  shooting from 194, 235
blizzards 295, 312
boats. *See also* canoes
  anchor for 40
  baling, with milk jugs 121
  camouflaging 176, 191
  distress call for 288
  freeing grounded 290
  trolling 125, 126, 128
bobbers, earplugs as 80
boots
  buying 22
  drying 41, 109
bowhunting. *See also* arrows
  with confidence decoys 196
  for deer 196, 210, 232
  grips and 197
  ground-blind shot 194
  loose servings and 195
  for pronghorn antelope 167
  sights for 169
  wax and 168
bowl, from duct tape 324
brownies, inside oranges 46
bug dope 6
bush hooking 111

C

cameras. *See also* photographs; videos
  point-of-view 178
  trail 181
camouflage
  for blinds 191
  for boats 191
  for gun stock 217
camping. *See also* cooking; fire; sleeping;
  specific equipment
  buying gear for 22
  insects and 6, 8

prepacking for 64
  under the stars 1
  in thunderstorms 9
cane pole, rigging 87
canoes
  bailing 121
  bent-shaft paddle for 108
  boat anchor for 40
  buying 84
  camouflaging 176
  features of 84
  paddle strokes for 105
  rigging 71
  seats on, from duct tape 107
canoe trips
  easy 85
  portage 39, 40
cans, opening 321
carpeting, indoor-outdoor
  as front porch for tent 33
  as wader changing mat 129
catfish, skinning 94
chiggers 6
chuck-'n'-duck cast 103
cinderblock pit cookers 275
climbing belts 257
climbing harness, emergency 309
clothes
  cleaning 262
  re-proofing waxed cotton 263
coffee cans
  catching bait leeches with 117
  emergency heater from toilet paper and 312
come-alongs 24
compasses
  air bubbles in 278
  importance of 294
confidence decoys 196
contour lines 277
cooking. *See also* fire
  biscuits 44
  brownies, inside oranges 46
  with cinderblock pit cookers 275
  cleaning up after 12, 15, 28
  dividing up responsibility for 12
  duck, with a stick 248
  Dutch oven 13
  fish 155, 323
  frogs 267
  gear for 28
  spices for 14
cotton, re-proofing waxed 263
coverboards 116
crappie, shooting docks for 150
crickets, as bait 122

cuts, superglue for 283
cutting boards 16

D

Dakota fire hole 52
declination 277
decoys
  confidence 196
  dove 206
  pronghorn antelope 167
  pulling in floating 209
  turkey 180, 196
deer
  approaching downed 164
  buck bed for 231
  calls 212
  confidence decoys and 196
  drags 205, 216
  field dressing 216
  hoisting 165
  looking for 210
  mounts 202, 214

photographs of 166, 182
pruning apple trees for 233
scents 211, 213, 234
steering, with buckets 232
tail, in lures and flies 147
tarsal glands of 213
DEET 6
distress call, maritime 288
docks, shooting, for crappie 150
dogs
  deskunkifying 35
  first-aid kit for 187
  removing porcupine quills from 36
  training 185, 186, 188
dog whistle, as duck call 177
dove decoys 206
drag washers, replacing 98
drinking water, collecting 313
dry ice 157
duck calls
  backward 208
  dog whistle as 177
  keeping clean 265
  making 207

tuning 175
duck hunting
  camouflaging canoe for 176
  decoys for 206, 209
  with duck flags 247
  floating table for 249
  shotguns for 250, 251
ducks
  cooking, on a stick 248
  diving wounded 188
  skull, European mount 174
  storing, in pantyhose 189
duct tape
  alternatives to 67
  bowl from 324
  butterfly bandage from 322
  for canoe seats 107
  carrying 68
  protecting lantern globes with 69
duffel bags, organizing 65
Dutch oven cooking 13
DWR (durable water repellent) 21

E

earplugs
    as bobbers 80
    for hunting 240
energy drink 43

F

field-dressing kits 216
finnsticks 219
fire
    burning gear in 53
    hanging pots over 54
    hauling wood for 50
    hole, Dakota 52
    log cabin council 55
    paper logs for 51
    splitting wood for 49
    starting 291, 300, 315, 318
    tips for 27
    wick 292

wild- 297
first aid
    for allergic reactions 286
    kit for dogs 187
fish
    cleaning 94, 96
    cooking, on a log 323
    frying oil, reusing 159
    grilling, with tree branch 155
    measuring 95
    photographs of 160
    shipping, with dry ice 157
    stringer for 132
fishing. *See also specific equipment*
    for bottom-dwelling predators 102
    bush hooks 111
    chuck-'n'-duck cast 103
    for crappie 150
    fly-casting practice 101
    with greased leader 81
    kids and 163
    for longnose gar 149
    on lunch break 90

at night 162
    photographs of 160
    for redbreast sunfish 151
    for smallmouth bass 144, 153
    tenkara 148
    with trigger snares 302
    trolling 125, 126, 128
    for trout 140, 158
    videos of 113
    with weirs 303
flares, starting a fire with 300
flash targets 252
flintlocks 253
fly rods
    buying 22
    making custom 78
    patching grip on 88
    rope-taping grip of 99
    spinning reel on 104
    for tenkara fishing 148
foam
    minicell 106
    tape 67

frogs
  gigging 266
  lures, hollow-body 145
  preparing 267
fuzz sticks 291

G

game boards, sleeping pads as 34
game trails
  marking, with glow sticks 204
  marking, with surveyor's tape 245
  recording, with GPS 179
  tracking blood 203
gar, longnose 149
garbage bags, as sand spikes 5
gathering guides, widening 136
gear. See also specific equipment
  burning 53
  buying 22
  for cooking 28
  hanging, inside tent 31
  keeping dry 42
  prepacking 64
gloves
  as bandolier 10
  for touchscreens 10
Gorilla Tape 67
GPS
  recording game trails 179
  saving backtrails with 281
guns. See also rifles; shotguns; target shooting
  buying used 172
  camouflaging stock of 217
  cleaning 173, 218, 228, 243
  customizing 171
  dry-fire practice with 172
  early 253
  fixing stock dings, with an iron 220
  jammed 225
  pistol shotshells 183
  ruining 173
  shooting, with two eyes 239
gun slings 171, 246
gunsmith box, building 243
guylines, reflective 2

H

hatchets. See axes and hatchets
heater, emergency 312
highwayman's hitch 25–26
hooks
  organizing 89
  Palomar knot for 91
  removing 138, 301
  treble, replacing 77
  World's Fair knot for 137

hunting. See also blinds; bowhunting; game
  trails; guns; specific game animals
  approaching downed animals 164
  camouflage 176, 191, 217
  cleaning clothes for 262
  grid system for binoculars 210
  photographs of 166
  on snowshoes 261
hydration bladders, sanitizing 38

I

insects
  blotter for 8
  repellents 6, 308
  stings from 285, 286

J

jerky 215

K

kids
  knives and 20
  teaching fly fishing to 163
knives
  blade shapes and grinds for 193
  carrying and drawing 17
  checking for nicks 284
  cleaning 19, 62
  cutting boards for 16
  kid's first 20
  pocket clips for 18, 299
  serrated 282
  sharpening 60, 63, 282
  sparking fire with 318
  testing, with newspaper 296
  tips for 19
knots
  arbor 120
  Bimini twist 86
  heaving-line 289
  highwayman's hitch 25–26
  orvis 161
  Palomar 91
  shear lashing 319
  World's Fair 137
Know-Nothing Shad Ball 146

L

lanterns
  maintaining 70
  night fishing with 162
  protecting globes of 69

laundry hamper, as stripping basket 142
layout blinds
  making 269
  shooting from 235
leaders, greased 81
leeches 117
lightning 9
lineman's belts 257
lines
  attaching, to reel 120
  dampening twist in 82
  marking 79
  red 83
  storing 131, 143
log cabin council fire 55
lunch, packing 45
lures
  cricket 122
  deer tail 147
  frogs, hollow-body 145
  Know-Nothing Shad Ball 146
  for longnose gar 149
  making 135, 139, 146, 154
  pork rind attached to 119
  red 83
  replacing treble hooks on 77
  for smallmouth bass 144
  supercharging, with a nail 74
  trimming 75
  for trout 158

M

machetes, sharpening 59
maps, topographic 277
matches
  shotshell case for 316
  waterproof 311
meat
  grinders 259
  storing 276
merit badge, for rifle shooting 237
milk jugs, bailing boats with 121
minicell foam 106
minnows, catching 156
mosquito netting, fixing torn 7

N

nets 93

O

oil, reusing fish-frying 159
oranges, brownies inside 46
orvis knot 161

P

paddles, bent-shaft 108
paddle strokes 105
painter lines 71
Palomar knot 91
pantyhose, storing a duck in 189
paper logs, rolling 51
paracord
    making camp table with 73
    rigging a pack with 72
    for signaling devices 280
    slings 171, 246
    snowshoes from 293
    wire from 314
percussion caps 253
photographs
    fishing 160
    hunting 166
    with point-of-view cameras 178
    with trail cameras 181, 182
picket stakes 3
pistol shotshells 183
pit cookers, cinderblock 275
"place" command 185
plywood bait farms 116
point-of-view cameras 178
pool noodle, sleeping with 32
Poop Tube 23
poppers, wooden dowel 76
Popsicle stick, as hook remover 138
porcupine quills 36
pork rinds, lures tipped with 119
portage 39, 40
potato tree 226
pots
    hanging, over fire 54
    scrubbing 15
pronghorn antelopes, decoys for 167

Q

quail hunting 241

R

rabbit gums, building 201
rain shell, re-waterproofing 21
rainy days, game boards for 34
recoil pads, removing 242
redbreast sunfish, fishing for 151
reels
    attaching line to 120
    on fly rods 104
    manual bail for 134
    replacing bearings of 100
    replacing drag washers of 98

rubberizing handle of 97
setting spool brake for 141
tips for casting with 133
Rescue Tape 67
ribbon leeches 117
rifles. See also AR rifles; blackpowder rifles
    bipods for 221
    brightening sights of 238
    camouflaging stock of 217
    cleaning 173, 218
    customizing 171
    fixing stock dings, with an iron 220
    merit badge for shooting 237
    PVC rest for 223
    ruining 173
ropes
    throwing 289
    whip finish for 66

S

salmon-egg bait 123
sand spikes
    for rods 152
    for tents 5
scent drippers 234
scent killers 258
scents, making 211, 213
Schmidt Pain Index 285
seines 118
servings, loose 195
shear lashing 319
shotguns
    camouflaging stock of 217
    cold-proofing 250
    double-barreled 241
    fixing stock dings, with an iron 220
    mounting 190
    pistols as 183
    recoil pads for 242
    waterproofing semiautomatic 251
signaling devices 280
sinkers 112
skunks 35
sleeping
    with pool noodle 32
    under the stars 1
    tips for 29
sleeping bags
    buying 22
    recommendations for 29
sleeping pads
    as game board 34
    integrated, into sleeping bags 29
slingshots 298
smallmouth bass
    lures for 144
    in small streams 153
smartphones, gloves for 10

snake bites, treating 279
snap caps 172
snowshoes
    hunting on 261
    improvising 293
social media, posting on 160
soda can pull tabs, as tent line tighteners 30
spice rack, from Tic-Tac boxes 14
spinners, making 135
spool brake, setting 141
squirrel
    calls 199
    hunting for 198, 200
stars, sleeping under the 1
stranded vehicles 295, 312
stringers 132
stripping basket, laundry hamper as 142
sumac berries, energy drink from 43
superglue
    for cuts 283
    for loose servings 195
surveyor's tape, dispenser for 245
survival kits 305–7
Swiss seat, making 309

T

tables
    camp 73
    duck hunter's floating 249
tapes, types of 67. See also duct tape
target shooting
    cheap targets for 184
    flash targets for 252
    potato tree for 226
    stand for 244
Tenacious Tape 67
tenkara fishing 148
tents
    fixing poles for 4
    front porch for 33
    garbage bags as sand spikes for 5
    hanging gear inside 31
    insects inside 8
    mosquito netting for 7
    one-man 29
    picket stakes for 3
    reflective guylines for 2
    soda can pull tabs as tent line tighteners 30
    zippers for 11
ticks 6, 192
tippets, protecting hair-thin 140
tires
    changing 127
    splitting wood with 49
toilet paper, emergency heater with 312
topographic maps 277
touchscreens, gloves for 10
trail cameras 181, 182

trailer jacks 127
trails. *See also* game trails
    saving, with GPS 281
    on topo maps 277
tread tape 67
treble hooks, replacing 77
trees
    apple, pruning 233
    buck bed from 231
    bucking fallen 48
triggers, cleaning 218
trigger snares 302
trolling 125, 126, 128
trout
    stickbaits for 158
    tippets 140
turkey calls
    box 273
    other bird calls for 272
    pot-style 268
    strikers, protecting 260
    wingbone 274
turkey decoys 180

V

vests, fishing 92, 130
videos 113

W

waders
    changing mat for 129
    drying out 109
    patching 110
water bottles, packing lunch in 45
wax, bowstring 168
weirs 303
whistle, from acorn cap 287
wildfire, escape from 297
wire, sources of 314
wood
    hauling 50
    splitting 49, 56
World's Fair knot 137
worm boxes 114

Z

Z-Drag 310
zippers
    fixing 11
    silencing 264

CREDITS

ILLUSTRATION COURTESY OF: *Conor Buckley:* Chapter Icons, 15, 22, 43, 61, 101–102, 126, 128, 138, 141–142, 270, 287, 290, 301–303, 322; *Hayden Foell:* 10, 41, 49–50, 105, 108, 175–176, 180, 186, 188, 206, 209, 214, 242, 248–249, 253, 266, 274, 293, 309; *Raymond Larrett:* 7, 24, 55, 111, 149, 194, 200, 231, 239, 275, 292, 310, 323; *Dan Marsiglio:* 86, 137, 161, 190, 282; *Samuel A. Minick:* 289; *Christine Meighan:* 46; *Robert L. Prince:* 6, 52, 77, 84, 90, 103, 139, 150, 155, 165, 171, 205, 206, 210, 223; *Paula Rogers:* 94, 133; *Jamie Spinello:* 132, 135, 152, 154, 202, 219, 262, 321; *Pete Sucheski:* 74–75; *Mike Sudal:* 54, 118–119, 153, 201; *Bryon Thompson:* 82; *Lauren Towner:* 3, 25–26, 56, 66, 71–73, 76, 78, 87, 96, 112, 120, 193, 224, 226, 234, 244, 251, 256, 259, 269, 296, 311, 318–319.

ALL TEXT BY T. EDWARD NICKENS, WITH THE FOLLOWING EXCEPTIONS: *Ryan Arch:* 316; *Scott Bestul:* 170; *Phil Bourjaily:* 250; *Jacob Campbell:* 30; *Eddie Crane III:* 50; *Joe Cermele:* 74, 75, 76, 78, 93, 103, 104, 122, 134, 140, 144, 145, 153, 158, 301; *Joe Doss:* 40; *Stephen Elliott:* 89; *Dave Hurteau:* 168, 232; *Ron Katzaman:* 230; *Tom Keer:* 110; *David Kretzschmar:* 80; *Greg Martin:* 15; *Keith McCafferty:* 62, 295, 312; *Michael McGilvrey:* 51; *Ron McLane:* 315; *John Merwin:* 86, 120, 137, 161; *Stephen Miller:* 143; *Tommy O'Conner:* 96; *David Petzal:* 220, 224, 225; *Kathy Zaborowski Richardson:* 31; *Todd Rockwell:* 228; *Michael R. Shea:* 191; *Terry Stoddard:* 260; *Ben Wagner:* 6

ABOUT THE MAGAZINE

In every issue of *Field & Stream* you'll find a lot of stuff: beautiful photography and artwork, adventure stories, wild game recipes, humor, commentary, reviews, and more. That mix is what makes the magazine so great, what's helped it remain relevant since 1895. But at the heart of every issue are the skills. The tips that explain how to land a big trout, the tactics that help you shoot the deer of your life, the lessons that teach you how to survive a cold night outside, told with authority and flair.

You'll find a ton of those skills in *The Total Outdoorsman Manual*, but there's not a book big enough to hold them all in one volume. Besides, whether you're new to hunting and fishing or an old pro, there's always more to learn. You can continue to expect *Field & Stream* to teach you those essential skills in every issue. Plus, there's all that other stuff in the magazine, too, which is pretty great. To order a subscription, visit www.fieldandstream.com/subscription.

ABOUT THE AUTHOR

T. Edward Nickens began his career writing a weekly outdoors column for the *Chapel Hill (N.C.) News* for 25 cents per column inch. He's been writing for *Field & Stream* since 2003 and has been one of the magazine's most prolific and wide-ranging authors. His work has won many national awards and has been collected in numerous "best of" anthologies. Nickens's first book for *Field & Stream*, *The Total Outdoorsman Manual*, has sold more than a quarter of a million copies worldwide. In addition to writing about hunting, fishing, and wilderness travel for *Field & Stream*, he

is host and field producer for *Field & Stream's Heroes of Conservation* web series, co-host of the brand's online *Gun Nuts* series, and for five years was host and field producer for the *Total Outdoorsman Challenge* on Outdoor Channel. He also writes for various other national magazines, for which he has reported on conservation issues from the rain forests of Nicaragua to the tundra forests of the Yukon. Nickens is based in North Carolina, where he chases ducks, deer, doves, trout, and squirrels—when he's not chasing them across North America for *Field & Stream*.

ACKNOWLEDGMENTS

This book is the culmination of work by two extraordinary teams: the staff at *Field & Stream* and the staff at Weldon Owen Publishing. I'm indebted particularly to Anthony Licata, Colin Kearns, and Joe Cermele at the magazine. *Field & Stream*'s approach to providing timeless editorial content to modern readers is unmatched. And my hat is off to the Weldon Owen gang: Mariah Bear and Conor Buckley especially, whose understanding of how to craft books that are as useful as readable—not to mention gorgeous—makes working on projects like this so exciting. Much has changed about hunting and fishing over the past few thousand years, but not this: We like to tell our stories and share our knowledge. It's been that way since we first gathered by a campfire with a rabbit taken with a club, and it's been that way now that we gather through social media. This book is only possible because of all the hunters, anglers, guides, writers, editors, and photographers, who showed me their stuff—and let me share it all with a big, broad world.

weldon**owen**

PRESIDENT, CEO Terry Newell
VP, PUBLISHER Roger Shaw
ASSOCIATE PUBLISHER Mariah Bear
EDITORIAL ASSISTANT Ian Cannon
CREATIVE DIRECTOR Kelly Booth
ART DIRECTOR William Mack
DESIGNER Allister Fein
ILLUSTRATION COORDINATOR Conor Buckley
PRODUCTION DIRECTOR Chris Hemesath
PRODUCTION MANAGER Michelle Duggan

Weldon Owen would also like to thank Jan Hughes for editorial assistance and Ken DellaPenta for the index; Meghan Hildebrand provided design expertise.

FIELD& STREAM

EXECUTIVE VICE PRESIDENT Eric Zinczenko
EDITOR-IN-CHIEF Anthony Licata
EXECUTIVE EDITOR Mike Toth
MANAGING EDITOR Jean McKenna
DEPUTY EDITORS Dave Hurteau, Colin Kearns, Slaton L. White
COPY CHIEF Donna L. Ng
SENIOR EDITOR Joe Cermele
ASSISTANT EDITOR Kristyn Brady
DESIGN DIRECTOR Sean Johnston
PHOTOGRAPHY DIRECTOR John Toolan
DEPUTY ART DIRECTOR Pete Sucheski
ASSOCIATE ART DIRECTORS Russ Smith, James A. Walsh
PRODUCTION MANAGER Judith Weber
DIGITAL DIRECTOR Nate Matthews
ONLINE CONTENT EDITOR Alex Robinson
ONLINE PRODUCER Kurt Shulitz
ASSISTANT ONLINE EDITOR Martin Leung

2 Park Avenue
New York, NY 10016
www.fieldandstream.com

Library of Congress Control Number on file
with the publisher
Flexi Edition ISBN 978-1-61628-807-5
Hardcover Edition ISBN 978-1-61628-866-2
10 9 8 7 6 5 4 3 2 1
2014 2015 2016 2017 2018
Printed in China by 1010 Printing Ltd
Field & Stream and Weldon Owen are divisions of
BONNIER